HEINEMANN COORDINATED SCIENCE · FOUNDATION

BIOLOGY

Arabella Stuart • Stephen Webster

Contents

How to use this book   1

SECTION A: THE ENVIRONMENT

CHAPTER 1: THE HOMES OF LIVING THINGS

1.1	The huge variety of life	2	1.3	Surviving on the rocky seashore	6
1.2	Finding out who's who	4	1.4	Some other interesting habitats	8

CHAPTER 2: FEEDING RELATIONSHIPS

2.1	Who eats who in the habitat?	10	2.3	Ecological pyramids	14
2.2	Wonderful webs	12			

CHAPTER 3: SURVIVING THE ENVIRONMENT

3.1	Adaptation on a rocky seashore	16	3.4	Only the best survive	22
3.2	In the Arctic and the desert	18	3.5	Predators and prey	24
3.3	Competing with your neighbours	20	3.6	Limits on population growth	26

CHAPTER 4: RECYCLING LIVING THINGS

4.1	Decomposers and decay	28	4.3	The carbon cycle	32
4.2	Microbes at work	30			

CHAPTER 5: INTERFERING WITH THE BALANCE OF LIFE

5.1	Growing beyond our limits	34	5.4	Feeding the world	40
5.2	The ozone layer and skin cancer	36	5.5	How to stop our polluting activities	42
5.3	Global warming	38			

SECTION A: QUESTIONS   44

SECTION B: LIFE PROCESSES AND CELL ACTIVITY

CHAPTER 6: THE ORGANISATION OF LIFE

6.1	Building blocks of living things	46	6.3	Tissues and organs	50
6.2	Plant cells are different	48	6.4	Organ systems	52

CHAPTER 7: A CLOSER LOOK AT THE CHARACTERISTICS OF LIVING THINGS

7.1	Feeding and excretion	54	7.3	Movement and sensitivity	58
7.2	Respiring, reproduction and growing	56			

SECTION B: QUESTIONS   60

SECTION C: GREEN PLANTS AS ORGANISMS

CHAPTER 8: HOW PLANTS LIVE

8.1	The parts of a plant	62	8.3	Transpiration	66
8.2	The plant finds water	64	8.4	The plant finds minerals	68

CHAPTER 9: HOW PLANTS FEED

9.1	Building food	70	9.3	Limiting factors	74
9.2	The leaf	72	9.4	After photosynthesis, what next?	76

CHAPTER 10: THE SENSITIVE PLANT

10.1	Knowing up from down	78	10.2	How to make plants behave	80

SECTION C: QUESTIONS   82

SECTION D: HUMANS AS ORGANISMS

CHAPTER 11: THE PATHWAY OF FOOD

11.1	Food for life	84	11.5	The food pipe and stomach	92
11.2	Vitamins and minerals	86	11.6	The small intestine	94
11.3	Completing your diet	88	11.7	The large intestine	96
11.4	The human gut	90			

CHAPTER 12: THE RESPIRATION SYSTEM

12.1	Why we breathe	98	**12.3**	Breathing in, breathing out	102
12.2	Gases in, gases out	100	**12.4**	Protecting your lungs	104

CHAPTER 13: UNDERSTANDING BLOOD

13.1	A transport system	106	**13.4**	Inside the blood	112
13.2	Your heart beat	108	**13.5**	Your healthy blood	114
13.3	Blood vessels	110			

CHAPTER 14: GETTING ENERGY

14.1	The 'fire' in your cells	116	**14.2**	The oxygen problem	118

CHAPTER 15: THE NERVOUS SYSTEM AND HORMONES

15.1	Making sense of things	120	**15.4**	The control centre	126
15.2	The eye	122	**15.5**	Chemical messages	128
15.3	How the iris controls 'dazzle'	124			

CHAPTER 16: DRUGS

16.1	Drugs which help sick people	130	**16.2**	The misuse of drugs	132

CHAPTER 17: KEEPING THINGS STEADY

17.1	Control of body temperature	134	**17.3**	Control by the kidneys	138
17.2	How do we warm up and cool down?	136			

CHAPTER 18: DISEASES

18.1	Avoiding disease	140	**18.2**	Fighting disease	142
SECTION D: QUESTIONS		144			

SECTION E: VARIATION, INHERITANCE AND EVOLUTION

CHAPTER 19: GENETICS AND INHERITANCE

19.1	Alone in a crowd	146	**19.3**	Boy or girl?	150
19.2	Passing the message	148	**19.4**	Genetic disease	152

CHAPTER 20: HUMAN REPRODUCTION

20.1	Girls	154	**20.4**	Fertilisation	160
20.2	Boys	156	**20.5**	The developing baby	162
20.3	Sexual intercourse	158			

CHAPTER 21: REPRODUCTION

21.1	Sexual reproduction	164	**21.2**	Reproducing without sex	166

CHAPTER 22: THE EVOLUTION OF LIFE

22.1	Life on Earth	168	**22.3**	Extinction	172
22.2	Fossils	170	**22.4**	New species	174
SECTION E: QUESTIONS		176			

Data Section	178	**Glossary**		180

Heinemann Educational Publishers
Halley Court, Jordan Hill, Oxford, OX2 8EJ
a division of Reed Educational & Professional
Publishing Ltd

MELBOURNE AUCKLAND
FLORENCE PRAGUE MADRID ATHENS
SINGAPORE TOKYO SÃO PAULO
CHICAGO PORTSMOUTH (NH) MEXICO
IBADAN GABORONE JOHANNESBURG
KAMPALA NAIROBI

© Arabella Stuart and Stephen Webster, 1996

Copyright notice
All rights reserved. No part of this publication may be reproduced, stored in a retrieval system, or transmitted in any form or by any means, electronic, mechanical, photocopying, recording, or otherwise without either the prior written permission of the Publishers or a licence permitting restricted copying in the United Kingdom issued by the Copyright Licensing Agency Ltd, 90 Tottenham Court Road, London W1P 9HE.

First published 1996

ISBN 0 435 58004 3

2000 99 98 97
10 9 8 7 6 5 4 3 2

Designed and typeset by Pentacor PLC,
High Wycombe, Bucks.

Illustrated by Phil Gibson, Tracy Hawkett, Kathy Lacey, and David Thelwell and Clive Spong (courtesy of Bernard Thornton Artists, London).

Cover design by Ken Vail Graphic Design.

Cover photograph by Oxford Scientific Films (Inset: Bruce Coleman).

Printed and bound in Great Britain by Bath Colour Books, Glasgow.

Acknowledgements
The authors and publishers would like to thank the following for permission to use photographs:

p 2: SPL. p 6: Heather Angel. p 7 Heather Angel. p 8 T, M & B: Bruce Coleman. p 9: Bruce Coleman. p 11 ML: NHPA. p 11 MR: Heather Angel. p16 Heather Angel. p 18 BL: O.S.F./Mickey Gibson. p 18 BR: Bruce Coleman. p 19: Bruce Coleman. p 20: Bruce Coleman. p 21: Bruce Coleman. p 23: NHPA/Stephen Dalton. p 25 T: NHPA/John Shaw. p 25 M: NHPA/T Kitchin. p 26: Garden Picture Library. p 29 R: Bruce Coleman. p 29 L: Roger Scruton. p 30: Roger Scruton. p 35: Bruce Coleman. p 36: Ace Photos. p 37: SPL p 40 T: Heather Angel. p 40 R: Bruce Coleman. p 42: Bruce Coleman. p 47: SPL. p 48: Biophoto. p 54 T: Bruce Coleman. p 54 B: Bruce Coleman. p 55: Ardea Ltd/Julie Bruton. p 56 BL & BM: The Garden Picture Library. p 56 BR: Bruce Coleman. p 57 L: Collections/Sandra Lousada. p 57 M: Bruce Coleman. p 57 R: Bruce Coleman. p 58 TR: Catherine Ashmore. p 58 TL: NHPA. p 58 BR: OSF. p 59 MR: O.S.F. p 59 M: Heather Angel. p 59 TR: Bruce Coleman. p 59 ML: Bruce Coleman. p 63 MR: Bruce Coleman. p 62 B: Bruce Coleman. p 62 T: Bridgeman Art Library. p 63 ML: Ardea Ltd/Alan Weaving. p 64: Zefa. p 65 TL&R: Harry Smith. p 66: Garden Picture Library. p 67: O.S.F./Daniel Cox. p 69: Holt Studios. p 70 T: Roger Scruton. p 70 M: SPL. p 71: SPL. p 74: The Garden Picture Library/Paul Windsor. p 74 TL&R: Roger Scruton. p 76: J. Allan Cash Ltd. p 77: NHPA. p 78: Bruce Coleman. p 79: The Garden Picture Library/Mel Watson. p 80: The Garden Picture Library/D. Askham. p 81: Bruce Coleman. p 84: Network/Mike Goldwater. p 85 TL: NHPA. p 85 BR: Roger Scruton. p 87 TR: SPL. p 87 BR: SPL. p 88: Anthony Blake/Joy Skipper. p 89: Bruce Coleman. p 93: SPL. p 95: SPL. p 97 TL: SPL. p 97 MR: SPL. p 99 M: SPL. p 99 TR: SPL. p 103: Ardea Ltd/Adrian Warren. p 104: SPL/Dr Gary Settles. p 105 TR: SPL. p 105 MR: Health Education Authority. p 106: Zefa. p 108: Biophoto. p 109 R&L: SPL. p 110: SPL. p 113 TL: SPL. p 113 TR: SPL p 114 BR: Biophoto. p 114 BL: Biophoto. p 115: SPL. p 116 BR: Bruce Coleman. p 116 BL: Allsport/Tony Duffy. p 119 D: Allsport/Jean Paul von Poppel. p 119 BR: Colorsport/Tavenier. p 121: J. Allan Cash Ltd. p 124: SPL. p 129: SPL. p 130: Roger Scruton. p 131: SPL. p 132: Shout. p133: headline from *Daily Mail* Saturday December 2 1995. p 136: Ace Photo. p 137: Wellcome Trust. p 139 TR: SPL. p 139 BL: Roger Scruton. 140 B: Wellcome Trust. p 140 T: SPL. p 141 T: SPL. p 141 B: SPL. p 143: SPL. p 146 T: Richard & Sally Greenhill. p 146 BL: Bruce Coleman. p 146 BR: Bruce Coleman. p 147 TL: Harry Smith Collection. p147 TR: NHPA. p 147 T: Hulton Deutsch. p 148 T: Richard & Sally Greenhill. p 148 T: SPL. p 148 B: Biophoto. p 150: SPL. p 152: SPL. p 153 T: SPL. p 153 B: SPL p 154: SPL/John Giannicchi. p 157: Biophoto. p159 L: Biophoto. p 159 R: SPL. p 162 T: NHPA. p 162 B: SPL/Petit Format/Nestle. p 163 R: SPL p 163 L: SPL. p 164 M: NHPA. p 164 B: NHPA. p 166: Bruce Coleman. p 167: O.S.F. p 169 T: Environmental Picture Library. p 169 M: N.S.P./C. Jones. p 169 B: Ardea Ltd/J. Mason. p 170 T&B: GeoScience Features Picture Library/Dr B. Booth. p 171 T: Hulton Deutsch. p 171 B: Natural History Museum. p 173 T: Bruce Coleman. p 174: Bruce Coleman. p 175: Bruce Coleman.

The publishers have made every effort to trace the copyright holders, but if they have inadvertently overlooked any, they will be pleased to make the necessary arrangements at the first opportunity.

Arabella Stuart teaches at Sevenoaks School, Kent. Stephen Webster teaches at The King Alfred School, Hampstead.

How to use this book

Heinemann Coordinated Science: Biology has been written for your GCSE course. It contains all the information you will need over the next two years for your exam syllabus.

This book has five sections. Each section matches one of the major themes in the National Curriculum.

What's in a section?

The sections are organised into double-page spreads. Each spread has:

Colour coded sections so you can quickly find the one you want.

Clear text and pictures to explain the science.

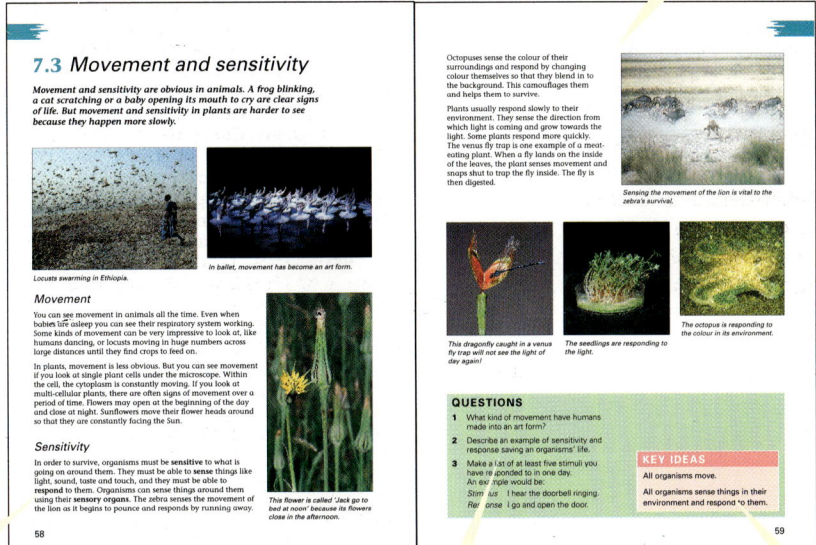

Scientific words printed in **bold** where they are first used in this book.

Questions to help check your understanding of the important ideas on the spread.

Key ideas boxes to highlight the most important ideas on the spread.

Section questions

At the end of each section, there is a double-page spread of longer questions. These are to help you find out if you understand the key ideas in that section. They can also help you revise.

Data section

There is also a double-page spread to help you with data handling skills, like plotting graphs.

Glossary

At the back of the book is a glossary. This contains an explanation for each of the scientific words printed in bold in the book. The words are arranged alphabetically.

Assessment and resource pack

All the answers for questions in this book are in the *Heinemann Coordinated Science: Foundation Biology Assessment and Resource Pack*.

CHAPTER 1: THE HOMES OF LIVING THINGS

1.1 *The huge variety of life*

How many different kinds of living things have you come across this week? Apart from humans and perhaps some pets, you have probably seen several insects and many different kinds of plant. There are millions of different kinds of living things in the world. How do biologists make sense of this great variety of life?

The study of living things or organisms and where they live is called **ecology**.

Living things can be found in every part of the world.

Grouping organisms

Organisms of the same kind are called **species**. There are about one and a half million known species in the world. Because there are so many, it is difficult to talk about them usefully unless we have a way of grouping them. Here you can see seven different kinds of animals. They all belong to different groups.

Look at these animals. Can you spot the important differences between them?

2

Some animal groups

Spiders

Spiders have four pairs of legs and do not have antennae.

Insects

Insects have three pairs of legs, one pair of antennae and wings.

Fish

Fishes are covered in scales and live in water. They lay their eggs in water.

Amphibians

The frog belongs to the group called **amphibians**. These have moist skin but do not have scales. Like fish, they lay eggs in the water. The eggs develop into tadpoles, which live in water, but the adults in most species of frog live on land and have lungs for breathing.

Reptiles

Reptiles have a dry, waterproof skin and most of them live on land. They lay eggs on the land. Crocodiles are reptiles.

Birds

Birds have wings and are covered by feathers.

Mammals

Mammals have hair. Their young usually grow inside the female and feed on her milk when they are born.

These animals are different from each other because each living thing is specially suited, or **adapted**, to living in one particular kind of place. For example, fish are adapted to living in water while birds spend most of their time in tree tops.

QUESTIONS

1 What is another word for living things?
2 Where are fish adapted to living?
3 What is the study of ecology?
4 How are:
   a insects different from spiders
   b fish different from reptiles
   c birds different from mammals?

KEY IDEAS

Ecology is the study of living things and where they live.

There are about ten million different species in the world.

Species can be sorted into groups according to what they are like.

1.2 Finding out who's who

Have you ever noticed a flower or insect and wondered what it is called? How would you go about finding out?

Describing organisms

In order to find out what group a particular organism belongs to, we often use keys. A **key** is a set of descriptions of what the different organisms are like. Here is an example of a key using the groups you have already come across.

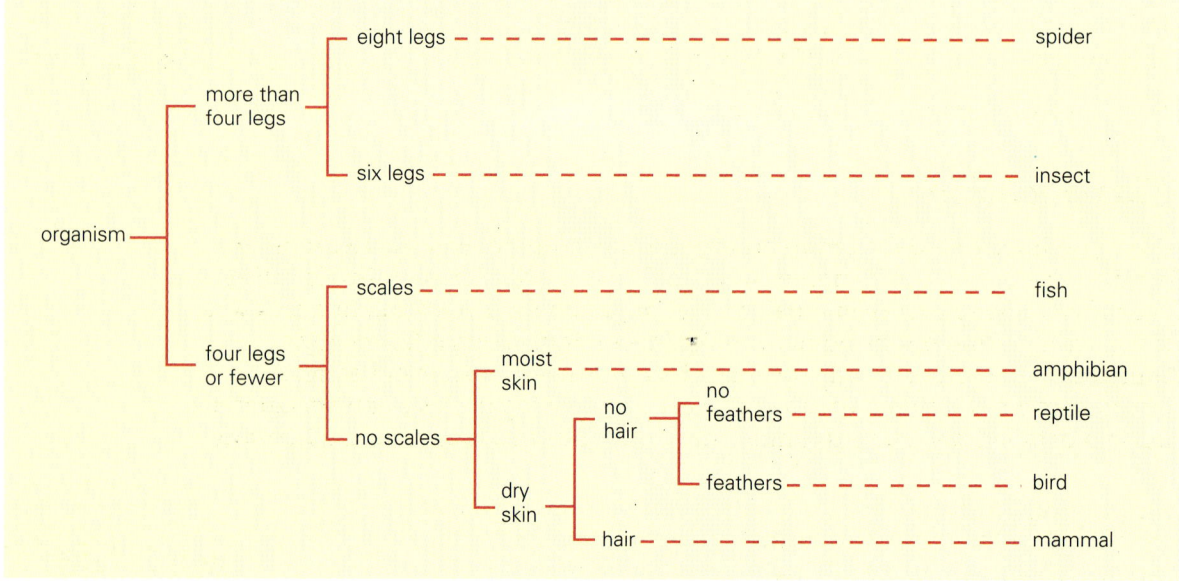

This key helps you to decide what kind of an animal an organism is.

Using a key

The place where an organism lives is called its **habitat**. Many different species can live in the same habitat. One example of a habitat is the rocky seashore. In the illustration on the page opposite you can see various organisms found in a rock pool. You can use the key above to find out what groups some of the animals living there belong to.

The animals that you can put into groups using this key are the mullet, herring gull, and human. The mullet has scales. So you can see from the key that it must be a fish. The herring gull has feathers so it must be a bird. Humans have hair so they are mammals.

Some organisms from a rocky seashore.

Classification

Once you have found the group an organism belongs to, you can use a more detailed key to find out its name. You can find out what an organism is called even if you have never seen it before. You might go for a walk and find a flower. If you want to find out its name, you could look it up using a flower key. Sometimes an organism is discovered which has never been seen before. A biologist can put it into a group quite easily by looking at the organism carefully, using a detailed key. Putting things into groups like this is called **classification**.

QUESTIONS

1. Give an example of a habitat.
2. Write down the names of five organisms which live in rock pools.
3. Look at this diagram of four kinds of animal. Use the key on this spread to find out which group each animal belongs to.

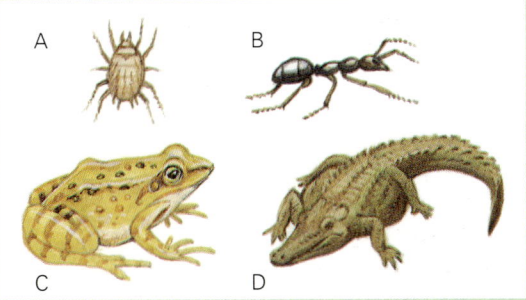

KEY IDEAS

The habitat is the place where an organism lives.

The rocky seashore is an example of a habitat where many different organisms live together.

Keys can be used to find out what a particular organism is called or the group to which a newly discovered organism belongs.

1.3 Surviving on the rocky seashore

Many different types of organism can survive on the rocky seashore. But what makes mussels or lugworms, rather than goldfish, tadpoles or earthworms survive here?

These organisms live side by side and are adapted in many different ways to the same habitat.

The rock pool habitat

Living things, or organisms, live in places that are especially well suited for them. The photograph above shows a rock pool. The organisms which live here have to survive some quite difficult living conditions. Rock pools are inter-tidal, which means that at some times during the day the rocks will be covered by the sea. At other times they will be pounded by the waves, or they will be in calm, shallow pools which can get quite hot in the sunshine.

The physical environment

The living conditions, like the temperature, amount of water and light, are called the physical **environment**. In the rock pool habitat, the environment is made up of water, but this water is salty. The temperature is fairly constant. For example, the water is very unlikely to freeze. But on a hot day, when the tide is out, the still water in the rock pool might get quite warm. The pounding of the waves is also part of the environment for the organisms, and they must be adapted so they are not washed away or crushed.

Communities and populations

All the organisms which live in a habitat like the rock pool make up the community of the rock pool. In any habitat there will be many different kinds of organism making up the **community**.

Look at the photograph of the mussels. You might find 200 mussels or more in one rock pool. The number of mussels in a rock pool is called the **population** of mussels. A population is a group of individuals of the same species living in a particular habitat.

Mussels are attached to the rock by thin threads to stop them being washed away by the sea when the tide comes in. The shell is closed tightly to stop the mussel drying out when the tide goes out again. They grow in clumps. The population of mussels in a rock pool can be quite large.

Mussels growing in Scotland.

QUESTIONS

1. What stops mussels being washed away by the sea?
2. Look at the diagram of the sea anemone. How is it adapted to suit its environment?
3. Describe the living conditions in the rock pool.

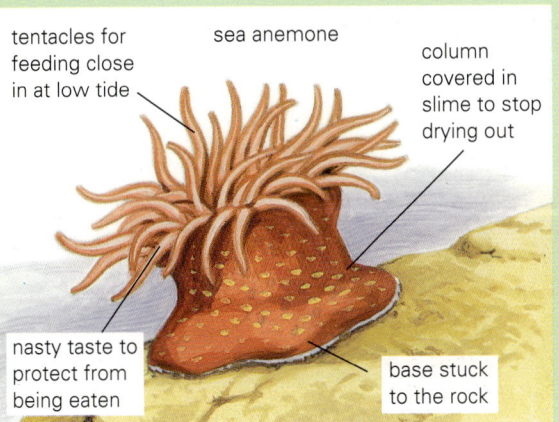

sea anemone
- tentacles for feeding close in at low tide
- column covered in slime to stop drying out
- nasty taste to protect from being eaten
- base stuck to the rock

KEY IDEAS

The environment is the living conditions of an organism.

The population is the number of one type of organism which lives in a habitat.

The community is made up of all the organisms which live in one habitat.

1.4 Some other interesting habitats

Organisms are found all over the world. Many habitats have very different environments. What are these environments like? How are the organisms which live there adapted to them?

The following photographs show some organisms living in four habitats from all over the world. The organisms survive because they are well adapted to their environment.

The desert

Desert plants live in an extremely dry environment so they have to be well adapted for saving water. It is also very hot during the day, and very cold at night.

If you look carefully at the cacti in the photograph of the desert, you can see that they have very fat stems, which is where they store water. They also have very waxy skins, which stops water leaving the cacti through their skins.

Some desert plants.

The Antarctic

In the Antarctic the air temperature is nearly always below freezing, even in the summer. In the winter there is very little light.

Penguins in the Antarctic build up thick layers of fat under their skin. This keeps them so warm that they don't even mind swimming in the freezing water to hunt for fish.

Penguins living in the Antarctic.

The tropical rain forest

In the tropical rain forest the environment is perfect for fast growth. The temperature is warm and there is plenty of moisture.

Plants growing in the tropical rain forest are adapted to grow very fast and produce large leaves to outshade other plants.

Tropical rain forest in Costa Rica.

Deciduous woodland

Deciduous trees loose their leaves in winter. Deciduous woodland is very common in the UK. The organisms which live in this environment will have to deal with warm summers and cold winters. There is usually plenty of water in the UK.

The trees in the deciduous woodland loose their leaves in winter when the days become shorter, and there is less sunshine.

The community of a particular habitat will be made up of organisms which are specially adapted, or suited, for that particular environment.

Deciduous woodland in Kent.

QUESTIONS

1. Write down the names of four different habitats.
2. This stick insect lives in a privet bush. How is it adapted to surviving here?

3. How are these organisms specially adapted to living in their environment:
   a trees in deciduous woodland
   b penguins in the Antarctic?
4. What features do cacti have that help them survive dry conditions?

KEY IDEAS

Every habitat has its own set of living conditions, or environment.

Organisms which live in a habitat will only survive and grow if they are well adapted to their environment.

CHAPTER 2: FEEDING RELATIONSHIPS

2.1 Who eats who in the habitat?

The Sun is the power station for the Earth. All energy for life on Earth comes from the Sun. We can feel the heat energy from the Sun but we can't use it in that form to grow. How is the Sun's energy changed into a form which living things can use?

Energy for all life comes from the Sun. It is trapped by plants which use it to make their own food. It passes from one organism to the next along what is called a **food chain**.

Producers and consumers

Every organism lives alongside many other kinds of organisms. In any habitat there will be organisms which can make their own food. These are called **producers**. There will also be organisms which can't make their own food but eat other organisms. These are called **consumers**. You can see the relationship between producers and consumers in the food chain shown in the diagram.

All green plants are producers because they make their own food using sunlight for energy, water and carbon dioxide. This way of producing food is called **photosynthesis** (see 9.1). In photosynthesis, the Sun's energy is changed into a form which can be used by living organisms.

Animals which eat green plants, like rabbits which nibble grass, are called **primary consumers**. Another name for these organisms is **herbivores** which means 'eating grass'. Animals which eat primary consumers, like foxes which eat rabbits, are called **secondary consumers**. Another name for these organisms is **carnivores** which means 'eating meat'. We can show the relationship between grass, rabbits and foxes like this:

grass ⟶ rabbits ⟶ fox

The grass uses the Sun to make its own food. The rabbits eat the grass and the fox eats the rabbit.

This is a food chain. You can find some more examples of food chains in the rock pool you studied earlier. The diagram here shows four organisms found in a rock pool and their feeding relationships.

The food chain for these would be:

seaweed ⟶ limpet ⟶ crab ⟶ herring gull

This food chain has four links. The herring gull is called the **tertiary consumer**, or top carnivore because it is found at the end of the food chain, and nothing eats it.

Food chain in a rock pool.

There are not normally more than five links in a food chain. Another food chain from the rock pool could be:

plants ⟶ mussels ⟶ starfish ⟶ herring gull

The herring gull is also the top carnivore of this food chain.

Carnivores at work

Carnivores are adapted to feeding on the different organisms in their particular environment. Starfish are carnivores and they have suckers under their arms. They attach themselves on to either side of the mussel and pull the shell open.

The young form of the great diving beetle is a carnivore found in ponds. It sinks its teeth into small live animals like tadpoles and sucks out the juices. It can get through as many as 20 tadpoles in an hour.

A starfish prises open the mussel to feed on it.

The young form of the great diving beetle feeding on a tadpole.

QUESTIONS

1 Look at the organisms in the picture of a food chain in a rock pool.
   Which is:
   a the producer
   b the primary consumer
   c the secondary consumer
   d a herbivore
   e a carnivore?

2 What is photosynthesis?

3 Explain how a carnivore, like a dog, gets the energy it needs to live.

KEY IDEAS

All green plants are producers. They make their own food.

Primary consumers feed on producers. They are called herbivores.

Secondary consumers feed on primary consumers. They are called carnivores.

2.2 Wonderful webs

Nearly all organisms eat quite a variety of foods. Humans eat plants, herbivores and carnivores. How does this fit in with the food chain idea?

Joining up food chains

You have looked at several food chains, including two from the rock pool you studied in 1.2. But the story is not quite as simple as that. The herring gull is the top carnivore for *two* food chains in the rock pool. Many of the organisms growing there either feed on several different species, or are eaten by several different species, *or both*. For example, limpets and mullet both feed on seaweed, while starfish and crabs both eat mussels.

Building a food web

Consumers usually have several different sources of food. Biologists can study a habitat to find out who feeds on what. Once they have discovered this by careful observation, they can build a diagram to show the pattern. They simply draw arrows from the food organism to the feeding organism. Because some of the lines cross over each other, you end up with something that looks rather like a spider's web. So it is called a **food web**.

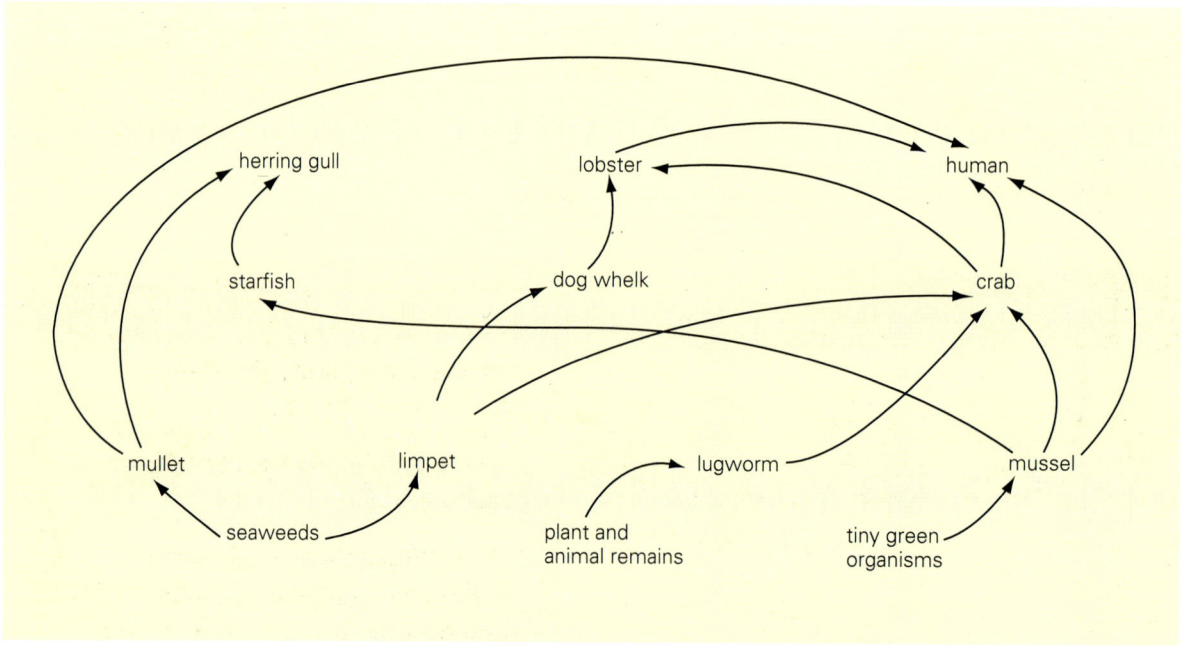

A food web showing the feeding patterns of some of the organisms which live in rock pools.

Who goes where?

If you look at the food web carefully, you can see that the producers (tiny green organisms and seaweed) are found at the bottom of the web. The next layer up are those organisms which feed on the producers. They are the primary consumers, or herbivores. Above them are the secondary consumers, or carnivores. The tertiary consumers are at the top. Some organisms can be at different levels in the food web. Humans eat lobsters, crabs, mullet and even seaweed, which are all at different levels of the food web. You can see that herring gulls also eat organisms from different levels of the food web.

When animals and plants die, their bodies still contain lots of food. Some organisms feed on their remains. So dead animals and plants in a community can be recycled.

A food web showing the feeding relationships in a woodland.

QUESTIONS

1. Look at the rock pool food web. Name:
   a two primary consumers
   b two secondary consumers.
2. Draw out two food chains you can see in the woodland food web.
3. Why must every food chain start with a green plant?

KEY IDEAS

In every community there are several food chains.

The food chains link up to form a food web.

A food web shows the feeding relationships in the community more accurately than a food chain.

2.3 Ecological pyramids

A cow will eat many times its own body mass of grass during its lifetime. Why does it need to eat so much grass? What does it use the grass for?

Organisms use up energy for lots of activities like growing, reproducing, moving, heating their bodies and repairing damage to themselves. As you move along the food chain, fewer and fewer organisms can survive as the number of organisms which can be supported gets smaller and smaller.

Pyramid of numbers

The diagram shows a food chain with four links.

leaves ⟶ caterpillars ⟶ shrews ⟶ hawk

As we move along the food chain, the number of organisms at each stage is going down. Why can't 100 caterpillars support 100 shrews or 10 shrews support 10 hawks? The organisms at each stage use up energy while they are living, so less and less energy is passed on to the next stage of the food chain.

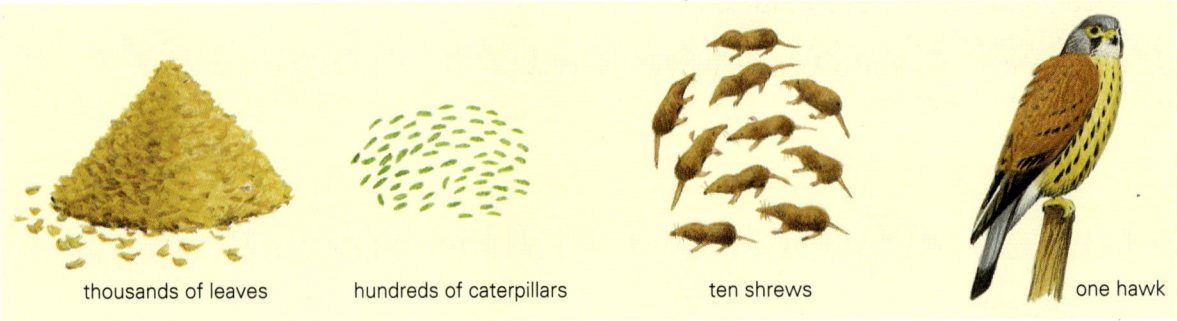

thousands of leaves   hundreds of caterpillars   ten shrews   one hawk

You can show up the number of organisms at each stage of the food chain in a diagram like the one shown here. The length of each bar depends on the number of organisms. Notice that the shape of the diagram is like a pyramid. This is why it is called a **pyramid of numbers**.

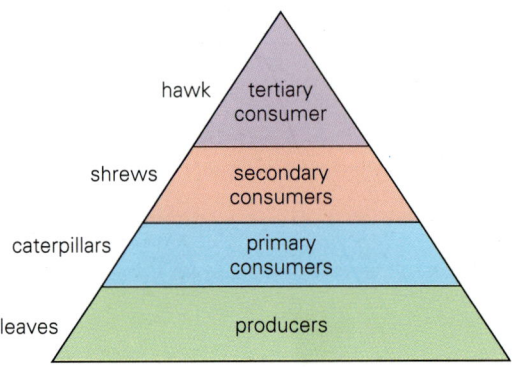

At each level of the food chain, the number of organisms gets smaller. The result is a pyramid of numbers.

But sometimes when you draw food chains as pyramids of numbers you get something which doesn't look very much like a pyramid.

Pyramid of biomass

The oak tree is a very big producer with thousands of leaves. It can support many caterpillars. But the fleas in the wheat pyramid are very tiny. One cat can support many fleas, as most cat owners have seen at one time or another. So the pyramid of numbers does not always show what is actually happening – that energy is lost from each level in the food chain. A better way of showing this would be to measure the mass of all the organisms in each level of the food chain, and then to plot a horizontal bar chart of the results.

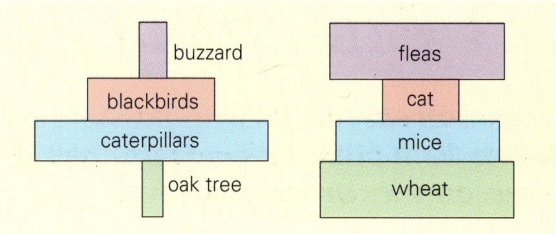

These do not look like pyramids. Can you think why not?

What happens if we use the mass of the organisms? The result is a pyramid shape again. This kind of pyramid is called a **pyramid of biomass** (the actual amount of living matter) because we have measured the biological mass of the organisms. The pyramid of biomass is often a better way of showing what happens in a food chain than the pyramid of numbers.

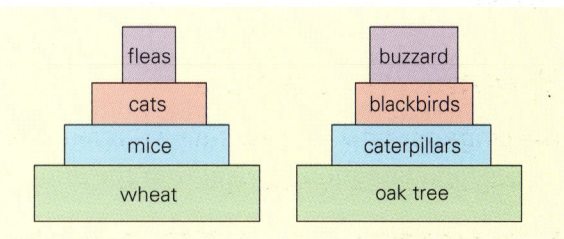

Pyramids of biomass for wheat and oak tree examples.

QUESTIONS

1. As you move along a food chain, what happens to the number of organisms which can be supported?
2. What is a pyramid of numbers?
3. **a** The oak tree pyramid of numbers does not look like a pyramid shape. Why is this?
   b The wheat pyramid of numbers does not look like a pyramid shape. Why is this?
4. What is a pyramid of biomass?

KEY IDEAS

Pyramids of number tell us how many individual organisms are found at each link of the food chain.

Pyramids of biomass tell us the total mass of the organism found at each link of the food chain.

CHAPTER 3: SURVIVING THE ENVIRONMENT

3.1 Adaptation on a rocky seashore

Organisms are faced with possible death each day. Death from predators or from their environment. How can they increase their chances of surviving?

In order to survive and grow, an organism must be well adapted to the environment around it. The rocky seashore has some difficult living conditions. The tide goes out twice each day. The organisms that live there are in danger of drying out, or overheating, and are easy targets for consumers. When the tide comes in the waves batter the organisms and could wash them away from their habitat. So you can see that it is not just any organism that can survive these conditions.

You have seen that there are many different animal and plant populations in the rocky seashore community. Each of these must have successful adaptations to deal with the difficult conditions described above.

The bladder wrack

The bladder wrack is a brown seaweed which is often found in rock pools. It is made up of a body with branched, flat fronds which are like leaves. At the end of the short stalk there is a holdfast which keeps the seaweed in place on the rocks and stops it being washed away. On its fronds are air filled sacs which are called bladders. These help the seaweed to float at the surface of the sea so that it can get as much light as possible to make its food.

The bladder wrack is floppy and slimy. These two adaptations protect it from the waves. It can bend easily in the water and the slimy surface stops it tearing as it crashes against the rocks. The slimy surface also protects the bladder wrack from drying out, although it is able to lose quite a lot of water before it dies. You can see that the bladder wrack is very well adapted for life in rock pools.

The bladder wrack.

Limpets

Limpets are also well adapted to life in rock pools. They have a hard shell which they stick firmly to the rock surface when the tide goes out. Their tough shells protect them from high and low temperatures, drying out at low tide, the action of the crashing waves as the tide is coming in, and any hungry carnivores.

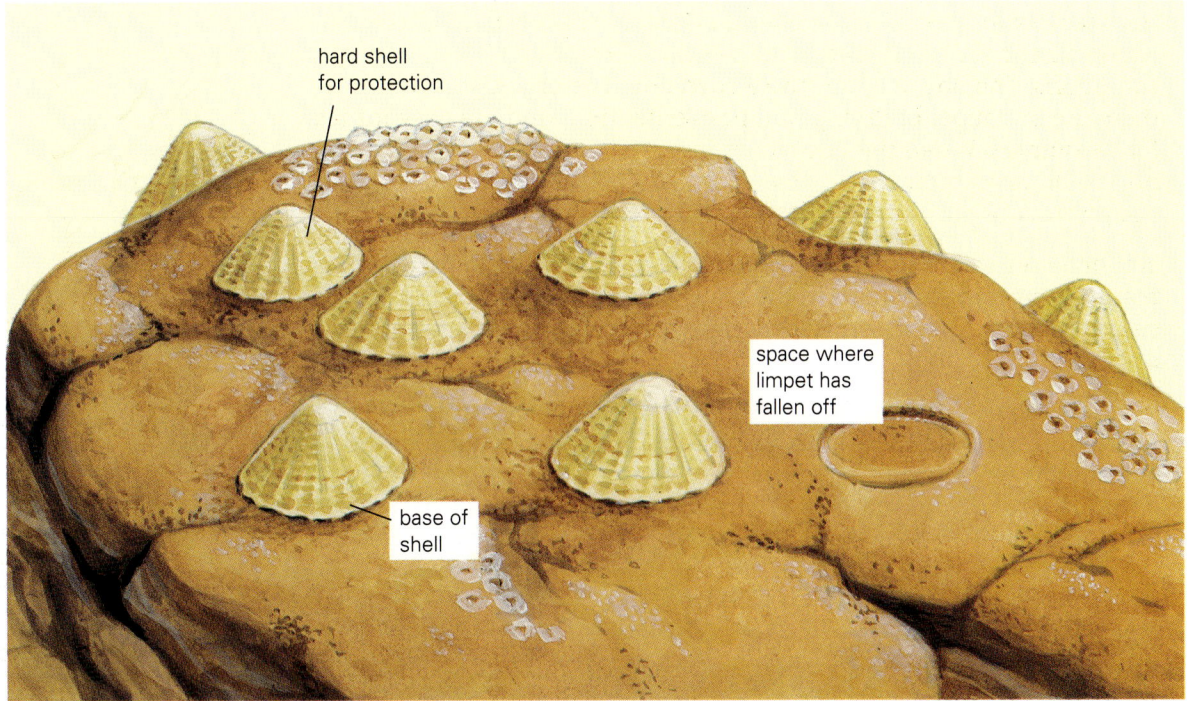

Limpets.

QUESTIONS

1. Give three environmental factors which organisms on the rocky shore must be adapted to.
2. Describe three ways in which bladder wracks are adapted to living in rock pools.
3. Limpets have a tough shell. Give three reasons why this shell makes them well adapted to living in rock pools.
4. Why is the rock pool a difficult habitat to survive in?

KEY IDEAS

All organisms in a community must be adapted to their environment in order to survive.

The environmental factors they must be adapted to include temperature, amount of light and amount of water.

3.2 In the Arctic and the desert

Camels and cacti are very different organisms, but they both have to survive the same harsh environmental condition – they live in habitats where there is very little water. How do they manage to do this?

In the Arctic the temperatures are always low, though they drop even further in winter. In the desert they are high in the day-time, but may drop at night. The amount of light is also different in these two habitats. In the Arctic in December there is practically no light all day, while in June there is daylight for 24 hours. Some organisms visit in the summer but travel, or **migrate**, south in the winter in order to escape the difficult living conditions. The desert is less affected by the seasons, and there is plenty of light for photosynthesis.

Water is a problem in both habitats. In the desert there simply isn't much rain and the very hot conditions mean that any water evaporates quickly. Interestingly, water is also a problem in the Arctic because most of it is frozen, particularly inland. So the Arctic could be seen as a frozen desert.

Some well-adapted organisms

Camels are very well adapted to living in the desert.

Cacti are desert plants with swollen stems in which they can store water. Their outer surface is waterproof and their leaves are small so there is less area from which to lose water.

- thick fur to keep the bear warm
- The Artic Polar bear is white so it is well camouflaged and blends in to the background. Polar bears are carnivores and they can hunt more easily because of this camouflage.
- small ears to prevent heat loss
- powerful leg muscles for digging in the snow
- large, strong paws for grabbing fish

The Arctic polar bear.

Good conditions for growth

In the desert and the Arctic, conditions are extreme. Few organisms are well enough adapted to survive there, so the total number of different species is quite low. In the tropical rain forest, conditions are very good for growth. The temperatures are warm, there is plenty of water, the light is strong. Here there are huge numbers of different species. In fact, over 600 new species of beetle have been discovered living in just one type of tree that grows in the rain forest in Costa Rica.

QUESTIONS

1. Name a plant that is successful in hot, dry places.
2. Why are polar bears successful in the Arctic?
3. Why are there so many more species in the rain forest than in the desert?
4. Think of an organism you haven't read about on these pages, and explain how it is adapted to its living conditions.

KEY IDEAS

In the desert and the Arctic, temperature, light and water are very important factors and organisms living there must be well adapted to them.

Some birds visit the Arctic during the summer months and migrate south when the temperatures drop.

3.3 Competing with your neighbours

Cane toads were introduced into Australia in 1935. They began to breed so fast that they outnumbered the native Australian toads. Why did this happen?

In sport, groups of people compete in order to win a game. A similar sort of thing happens in the living world. Organisms compete with each other for things like space to live in, food and water, and light for plants. There is **competition** between the organisms.

Competing plants

Gardeners spend a lot of time weeding their flower beds. This is because they want to give the plants they have planted enough space to grow well. Plants need water and minerals, or **nutrients**, from the soil. They also need plenty of light. The trouble is that weeds often grow very fast. Their roots spread out quickly to take in water and minerals and they grow tall so that they can get more light. They are good at competing with the gardener's plants, and they tend to take over if no weeding is done.

These weeds compete well with the garden plants!

Rhododendrons have not always grown in the UK, they are not native. They were brought from abroad by travellers in the last century. They compete very well with many species in the environment because their roots are wide spreading and they give out a poison which kills other plants. Rhododendrons are doing so well in the wild that they are becoming a pest.

One of our own plants, native in the UK, is the bluebell. This plant can grow in the shade of trees. Most plants are not able to survive in woods because they would not get enough light. This is why there is usually some space on the floor of woods. The bluebell grows fast and flowers in the spring before the leaves have grown on the trees to make shade.

These rhododendrons may look pretty but they are taking the place of many other species in the UK.

Bluebells growing on the floor of a deciduous wood.

Competing animals

Animals of different species can also compete for food. Often different animals feed on the same food. We can see in the rock pool food web that crabs and starfish both feed on mussels (see 2.2). The crabs and the starfish are in competition for the mussels, and the animal that competes best will grow faster and reproduce faster. Animals also compete for territory, shelter and nesting sites.

In Australia cane toads compete well against native animals because cane toads breed quickly in any warm, wet environment, producing large numbers of eggs. Their skin contains poison, so they have very few predators.

QUESTIONS

1. Write down the sort of things that animals and plants compete for.
2. Why is the rhododendron particularly good at competing?
3. Explain why bluebells can live in woodland where it is too shady for many other plants to grow.

KEY IDEAS

Organisms of different species compete with each other.

Plants compete for space, light, water and nutrients.

Animals compete for space, food and water.

3.4 Only the best survive

Each poppy produces tens of thousands of seeds every time it reproduces. What happens to all these seeds? Why don't they all grow into mature poppies?

In 3.3 you looked at competition between organisms of different species. But members of the same species also compete. For example, if you were to plant ten acorns in a pot of earth, they might all **germinate**, that is begin to grow into plants. But they would not all grow to be mature oak trees. The acorn seedlings compete with each other for water and light and nutrients from the soil. The seedling which grows the fastest will shade the other plants and will survive while the others die out.

In nature, plants and animals often produce more offspring than their habitat can support. Only some of the offspring will survive because there simply isn't enough food, water and space for all of them to grow properly. This means that there is competition and only those plants or animals which are best adapted will survive and reproduce.

One seedling is outcompeting the others.

The diagram shows two cacti living near each other in the desert during the dry season. The cactus with the long roots will be able to reach down to the water and survive. It will reproduce to make more cacti with long roots. The cactus with short roots will die.

These cacti are fighting for survival in the desert.

Survival of the fittest

Competition between members of the same species leads to the best adapted members surviving while the rest die out. Since the best adapted will be the only ones to reproduce, the next generation will also have the good adaptations. This process is called the 'survival of the fittest'.

Another example of 'survival of the fittest' can be seen in moths. One species of peppered moth exists in two forms – a sooty one and a pale one. In the countryside the bark of the trees is pale brown. Here the pale moths can't be seen by birds which feed on them. But the sooty ones can. So the sooty ones are eaten and their population goes down. In industrial areas where the bark of trees is black, the opposite happens. There the pale moths can be seen, and they are the ones that are eaten.

The pale moth is more likely to be eaten.

QUESTIONS

1. What do acorn seedlings compete with each other for?
2. Explain what feature of a cactus will help it reach water in the dry season in the desert.
3. Which form of peppered moth will survive best on a tree in the countryside? Explain why.

KEY IDEAS

Competition happens between members of the same species.

The best adapted, or fittest, members of the species survive while the rest die out.

3.5 Predators and prey

The foxes in a habitat will never eat all the rabbits in that habitat. Why is this? What happens to the numbers of foxes when the numbers of rabbits gets very low?

Predators are animals that catch and kill other animals called **prey**. So predators will have an effect on the population of the prey. But the number of prey will also have an effect on the population of the predators because if there are not enough prey, then some of the predators will starve and die.

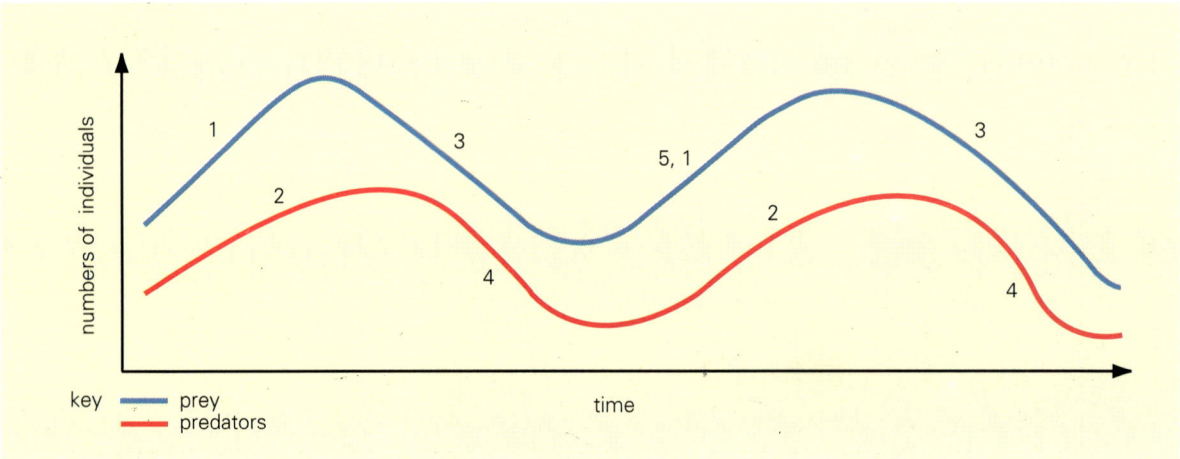

This graph shows the cycle of numbers of predators and prey.

The cycle of predators and prey

As you read through 1 to 5 below, follow the numbers on the graph above.

1 If there is plenty of food, the prey will reproduce and their numbers will go up.

2 Now there are more prey for the predators to feed on. So the predators will grow and reproduce and their numbers will increase.

3 This means that there are more predators around, so the amount of prey eaten will increase. The numbers of prey will therefore go down.

4 Now there is less food for the predators, so many predators starve to death.

5 With fewer predators around to eat them, the numbers of prey increase again and the whole cycle begins again.

The lynx and the snowshoe hare are examples of organisms which follow the cycle of predator and prey which is outlined opposite. With predators who feed on many different kinds of prey, the pattern would not be so obvious.

Predators who become too good at catching their prey may make their prey numbers so low that they end up starving.

The snowshoe hare and the lynx.

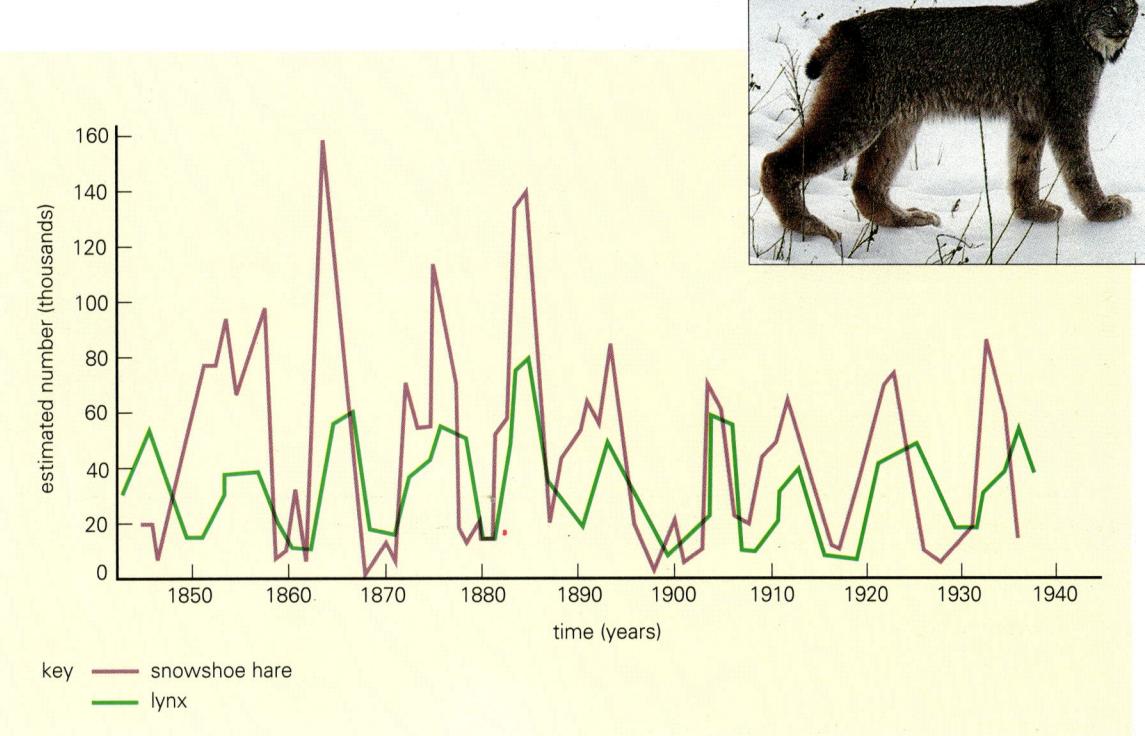

The graph shows the cycle of predator/prey for the lynx and the snowshoe hare.

QUESTIONS

1. What is the name for animals that catch and kill other animals?
2. What are prey?
3. Describe what happens to the population of predators if there are:
   a lots of prey
   b very few prey.

KEY IDEAS

In a cycle of predator/prey, the population of a particular species goes up or down, depending on the amount of prey.

3.6 Limits on population growth

If all the offspring of one female greenfly survived and reproduced, she could be the ancestor of 600 000 000 000 greenfly in one year. Why isn't the world covered with greenfly?

The greenfly population on roses can increase very quickly under the right conditions.

Birth rates and death rates

The size of a population depends on the birth rate and the death rate. The birth rate of greenfly is enormous, but so is their death rate. Many greenfly are eaten by ladybirds and birds, or sprayed by gardeners. Their birth rate and death rate is about the same, so the population of greenfly stays about the same.

Population size is affected by other things too. The amount of food is very important. If there isn't enough food to support the offspring, many will starve. In crowded conditions, disease spreads quickly, so large populations may mean deaths from disease. And enough space to live is also important. If there isn't enough space on the rock for a limpet to stick itself down, it will be washed out to sea.

Nearly always, the population of an organism is affected by many factors working together. The population of rabbits in a habitat will depend partly on the number of foxes around to eat them. But food, space for burrows, and infection with a disease called myxomatosis are all also important for keeping population numbers down, or controlling the population.

The human population

The rabbit population shown in graph **A** has increased quickly, but then it levels off because of the factors affecting death rate you have read about. But the pattern for the human population in graph **B** is different.

The human population is increasing very quickly because the human death rate has decreased. The number of people dying from disease is much smaller than it used to be because of better hygiene in our water supply, sewage and food handling.

Children are vaccinated against diseases like polio and meningitis. The discovery of antibiotics means that most diseases caused by bacteria can be treated.

As the human population increases more land must be taken for farming to produce extra food. In this way wild habitat is destroyed.

In order to control the population increase, we must decrease the birth rate. Efforts are being made to educate people about family planning. If we don't control our population, famine, war or disease may increase the death rate in the future.

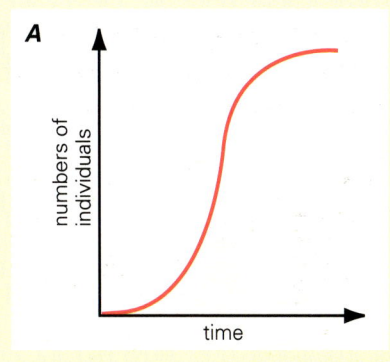

A The normal pattern for a population. It levels off because of the environmental factors you have been looking at.

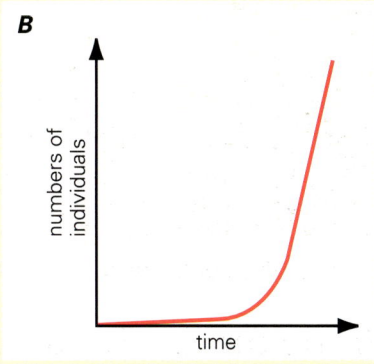

B The increase of the human population on Earth.

QUESTIONS

1. What happens to many greenfly to control their population?
2. What factors would make the rabbit population:
   a increase
   b decrease?
3. Give three reasons why the human death rate has decreased in Europe in the past 200 years?

KEY IDEAS

The size of a population depends on the birth rate and the death rate.

The size of animal and plant populations are affected by many factors.

These factors include food, space, disease and predators.

CHAPTER 4: RECYCLING LIVING THINGS

4.1 Decomposers and decay

Have you ever wondered what happens to living things when they die? They must be broken down and recycled.

When plants grow, they take in water from the soil, carbon dioxide from the air and they use the Sun's energy to make food. Plants also take in chemicals from the soil. These chemicals become part of the plant's body. If the plant is eaten, the chemicals are passed on to a herbivore. If the herbivore is eaten, they are passed on to a carnivore. In this way, chemicals make up parts of the bodies of the plants and animals in the food chain. These plants and animals then die.

Decomposers

If this were the whole story, two things would happen. First, the chemicals in the soil would run out and second, the world would be covered in heaps of dead organisms. Fortunately, in every food web there are organisms called **decomposers**. These feed on the dead organisms and break them down into chemicals again. The chemicals go back into the soil and the whole cycle begins again. We say that the plants and animals have decomposed. The two most important groups of decomposers are **fungi** and **bacteria**, which are both microbes.

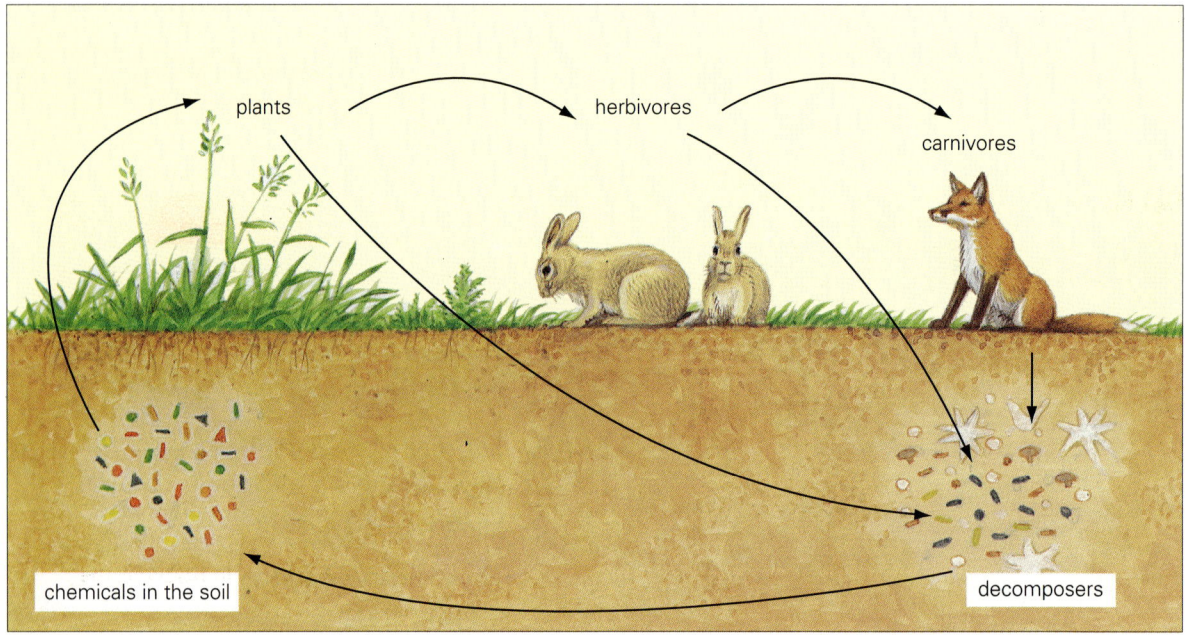

Dead organisms are decomposed.

Decomposition in a stable community

In a stable community, the amount of chemicals taken from the soil is the same as the amount of chemicals returned to the soil. The process of decomposition happens very fast. Leaves which fall from trees in the autumn will have decomposed by the following summer.

These strawberries are being decomposed by bacteria and fungi.

All these leaves will decompose in a few months.

QUESTIONS

1. What do plants need from their environment in order to grow?
2. What happens to the dead bodies of plants and animals?
3. Name the two most important groups of decomposers.
4. Explain why we are not knee deep in dead organisms.

KEY IDEAS

Living things remove chemicals from the soil which are passed along the food chain.

Dead organisms are broken down by decomposers, like bacteria and fungi, in a process called decomposition.

The chemicals from the bodies of dead organisms are returned to the soil. They are recycled.

4.2 Microbes at work

If you leave food in a warm, moist place it soon begins to break down into a smelly liquid. What kind of organisms are breaking the food down? Why doesn't food break down quickly when you put it into a fridge?

The two main groups of decomposers are the fungi and bacteria. These sorts of organisms are called **microbes**, which means 'small life'. Their **spores**, from which they grow, are so tiny that they float around in the air. After an animal or plant dies, it isn't long before spores land on it and begin to grow into mature bacteria and fungi. Then they spread right through the dead organism. A teaspoon of rotting plant material can contain over 1 000 000 000 (one thousand million) bacteria.

Mummies

Like any organism, bacteria and fungi need moisture and warmth in order to feed and grow. Most of them also need oxygen. Moisture is needed for the spores to develop into fungi or bacteria. A dead body which is kept completely dry will not decompose. The ancient Egyptians used to preserve the bodies of their kings in this way. Keeping them completely dry meant that the bodies would shrivel up. The process is called mummification.

Mammoths

Microbes multiply much more quickly in warm conditions, and so decomposition happens fastest in the warmth. We keep food in fridges to slow down decomposition by microbes. If the temperature is well below freezing, no decomposition will happen at all. The bodies of mammoths which died in Siberia thousands of years ago have been dug up with their flesh preserved and so fresh that the local people cooked mammoth steaks!

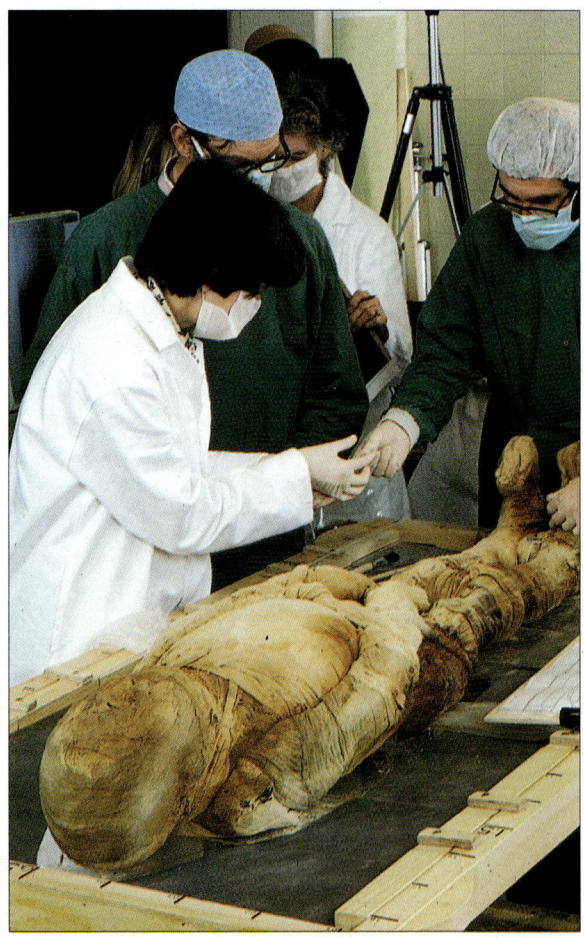

Removing the wrapping from a mummy shows the body has not decomposed.

Uses of microbes

Humans have found ways of using microbes to break down their wastes. Microbes are very important in sewage works. Bacteria break the sewage down into simpler chemicals. The sewage is then treated before it can be put back into the environment.

Gardeners use microbes to break down their garden waste. The waste is piled on to a compost heap. The compost heap is raised on bricks so that air can circulate under and through it, and the microbes have plenty of oxygen. The compost heap must be quite small because the activity of the microbes makes heat. In a large compost heap the temperatures can get so high that the microbes are killed. The decayed plant material is full of chemicals and can be used by the gardener as fertiliser.

A compost heap.

QUESTIONS

1. What conditions help microbes to decompose materials quickly?
2. Explain how compost heaps are built to make them work efficiently.
3. Explain:
   a what mummification is
   b how mummification helps preserve dead bodies.

KEY IDEAS

Microbes decompose materials faster in warm, moist conditions. Most need oxygen too.

People use microbes to break down sewage and garden waste.

4.3 The carbon cycle

Plants all over the world are taking in carbon as carbon dioxide during photosynthesis. Why doesn't the air run out of carbon dioxide after a time?

Carbon from carbon dioxide

You have seen how the chemicals that make up the bodies of living things travel from the soil to living things and back to the soil again. One very important chemical is **carbon**. The bodies of all living things contain carbon. Carbon comes from carbon dioxide in the air. Plants take in carbon dioxide and use some of the carbon from it during photosynthesis to make large chemicals for growth. These body-building chemicals are added to the body of the plant as it grows.

When plants respire, they return some of the carbon back to the air as carbon dioxide. If a herbivore eats the plant, some of the carbon, is used to build the herbivore's body. As the herbivore breathes, it also releases some of the carbon back into the atmosphere as carbon dioxide.

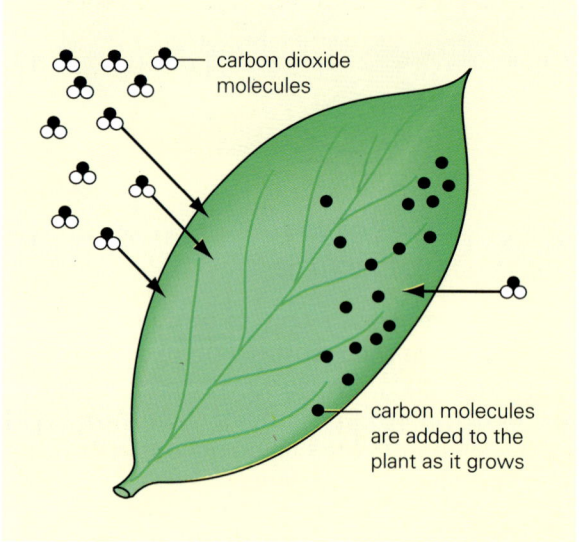

The plant is taking in carbon dioxide during photosynthesis and using carbon to make large chemicals for growth.

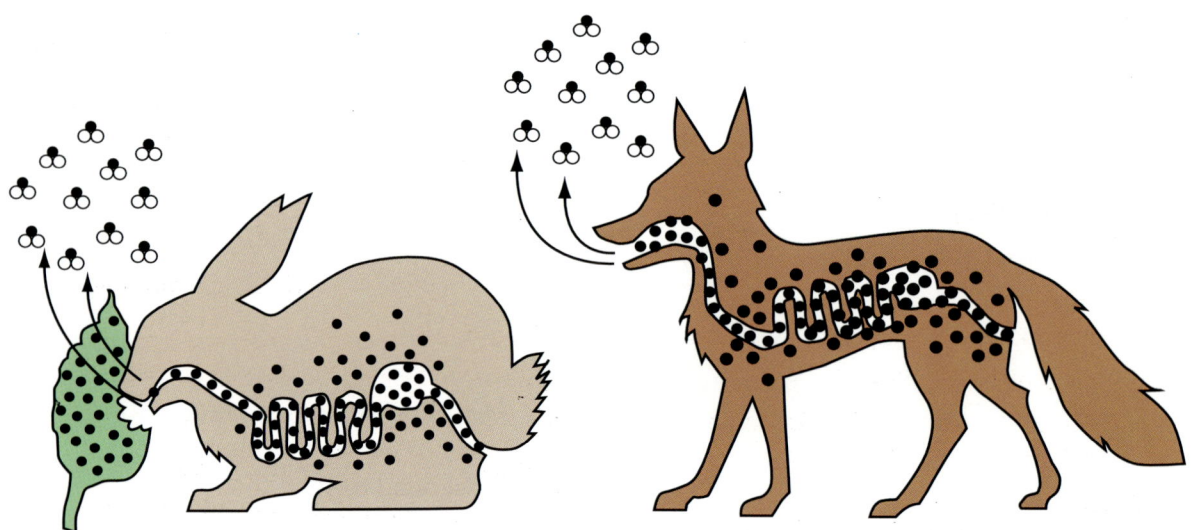

As the rabbit nibbles the grass, it takes in the carbon. It uses carbon for growth. It breathes out carbon dioxide.

If the fox eats the rabbit, the carbon is passed to the fox. Some carbon is used for growth, some is breathed out as carbon dioxide.

Coal

When plants and animals die, microbes decompose their bodies. These microbes give out carbon dioxide when they respire. Over many thousands of years, the carbon in plant materials in the soil was turned into coal. This coal has been mined and is burned in factories. When the coal burns, the carbon in it is changed into carbon dioxide which returns to the air. Other fuels, like gas, oil or petrol also release carbon dioxide when they are burnt.

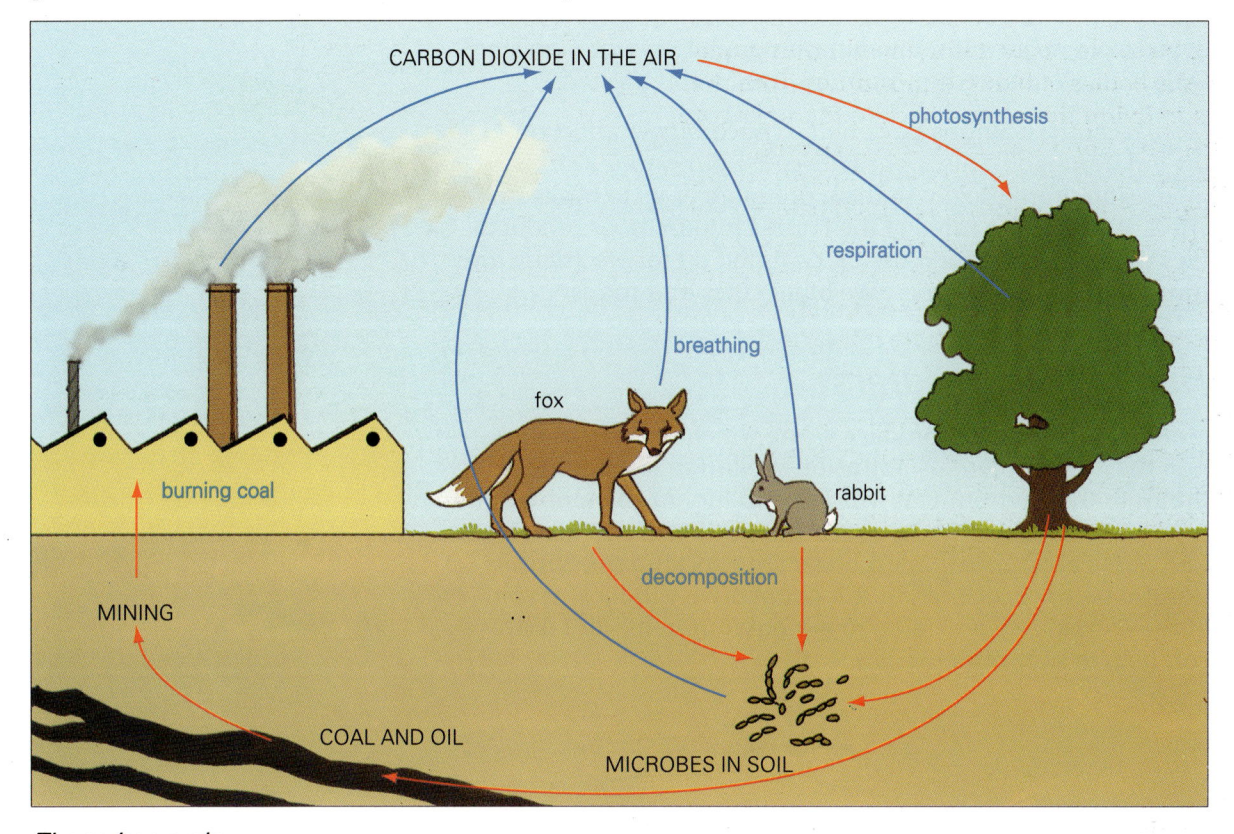

The carbon cycle.

QUESTIONS

1. In what chemical do we find carbon in the air?
2. How do plants use the carbon they take in during photosynthesis?
3. How does the carbon in dead animals and plants get back into the air?
4. What do you think would happen if the carbon was not recycled by microbes?

KEY IDEAS

Carbon comes from carbon dioxide in the air.

Carbon dioxide is taken in by the plant during photosynthesis.

Carbon dioxide returns to the air during breathing and respiration by living organisms and during the burning of coal.

CHAPTER 5: INTERFERING WITH THE BALANCE OF LIFE

5.1 *Growing beyond our limits*

There are 5 300 000 000 people in the world today, and every one of them adds waste to the environment in one way or another. What effect is all this having on the environment? What can we do to reduce the effect?

Humans have been changing the environment for thousands of years. To begin with, the human population was very small. Only the few areas where humans lived were affected.

More recently, humans have had a much bigger effect on the environment. This is partly because our population is increasing dramatically so there are more of us to make an effect. Also, we use more of the Earth's resources, or products. We cut down forests and use up coal and oil for electricity and running cars and factories. We build cities and roads.

Humans as polluters

Many of our activities produce waste which often goes back into the environment as **pollution**. Pollution is when we add things to the environment which harm life. At the moment the future is not looking good, as our population is still growing so fast. Some ecologists think that we are wrecking the Earth's natural balance for ever. In this chapter we will look at some of the damage we are doing to our environment, and how we can help to save our environment.

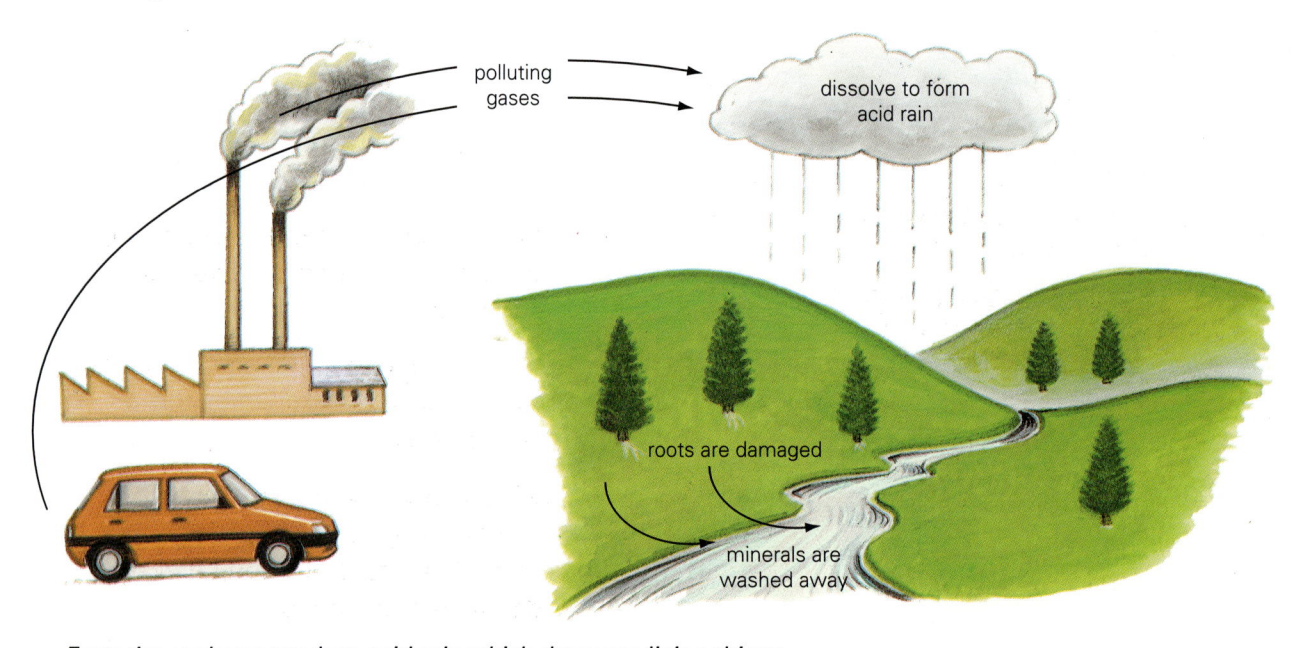

Factories and cars produce acid rain which damages living things.

Acid rain

When fuel, like oil, petrol, coal and gas is burned in power stations, factories and motor vehicles, smoke and gases are given off. Some of the gases are carbon dioxide, sulphur dioxide and nitrogen oxide. All these gases are **acidic**. This means that when they dissolve in water, they produce acids. As the gases rise up into the air, they meet water vapour and they dissolve to form acid rain. Acid rain falls on to soil and affects the minerals in the soil. The roots of plants are damaged. Important minerals dissolve because of the acid and they are washed away. The plants die from diseased roots and not enough minerals.

In order to stop the problems of acid rain, we must cut down the amounts of acidic gases we release into the air. The number of coal burning power stations is falling and more are using gas instead, which produces less sulphur dioxide.

These trees have been damaged by acid rain.

QUESTIONS

1. In which ways are we using up more of the Earth's resources?
2. Name three gases which are given off when we burn oil, petrol, gas and coal.
3. Describe how these gases can damage plants.

KEY IDEAS

With a growing human population, our effect on the environment is increasing.

We are using up the Earth's natural resources, like coal, oil and space very quickly.

We are polluting the environment with acidic gases from factories and cars. These make acid rain which damages living things.

5.2 The ozone layer and skin cancer

If you sunbathe without using protective sun cream, you can get very badly sunburned. Later in life, this can lead to skin cancer. What causes sunburn? Why is sunburn becoming more common?

The importance of ozone

About 25 to 30 km above the surface of the Earth, there is a layer of a gas called **ozone**. This layer is about 5 km thick and surrounds the whole Earth. It stops some of the Sun's harmful **ultraviolet** rays of light from reaching the Earth. These ultraviolet rays cause skin cancer if the skin is exposed to them for a long time. So the ozone layer is very important to humans.

Scientists believe that the ozone layer is getting thinner. The thinner it gets, the more ultraviolet rays reach the Earth, and the more dangerous it is for our skin, as well as our crops.

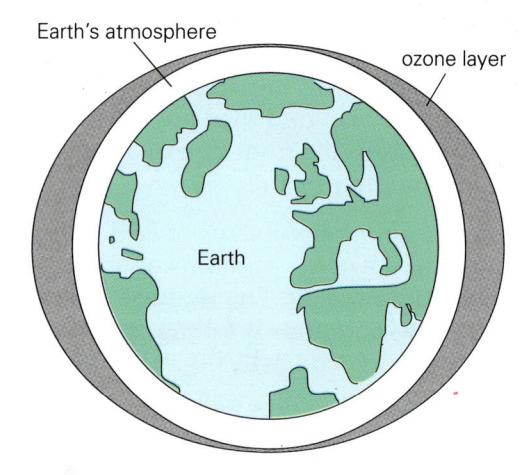

The ozone layer is thicker at the equator and thinner at the poles.

Ultraviolet rays cause sunburn unless you use protective sun cream.

CFCs

We have discovered that ozone is broken down by **chlorofluorocarbons**, or **CFCs**. These chemicals are used in fridges, air conditioning and aerosol sprays. They are also found in certain types of plastic packaging. They are released into the air from disused fridges when they are destroyed or from aerosols when they are sprayed. Gradually they find their way up to the ozone layer. In the ozone layer, the CFCs are broken down by the ultraviolet light into chlorine and other gases. The chlorine breaks down the ozone so there is less ozone in the ozone layer.

Thinning of the ozone

We can see from satellite pictures that the areas over the North and South Poles have very little ozone in the air. This means that more ultraviolet light can reach the Earth's surface to harm our skin and to damage crops.

It is clear that we must stop using CFCs so that we can prevent further thinning of the ozone layer. We can all help by buying only aerosol cans labelled 'ozone friendly'. But even if CFCs were totally banned today, it would take about 100 years to replace the ozone that has already been broken down.

An 'ozone friendly' label on an aerosol means that it does not contain CFCs.

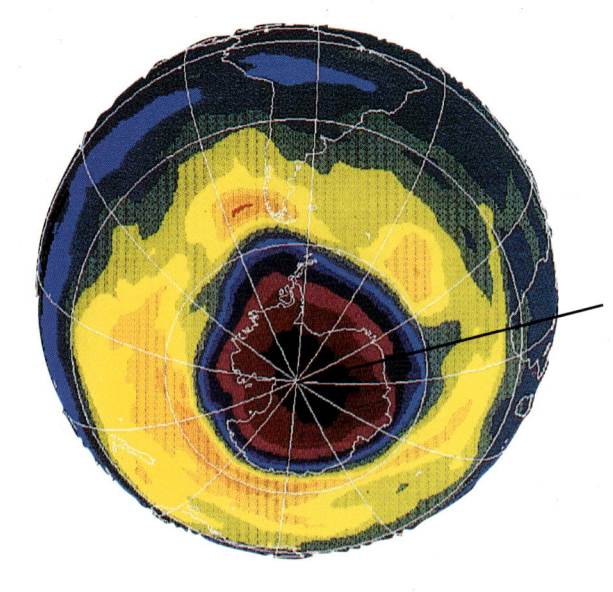

South Pole; the ozone layer is thinnest here

Is the ozone layer getting thinner? Many scientists believe that it is.

QUESTIONS

1. What are the Sun's harmful rays called?
2. What does ozone do to ultraviolet rays?
3. Name two products that use CFCs.
4. Predict what could happen if the ozone layer gets thinner.

KEY IDEAS

The ozone layer absorbs the Sun's harmful ultraviolet rays.

CFCs, which are used in aerosols and fridges, break down ozone.

With less ozone, more ultraviolet rays reach the Earth's surface, so there is a bigger risk of skin cancer and crop damage.

5.3 Global warming

If you have been into a greenhouse when the Sun is shining, you will have noticed that it gets very warm. How does the 'greenhouse' effect work, and how is it linked to global warming?

The air around the Earth acts in a similar way to the glass in the greenhouse and warms the Earth. We call it the greenhouse effect. If this did not happen, the Earth's surface would be about −40°C.

The greenhouse effect

The Sun's rays are strong and can easily pass through the glass into a greenhouse. When the rays are reflected from the plants, they are weaker and cannot pass out of the greenhouse. So the greenhouse warms up.

The air around the Earth works a bit like a greenhouse. The strong rays from the Sun pass through the air to the Earth. But the rays that are reflected back from the Earth are weaker. They are absorbed by carbon dioxide, water vapour and methane. This keeps the Earth warm.

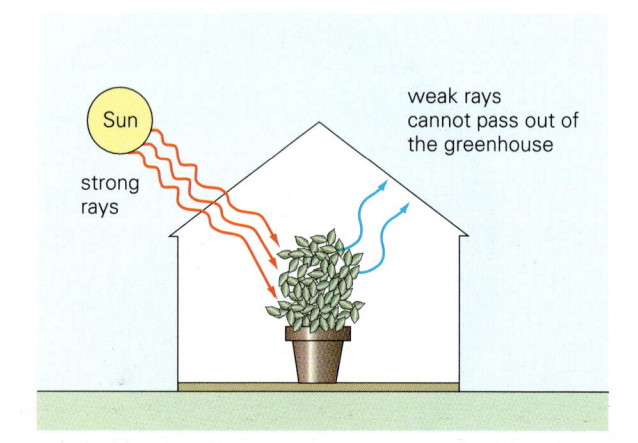

The greenhouse effect.

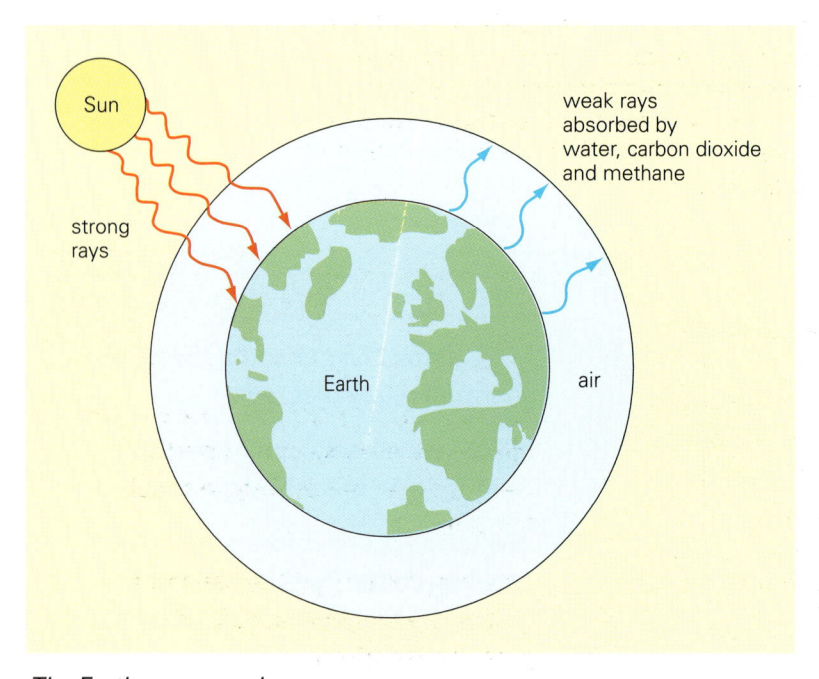

The Earth as a greenhouse.

Global warming

Some people are worried because the Earth's surface is gradually warming up. This is called **global warming**. No one is sure why this is happening, but it could be because the amount of carbon dioxide and methane in the air is increasing. More of these gases will trap more of the rays. If the temperature of the Earth carries on increasing, there could be some dramatic effects.

The possible effect of another 200 years of global warming. The ice caps may melt and the sea level may rise worldwide.

The carbon dioxide increase comes from burning fossil fuels like coal and oil. The methane comes from decaying plant matter in waste tips, and natural gas leaks. Although we are not sure that these gases are causing the global warming, many people think we should not take any chances. We should try to cut down on the amount of fossil fuels we burn, so that less carbon dioxide is released into the air.

QUESTIONS

1. Which gases absorb light rays given off by the Earth?
2. What dramatic effects might be seen on the Earth if global warming carries on for 200 years?
3. The amount of carbon dioxide in the atmosphere is increasing. Where is the extra carbon dioxide coming from?
4. Why might extra carbon dioxide in the air cause global warming?

KEY IDEAS

The amount of carbon dioxide in the atmosphere is increasing partly because we are burning so much fossil fuel.

This may be part of the cause of global warming because of the greenhouse effect.

5.4 Feeding the world

In 1990 there were twice as many people in the world as in 1950. In order to feed all these people, farming has become more efficient. But how can farmers produce more food from the same amount of land?

Imagine how much more space there would be for crops if all the hedgerows were removed.

Hedgerows

If you look at the old methods of farming, you can see that there was a lot of waste. Fields were quite small with hedgerows around each one. In each field, the space at the edges was wasted.

Farmers now tend to have much bigger fields so less space is wasted. But the hedgerows act as windbreaks. When they are removed, the wind can blow away the fertile top layer of soil.

Hedgerows are a habitat for lots of animals and plants. Since 1945, 200 000 km of hedges have been removed in England and Wales. This is an enormous loss of habitats and many of the animals and plants which lived in hedges have become rare now.

Fertilisers

Another change in farming methods has been the addition of chemicals, called **fertilisers**, to the fields. Fertilisers add nutrients to the soil so that plants can grow faster. They may be washed away into lakes and rivers where bacteria begin to grow very fast because of all the nutrients in the water. The bacteria use up so much oxygen that fish can no longer survive in the water. Fertilisers have polluted many lakes and rivers.

Salmon can only survive in water with lots of oxygen. Their numbers drop quickly when water becomes polluted.

Pesticides

Insects, weeds and plant diseases slow down the growth of crops. They are called **pests**. In order to increase food production, many farmers use **pesticides** which kill the pests without harming the crops.

Pesticides can kill useful insects as well as pests and so the number of useful insects may go down. Many of the pesticides which have been used in the past are dangerous to animals. **DDT** was used a great deal in the 1940s and 1950s. It worked very well as a pesticide. But DDT is stored in fatty tissue. At each level of the food chain, more and more organisms containing DDT are eaten. So the amount of DDT stored in the fat builds up, until the top carnivore has so much DDT in its fat stores that its survival is affected.

A decrease in the numbers of birds of prey in many ecosystems led to the discovery that these birds had high levels of DDT in their bodies. They could not reproduce well as their eggshells became thinner. This pesticide has now been banned in the USA and Europe.

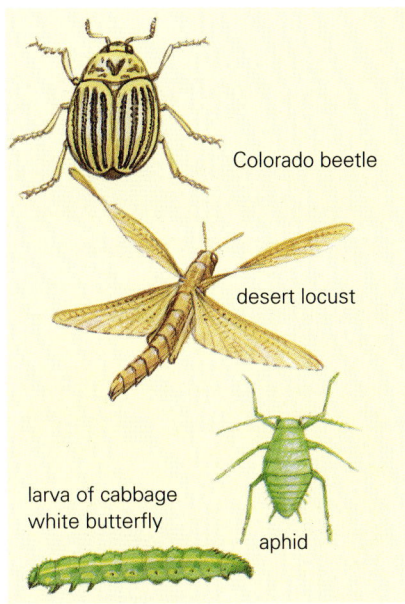

Some pests of crops.

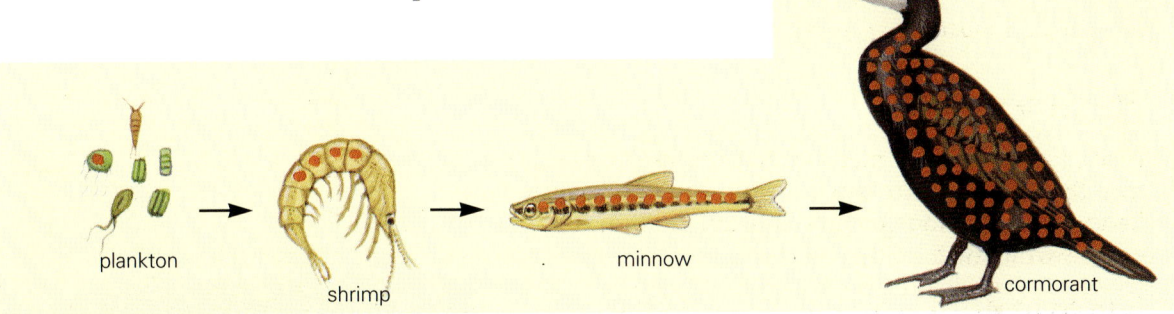

The amount of DDT stored in fatty tissue in the body increases at each level of the food chain. (The red dots represent DDT.)

QUESTIONS

1. Name the habitat which has been removed by modern farming methods.
2. What are the problems of having large fields?
3. How do fertilisers affect fish in lakes?
4. Explain:
   a the uses of pesticides
   b the harmful effects of pesticides

KEY IDEAS

Farming has become more efficient with the use of pesticides, fertilisers and larger fields.

Larger fields cause soil erosion and the loss of habitat.

Fertilisers can cause changes to the oxygen level of lakes and rivers so fish cannot live in them.

Pesticides can reach dangerously high levels in the food chain.

5.5 How to stop our polluting activities

In this chapter we have seen how our society is damaging the environment in many different ways. Many ecologists believe that we may soon do so much damage that it can't be repaired.

Of course, we would all like our environment to be clean and beautiful, but we can't stop all our polluting activities at once. What *can* we do to limit the damage?

Over many years, our society has grown to depend on things like cars, electricity, fast-growing crops, and packaging around food. If we were to go back to less polluting ways of life, our society would have to change. People would be less able to travel long distances to get to work, and we wouldn't be able to transport food around the country in big lorries. Without fertilisers we would find it hard to produce enough food to feed ourselves. Without power stations burning fossil fuels we would not have enough electricity for our homes at night. Many governments are not prepared to use different ways of producing electricity because they think it would cost too much.

The destruction of the forests

Deforestation, or destroying forests, is an example of how difficult it is to encourage people to make decisions which will help our environment. People have always cut down trees for building and firewood, but now the rate of deforestation is enormous in some parts of the world.

Destroying forests is bad for the environment for several reasons:

- there are fewer trees to carry out photosynthesis which uses up carbon dioxide (see 9.1)
- when the trees are burned more carbon dioxide goes into the atmosphere and this may be adding to the problems of global warming
- the rain forest soil is very thin and without the roots of trees to bind it, it is quickly washed away by the rain making it very difficult for anything to grow there again
- the climate becomes drier because the trees which helped to keep the air moist have disappeared
- millions of species of animals and plants which live in the rain forest have lost their habitat.

This used to be a tropical rain forest.

The reason people cut down the rain forest is to sell the timber and to make space for growing food. If they could learn about other ways of getting food, and about how to control their population, less deforestation would be necessary.

What can you do?

There are things that each person can do which would slow down the pollution of our environment.

buy organic foods that are produced without the use of fertilisers or pesticides

recycle paper, tin cans and bottles

walk or cycle, if possible

buy ozone-friendly spray cans

fit a catalytic converter to your car

re-use plastic bags

turn off lights when you don't need them

Some ways you can help to save our environment.

QUESTIONS

1. Write out some polluting activities that we have come to depend on.
2. Why is tropical rain forest being destroyed?
3. Write down five different things you could do which would help to save our environment.

KEY IDEAS

We are polluting our environment to a dangerous level.

There are many ways we could slow down or stop polluting the environment.

It is difficult to stop some kinds of pollution because it would mean spending more money.

SECTION A: QUESTIONS

1 The shells shown below are all common on seashores in the UK.

a Use the key to find out the name of each shell.

b How are shells in general well adapted to living on the seashore?

2 Look at the food web shown here.

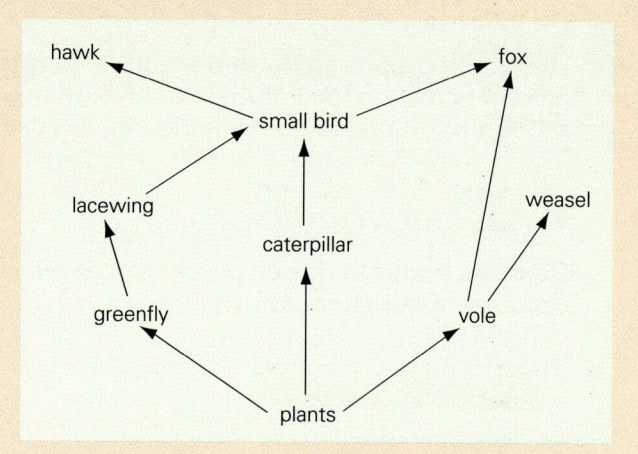

a Write down the name of **a** a herbivore and **b** a carnivore in the food web.

b How do producers get their food?

c Draw two food chains using the food web. One should have three levels and one should have five levels.

d Predict what a pyramid of biomass for your three-level food chain would look like.

e If the small bird population dropped suddenly, what do you think would happen to the population of hawks? Why would this happen?

3 100 cress seedlings were planted in moist soil in a small plant pot and 100 cress seedlings were planted in moist soil in a large seed tray. The numbers of seedlings were counted every four weeks for 20 weeks. The results are shown in the table.

Number of live seedlings	Time (weeks)					
	0	4	8	12	16	20
in small plant pot	100	95	85	70	50	20
in seed tray	100	100	100	100	100	100

a Plot a graph which shows these results.

b What happens to the number of seedlings in the seed tray during the 20 weeks? What happens to the number of seedlings in the small pot?

c What things might the seedlings in the small pot be competing for?

d Suggest how you could help more cress seedlings survive in a small pot.

4 Camels are well adapted to living in deserts and polar bears are well adapted to living in the Arctic.
  a Describe what the environment is like in the desert.
  b Give two ways that the camel is well adapted for living in these conditions.
  c What is the environment like in the Arctic?
  d Give two ways that the polar bear is adapted for living in these conditions.

5 Gardeners often use compost heaps to get rid of their garden waste.
  a What is the name given to the process of breaking down dead organisms?
  b Name two groups of organisms which carry out this process.
  c What three conditions must be present for the breaking down process to work in the compost heap?

6 Look at the diagram of the carbon cycle.

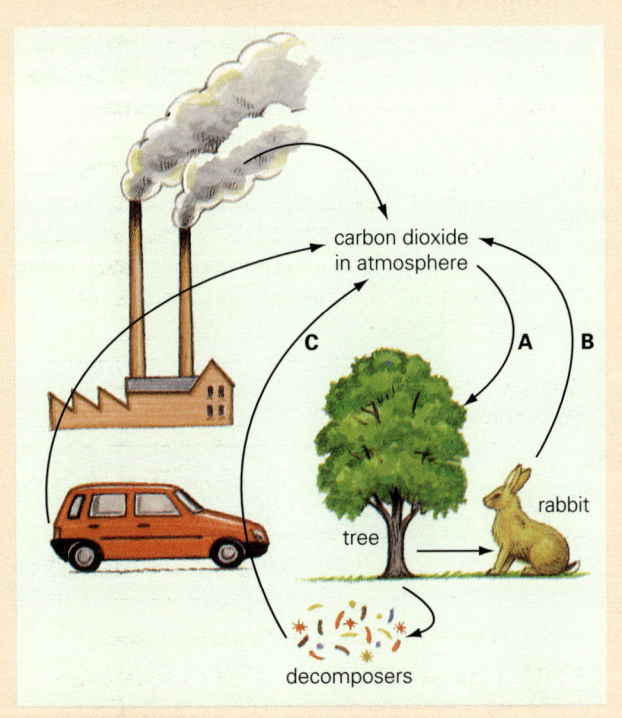

  a What is the name of the process which is going on at **A**.
  b Name the process by which carbon dioxide goes back into the atmosphere at **B**.
  c What sort of things which give off carbon dioxide are burned in factories and cars?

7 Gases given out by cars and factories can cause damage to living things many miles away, when they form acid rain.
  a Name three gases which form acid rain.
  b How do the gases change into acid rain?
  c What effect does acid rain have on trees, and why?

8 Write down three things we can do to help stop our environment from being polluted. In each case, say how the activity would help.

9 Look at the graph below which shows the population rise in a country in the developing world.
  a What was the population in 1850?
  b What is the population now?
  c Read off from the graph what the population is likely to be in 2020.
  d Give three reasons why more people mean more pollution.
  e What can we do to slow down the population increase?

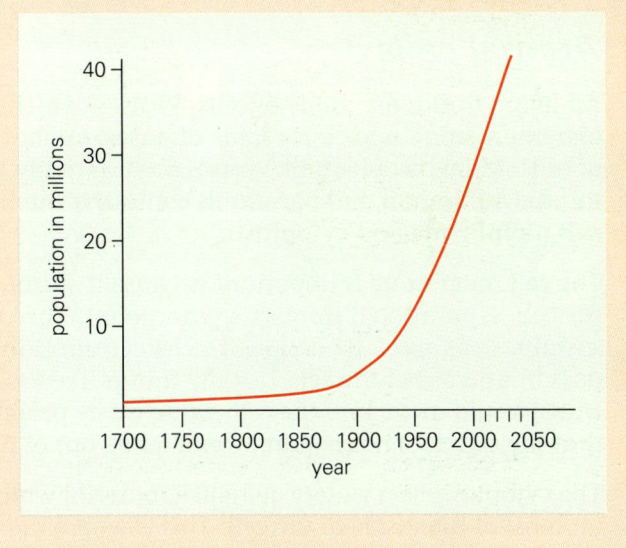

CHAPTER 6: THE ORGANISATION OF LIFE

6.1 Building blocks of living things

*Organisms are all different shapes and sizes.
So what do you, as a human, have in common with a house fly or a geranium? What is it that makes something alive?*

In order to stay alive all organisms carry out the following **life processes**:

1 they reproduce

2 they feed

3 they respire, which means releasing energy from their food

4 they grow

5 they excrete, or get rid of substances they don't want

6 they move

7 they are sensitive to changes in their surroundings.

Some living things are made of one cell. They are called **single-celled organisms**. Others are made of many cells and are called **multi-cellular organisms**.

Animal cells

All living things are made of cells. Viruses, which are extremely small and cause some diseases, are not made of cells. Many people think viruses are not really living things. All animal and plant cells contain a **nucleus**, **cell membrane** and **cytoplasm**.

The cell membrane is important because it surrounds the cell, separating it from its environment. The cell membrane is specially designed to let certain things pass in and out of the cell. Usually things like food and water would move into the cell, while waste products that the cell does not require would move out of it.

The cytoplasm is a watery, jelly-like material which fills up most of the inside of the cell. This is where the chemical reactions take place which help the cell to grow, reproduce and give it energy.

In the nucleus there are some long, thread-like materials called chromosomes. The chromosomes are made up of genes which control what the cell is like.

In organisms made of one cell only, all the life processes mentioned above happen in one cell. In bigger organisms which are made of more than one cell, there will be different kinds of cells for doing different jobs in the organism. The cells are **specialised**.

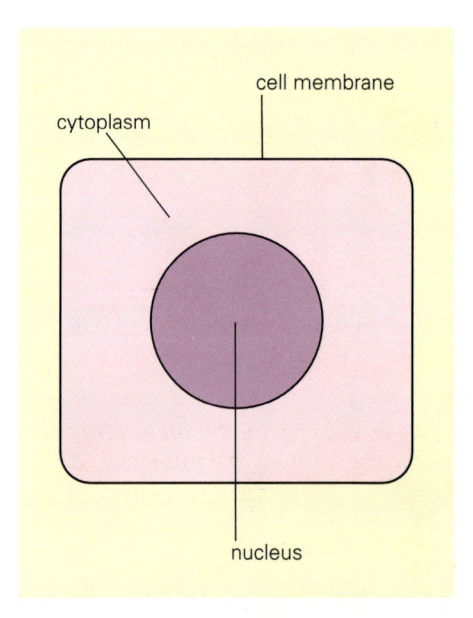

An animal cell.

Specialised animal cells

You can see some examples of different kinds of animal cells in the diagrams. Notice that they all contain a nucleus, cytoplasm and a cell membrane, but they look very different from each other. They do different things in the body. These cells are all specially designed for a particular job in the body.

The sperm cell is the male sex cell (see 20.2). It has to swim to the female's egg to try and fertilise it. It is well suited for the job because it has a tail with which to swim. Nerve cells send messages (see 15.4). They have a long axon along which the messages can travel.

You can see from the diagrams how red blood cells (see 13.4) and muscle cells are designed for their jobs.

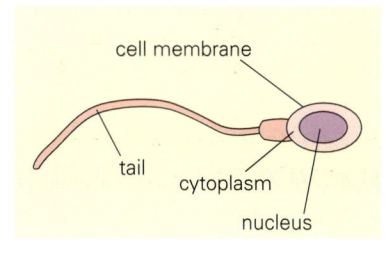

A sperm cell.

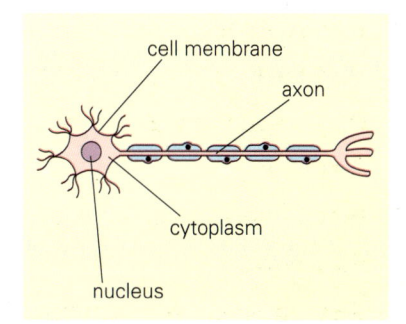

A nerve cell.

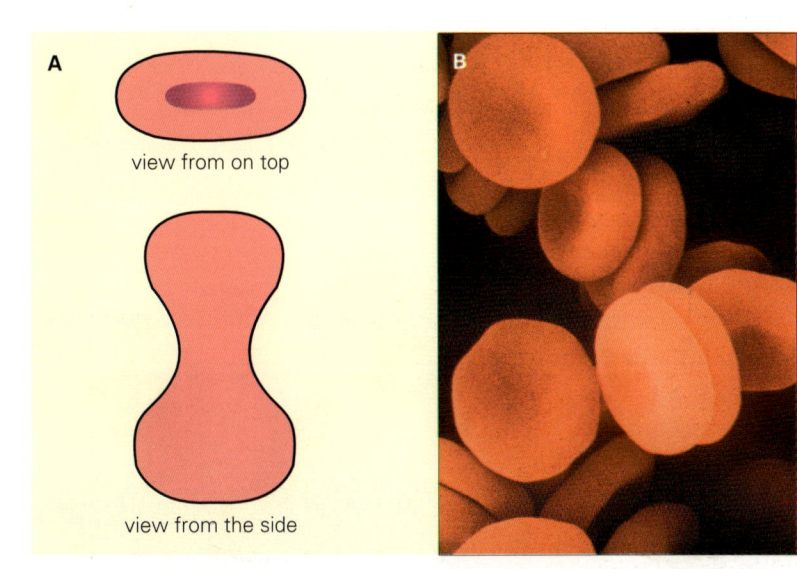

muscle cells are adapted for movement in the organism

A muscle cell.

A The shape of a red blood cell means more oxygen can get into the cell than if it were completely round. **B** Red blood cells.

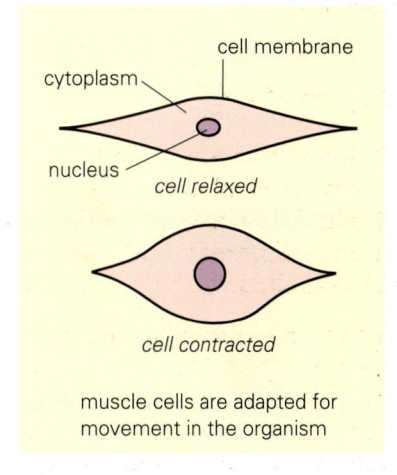

QUESTIONS

1. What three things do the cells of all plants and animals contain?
2. What are the functions of these three things?
3. Explain how a sperm cell is well-suited for its function.
4. Why aren't cells all identical?

KEY IDEAS

All living things are made up of cells.

All animal and plant cells have a cell membrane, a nucleus and cytoplasm.

Different cells have different functions.

6.2 Plant cells are different

What makes plants look green?
How are plant cells different from animal cells?

Like animal cells, plant cells have a cell membrane, nucleus and cytoplasm. But they have some other features too. They have a **cell wall**, a **vacuole** and many, though not all, have **chloroplasts**. The palisade cell in the diagram of a plant cell is the sort of cell which would be found in a leaf of a plant. It helps to make food for the plant.

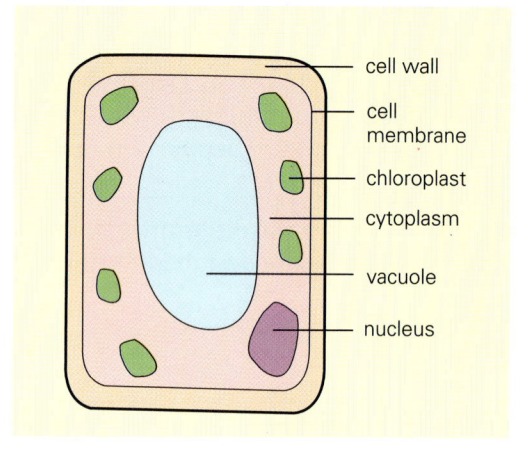

The cell wall of a plant cell is made of a strong material which helps to protect and support the cell. The cell wall has holes in it to let food and waste products through.

A vacuole is an area in a cell which is surrounded by a membrane. There is a solution of sugars and other things inside the vacuole which is called the cell sap.

Chloroplasts are found in the cytoplasm of the plant cell. It is the chloroplasts which make the plant look green. Chloroplasts are very important because they trap energy from the Sun so that the plant can make its own food. Chloroplasts are only found in the parts of a plant which are above the ground.

Some plants are single celled. This means that all the functions for life happen in the one cell. An example of a single-celled plant is an alga (plural, algae).

A plant cell.

Specialised plant cells

Multi-cellular plants are made up of different kinds of cells. Just as in animals, different parts of the plant have different functions. So there are different kinds of cell (see diagrams opposite for some examples). Root cells have root hairs which make them well-suited to absorbing water and minerals from the soil (see 8.4). Plants have tiny holes all over their surface called stomata. The guard cells of the stomata can open and close.

When xylem cells grow, they have a nucleus and cytoplasm. They lose these later as they become hollow tubes, like straws, for carrying water.

The pond water looks green because of all the chloroplasts in the algae which live here.

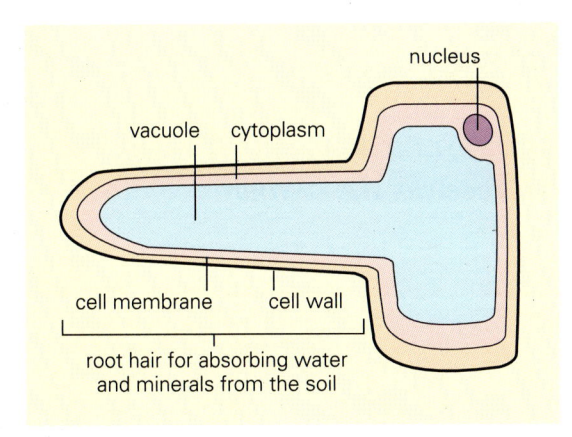

A root cell.

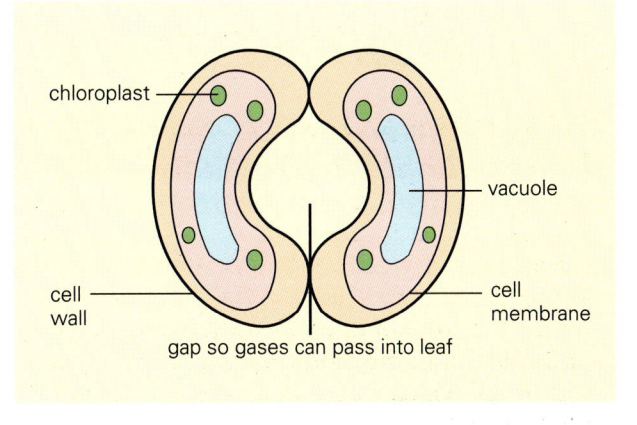

Guard cells have a gap in the middle so that gases can pass in and out of the plant.

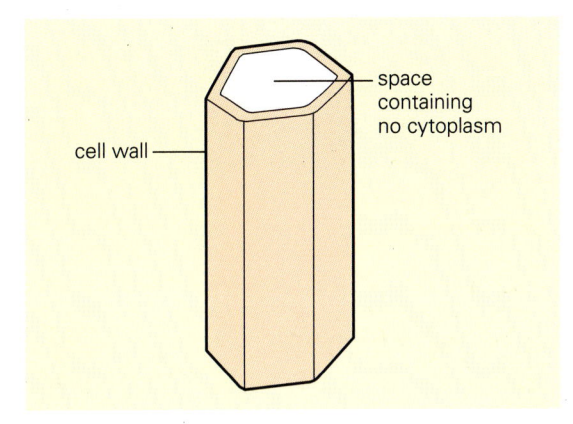

Xylem cell.

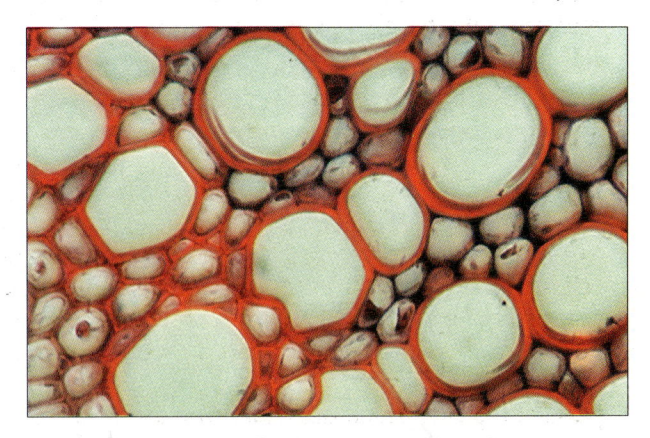

Xylem is made up of hollow, straw-like tubes.

QUESTIONS

1. Name three structures found in plant cells but not in animal cells.

2. Look at the diagram of a bacterium. This is neither an animal nor a plant. Say how it is similar to animal and plant cells, and how it is different.

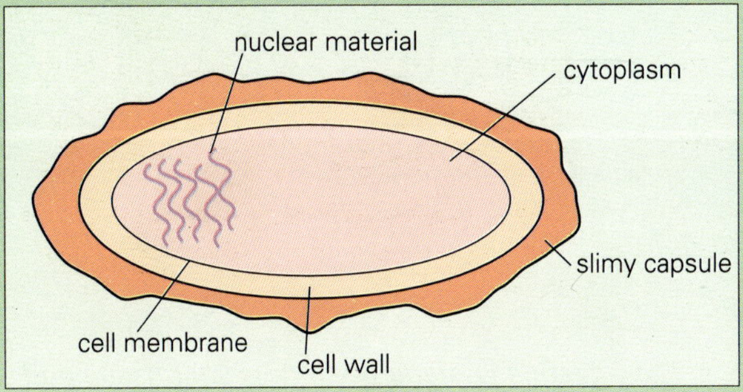

3. What makes a plant look green? What is the purpose of this structure?

4. How is a root cell well suited for its function?

KEY IDEAS

As well as a nucleus, cell membrane and cytoplasm, plant cells also have chloroplasts, a cell wall and a vacuole.

Plant cells are different from each other according to their function.

6.3 Tissues and organs

An adult human is made up of about 100 000 000 000 000 cells! How are all these cells organised so that each receives the oxygen and nutrients needed for life?

Tissues

In multi-cellular organisms, the same type of cells are grouped together to make a **tissue**. The cells in the tissue work together to carry out that tissue's function.

Plants and animals are very well organised, with different tissues carrying out different jobs. But one tissue cannot do very much on its own. Usually, two or more types of tissue must work together to do a job.

The small intestine

In the human body, digestion of food happens in the small intestine (see 11.6). The food must be moved along, and to do this, two types of tissue are needed. Glandular tissue produces mucus to make the food slimy so it moves along the intestine more easily. Cells lining the intestine have small hairs, called cilia, which help pass the food along. Muscle tissue moves the food along.

Muscle cells can shorten. This is called **contracting**. If a whole sheet of muscle cells contracts, there will be quite a large movement. If a tube of muscle tissue like the intestine contracts, the food inside will be squeezed along it. It works a bit like toothpaste squeezed from a toothpaste tube.

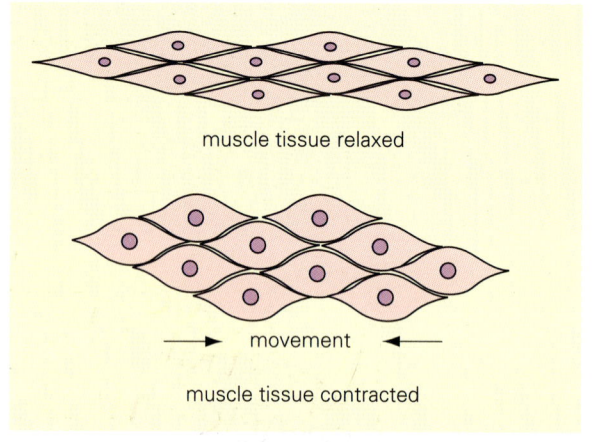

Muscle tissue before and after contracting.

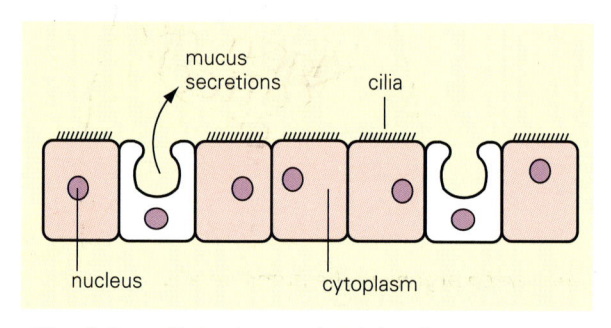

Glandular cells make up glandular tissue.

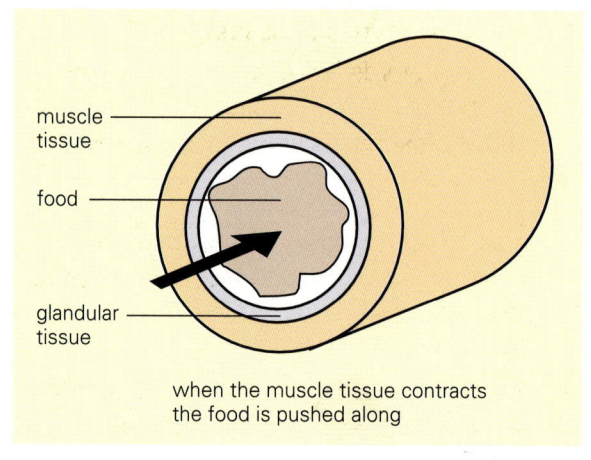

The intestine is made up of muscular tissue and glandular tissue working together.

Groups of tissues

Groups of tissues working together to do a specific job are called **organs**. The small intestine is an organ. The body has many different organs, and most of them are made up of several kinds of tissues. The diagram shows some of the main organs in the human body.

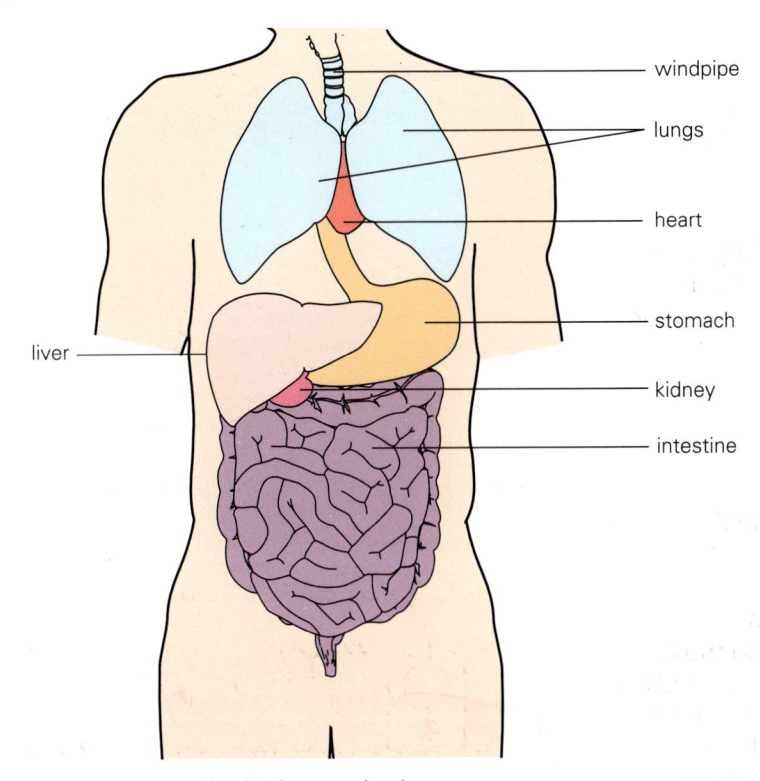

Some of the organs in the human body.

QUESTIONS

1. Name two types of tissue.
2. Use the words below to complete the paragraph:

   cells   tissues   organs   organisms

   In multi-cellular _____, large numbers of _____ that have the same structure and function are grouped together to form _____. These are usually grouped together to form _____ which have a particular job to do.
3. Explain how two tissues work together to carry out the same job in the small intestine.

KEY IDEAS

Cells of the same kind join together to make tissue.

Different types of tissue join together to make organs.

Organs carry out a particular job in the body.

6.4 Organ systems

You may have heard of the heart–lung system, the respiratory system or the excretory system. What are these systems, and how are they made up?

In 6.3 you looked at the intestine as a organ. But digestion doesn't just happen in the intestine – many other organs are involved. The liver, gall bladder and pancreas are especially important in digestion. An **organ system** is a collection of organs which together carry out an important job in the body.

The diagram shows the digestive system, the respiratory (breathing) system and the excretory, or urinary system. There are other organ systems in the human body; the main ones are outlined in the table.

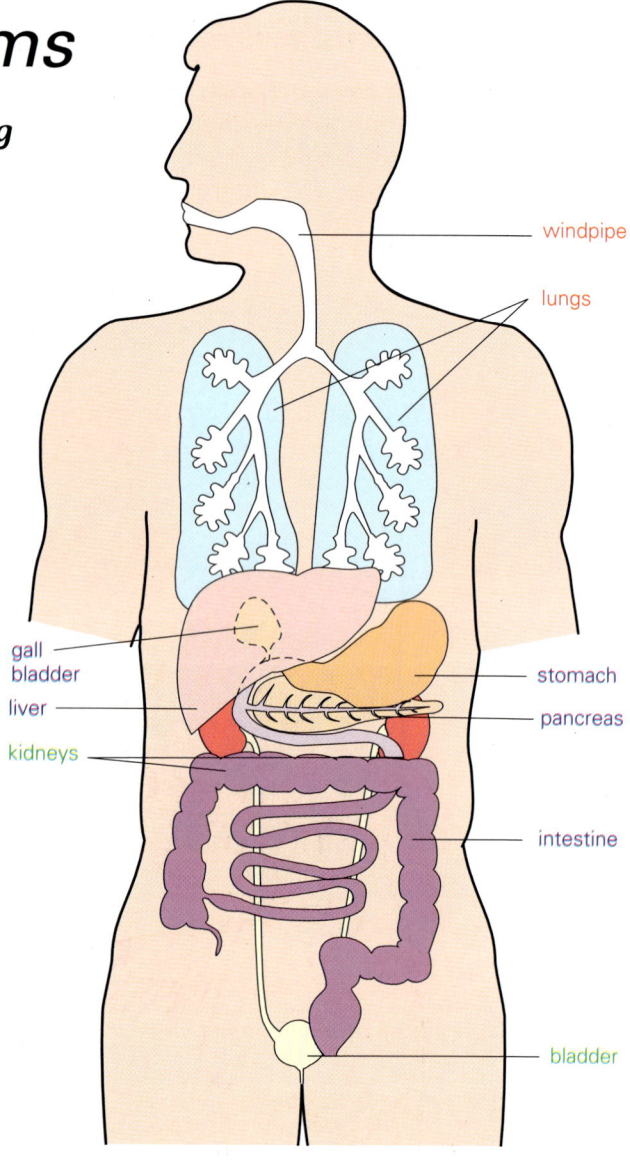

Key
— digestive system
— respiratory system
— excretory system

Some organ systems in the human body.

Name of organ system	Main organs in the system	What they do
digestive	gut, liver, pancreas	digest and absorb food
respiratory	windpipe, lungs	take in oxygen and remove carbon dioxide
circulatory	heart, blood vessels	carry oxygen, carbon dioxide and food around the body
excretory	kidneys, bladder	remove waste
nervous	brain, spinal cord	carry messages from one part of the body to another

Some of the main organ systems found in humans.

Building up an organ system

The diagram shows how an organ system is built up. This summarises what you have learnt in this chapter.

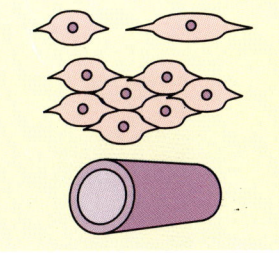

Function
muscle cells can contract and relax

muscle tissue can move food along

the small intestine digests food

Building an organ system
cells are the building blocks of organisms

tissue – group of cells with a similar function

several tissues may combine to form an organ. In the intestine muscle tissue and glandular tissue work together with nerves and blood

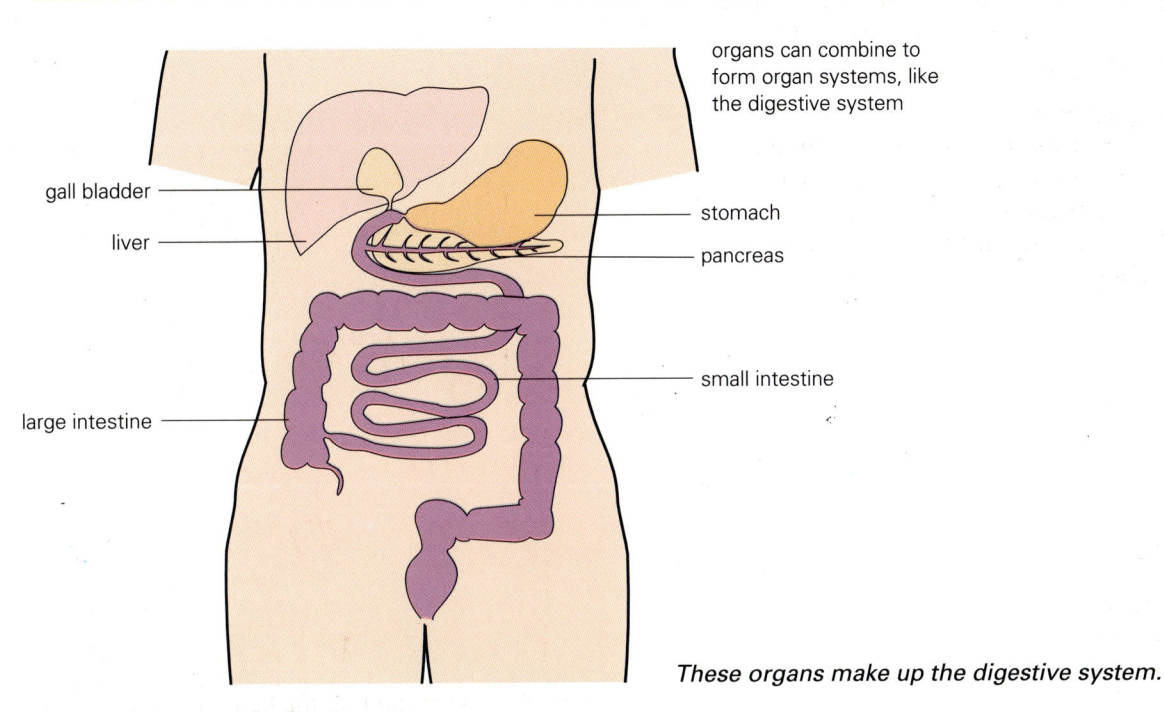

organs can combine to form organ systems, like the digestive system

- gall bladder
- liver
- stomach
- pancreas
- small intestine
- large intestine

These organs make up the digestive system.

QUESTIONS

1. Give an example of an organ system and name its function.
2. To which organ systems do the following organs belong:
   lungs, kidneys, liver, windpipe, bladder, pancreas?
3. Why is it important for a large, multi-celled organism to have division of labour?

KEY IDEAS

A group of organs working together form an organ system.

An organ system is responsible for carrying out an important task for the body.

CHAPTER 7: A CLOSER LOOK AT CHARACTERISTICS OF LIVING THINGS

7.1 Feeding and excretion

You share the same basic cell type as a mosquito. You also share the fact that you carry out seven basic life processes. How do organisms as varied as algae and elephants carry out these processes?

Things that all organisms do

All organisms have to do certain things in order to survive. These things are feeding, growing, respiring, moving, being sensitive to the environment, excreting and reproducing. In this chapter you will be looking at the ways different organisms carry out these life processes.

Feeding

All organisms must feed. Feeding means taking substances into the body which can be used for energy and building up the body. The food is broken down using the **digestive system**.

Feeding in animals

In animals, taking in food is quite easy to see. Many animals feed on plants; these are the herbivores.

Carnivores feed on other animals that they catch. Lions live in the same habitats as zebras, and hide in long grass. They chase and kill the zebras.

Feeding in plants

It is harder to see how plants feed. Plants can't catch food, so they have to make their own. They do this by a process called **photosynthesis**. They use energy from the Sun to change chemicals into useful food. They use the food for energy and growth just like animals do.

After this meal, the lion won't need to eat for several days.

Plants need the Sun's energy to grow.

Excretion

All cells produce waste materials, some of which are poisonous. The organism must get rid of them. The way they get rid of them is called **excretion**. The organ system used in humans and other mammals is the **excretory system**, which produces urine. Urine contains the poisonous substance urea.

Plants also have to excrete their waste materials. One of the ways they do this is to transport all the poisonous waste to the leaves when the leaves are being lost in autumn.

Chimpanzees urinate to remove waste products from their bodies.

Poisonous waste products are moved up the stem and into the leaves before they fall.

QUESTIONS

1. What is
   a a herbivore
   b a carnivore?
2. How is feeding in animals different from feeding in plants?
3. What do you call the process by which living things get rid of their poisonous waste?
4. Give one example of the way plants get rid of their poisonous waste.

KEY IDEAS

All organisms carry out the seven life processes.

All organisms feed.

All organisms get rid of poisonous waste products by a process called excretion.

7.2 Respiring, reproduction and growing

How do organisms get the energy they need for growth and reproduction?

Respiration

The food taken in by the organism is broken down into chemicals by its **digestive system**. These chemicals are carried around the body to the cells.

Some of the digested food carried around the plant or animal body to every cell is used by the cell for its work. The digested food supplies the energy for this work. Cells need oxygen to get the energy out of the food, so all organisms must respire to get oxygen into their body. Humans take oxygen out of the air by breathing using the **respiratory system**. Many animals which live in water have special organs to get the dissolved oxygen out of the water. Fish have gills, for example.

Plants also take in oxygen, through tiny holes, or **stomata**, all over their surface. Even their roots take in oxygen.

Many organisms can absorb oxygen which is dissolved in water.

Reproduction

All organisms reproduce to make more of their own kind. This makes sure that their species survives and does not die out and become **extinct**.

Some organisms can reproduce without a partner. This is called **asexual reproduction** (see 21.2).

A male and female of the same species are needed for **sexual reproduction** (see 21.1). They must combine their genes to make the offspring. This process is called **fertilisation**. In animals this is called mating. They use their **reproductive system** for mating (see Chapter 21). In plants, the flower is the reproductive system. After fertilisation, seeds are formed which later grow into new plants.

Two sunflowers, one before fertilisation (A), the other with ripening seeds (B).

Rhinoceroses mate in order to combine their genes.

Growth

Organisms grow by making more cells. Growth happens when cells divide into two and each gets bigger.

Many organisms, like humans, stay basically the same shape as they grow, though they get bigger and heavier. Others may change shape completely, like the caterpillar, as well as getting bigger and heavier.

Plants begin life as a small seed which **germinates** into a seedling. The seedling grows into a plant.

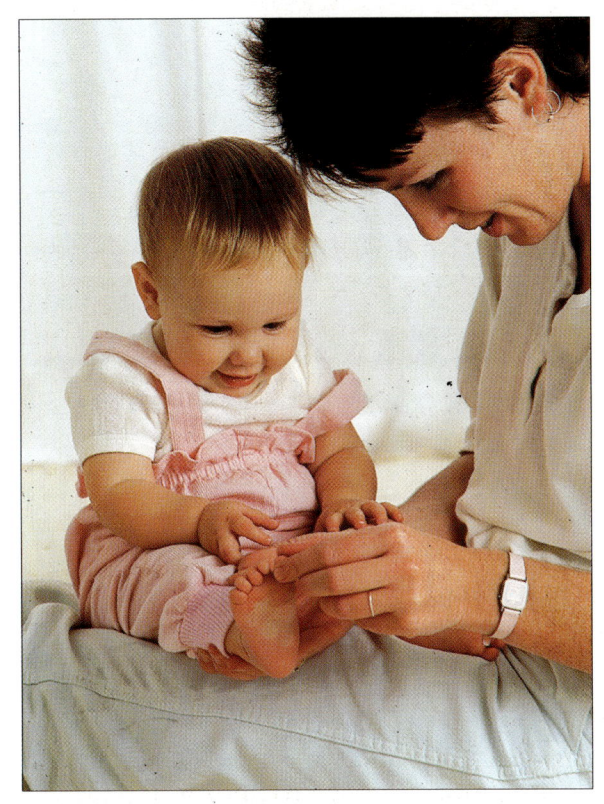

The baby girl will grow into a woman in about 15 years.

Caterpillars change into butterflies.

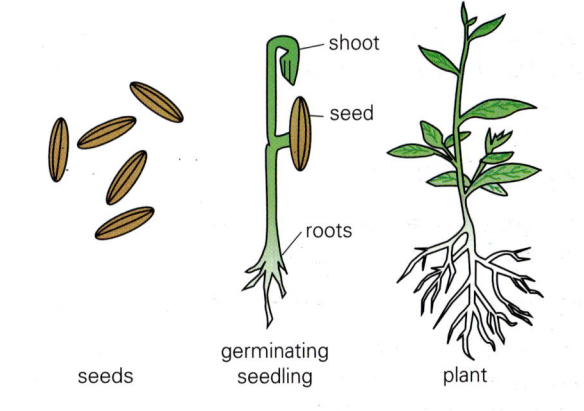

Plants begin their lives as seeds.

QUESTIONS

1. What do cells use oxygen for?
2. Many fish fertilise thousands of eggs each time they reproduce. Humans usually only fertilise one. Why do you think fish do this?
3. Explain how
   a humans, b caterpillars and c plants change during growth.

KEY IDEAS

Respiring is taking oxygen into the body, which is used to release energy from the food.

All organisms reproduce so their species does not become extinct.

All living organisms grow and breathe.

7.3 Movement and sensitivity

Movement and sensitivity are obvious in animals. A frog blinking, a cat scratching or a baby opening its mouth to cry are clear signs of life. But movement and sensitivity in plants are harder to see because they happen more slowly.

Locusts swarming in Ethiopia.

In ballet, movement has become an art form.

Movement

You can see movement in animals all the time. Even when babies are asleep you can see their respiratory system working. Some kinds of movement can be very impressive to look at, like humans dancing, or locusts moving in huge numbers across large distances until they find crops to feed on.

In plants, movement is less obvious. But you can see movement if you look at single plant cells under the microscope. Within the cell, the cytoplasm is constantly moving. If you look at multi-cellular plants, there are often signs of movement over a period of time. Flowers may open at the beginning of the day and close at night. Sunflowers move their flower heads around so that they are constantly facing the Sun.

Sensitivity

In order to survive, organisms must be **sensitive** to what is going on around them. They must be able to **sense** things like light, sound, taste and touch, and they must be able to **respond** to them. Organisms can sense things around them using their **sensory organs**. The zebra senses the movement of the lion as it begins to pounce and responds by running away.

This flower is called 'Jack go to bed at noon' because its flowers close in the afternoon.

Octopuses sense the colour of their surroundings and respond by changing colour themselves so that they blend in to the background. This camouflages them and helps them to survive.

Plants usually respond slowly to their environment. They sense the direction from which light is coming and grow towards the light. Some plants respond more quickly. The venus fly trap is one example of a meat-eating plant. When a fly lands on the inside of the leaves, the plant senses movement and snaps shut to trap the fly inside. The fly is then digested.

Sensing the movement of the lion is vital to the zebra's survival.

This dragonfly caught in a venus fly trap will not see the light of day again!

The seedlings are responding to the light.

The octopus is responding to the colour in its environment.

QUESTIONS

1. What kind of movement have humans made into an art form?
2. Describe an example of sensitivity and response saving an organisms' life.
3. Make a list of at least five stimuli you have responded to in one day.
   An example would be:
   Stimulus   I hear the doorbell ringing.
   Response   I go and open the door.

KEY IDEAS

All organisms move.

All organisms sense things in their environment and respond to them.

SECTION B: QUESTIONS

1. Copy out the table below. Put a tick (✓) if the cell structure on the left is present and a cross (✗) if it is not.

Cell structure	Animal cell	Plant cell
cell wall		
nucleus		
vacuole		
chloroplast		
cell membrane		
cytoplasm		

2. Which of the structures in the table in question 1:
   a controls the development of the cell
   b traps the Sun's energy
   c surrounds the cell and separates it from its environment
   d is the place where the cell's chemical reactions happen?

3. Look at the cells in the diagram below.

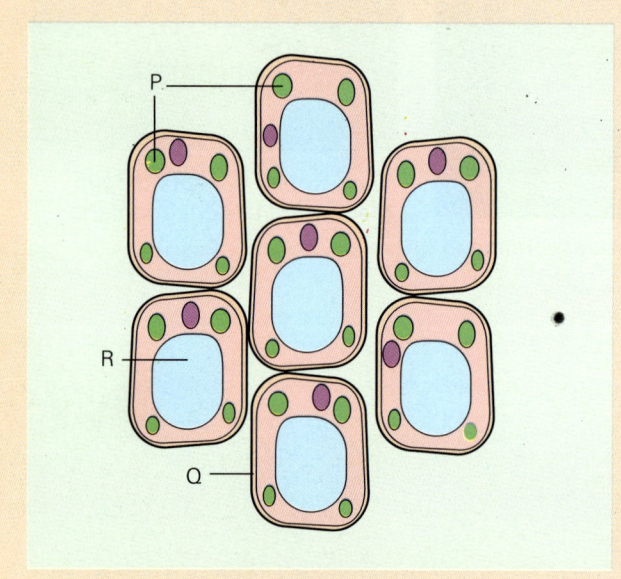

   a What are the structures P, Q and R?
   b Do they come from an animal cell or a plant cell?
   c Give three reasons for your answer.

4. Look at the cells in the diagram below.

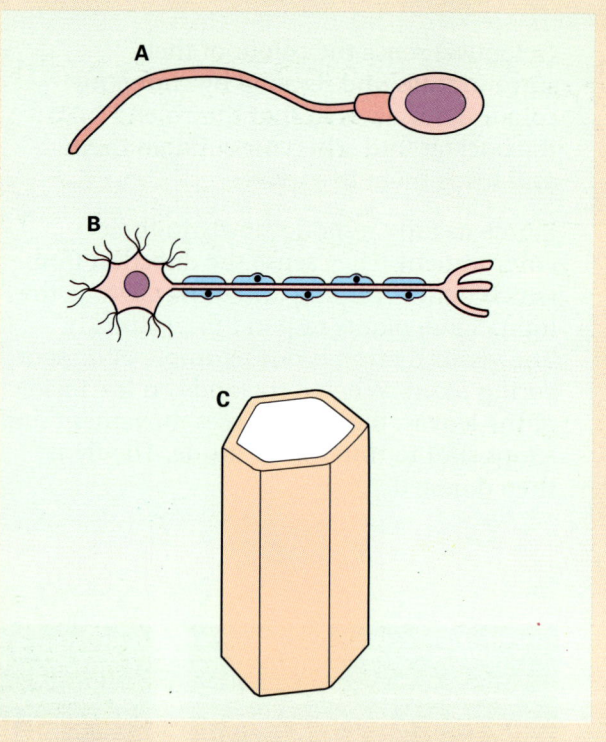

   a What type of cells are cells A, B and C?
   b How are each of these cells well suited to their function?

5. Look carefully at the cells shown in the diagram below.

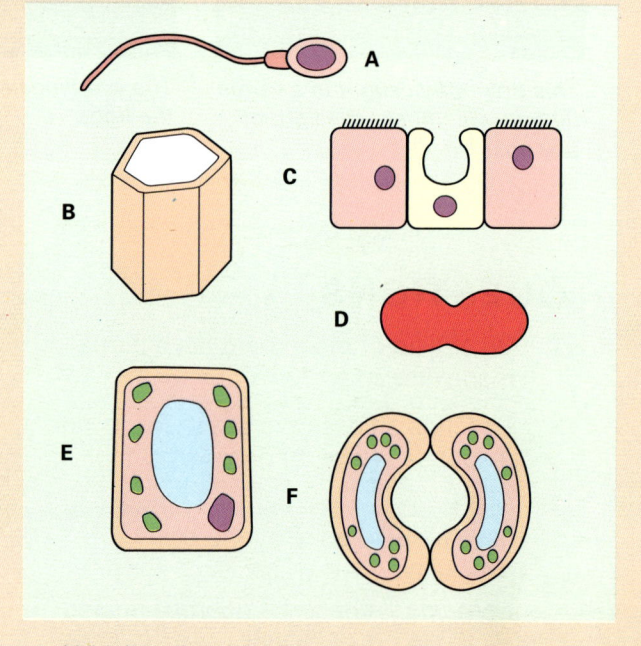

   a Which cells are surrounded only by a cell membrane?

60

b Copy and complete the following table using the cells shown in the diagram.

Name of cell	Special role of cell	One way in which it is different from typical animal or plant cell	Reason for the difference

6 A tree is a living organism but a car is not. Using these as your examples, explain the differences between living and non-living things.

7 Look at the diagrams below. Which diagram matches up with which life process 1 to 7?

1   respiration
2   growth
3   feeding
4   sensitivity
5   reproduction
6   excretion
7   movement

CHAPTER 8: HOW PLANTS LIVE

8.1 The parts of a plant

Why do plants have different parts? What is important about roots?

The plants shown in this illustration have a stem, some leaves and roots. The **stem** stretches towards the light so that the leaves can make food. Water and minerals are carried along the stem to the leaves. The roots anchor the plant and can bend towards water. The leaf is held in the light and collects the Sun's energy, so that the plant can make its own food by **photosynthesis**.

The stem

The rain forest shown in the photograph is a community of many different plants. Each plant is using its leaves to catch the light. The biggest plants are the trees. They use their huge stems or trunks to hold the leaves high up in the light.

A forest looks peaceful. But each plant is struggling to keep its share of light and essential supplies of water and minerals. Plants with small stems may stay in the shadow of large trees, and die from lack of light. Other plants, like ivy, reach for light by tangling their stems up tree trunks.

Surviving in the shade

Some plants can live in the shade, and even prefer it. They may be adapted for living in less bright areas by having very large leaves, which collect as much of the light as they can.

The structure of a plant.

The stems of plants help them reach towards the light.

Roots

Roots have two main jobs.

1 They *anchor* the plant firmly in the ground. This stops the plant toppling over.

2 They take in water and minerals. Most roots are too small to see. These are the **root hairs**.

The roots of trees and plants help to prevent soil **erosion**. The photograph shows land where all the trees have been cut down. There is now a danger of erosion. Erosion is when the soil is washed away, leaving bare rock. It happens because there are no roots to help stick the soil together.

Roots prevent erosion of the soil.

The roots spread through the soil.

QUESTIONS

1 List three main parts of a plant.
2 Which part of a plant carries water to the leaves?
3 Which part of a plant captures the light?
4 Name two jobs of roots.
5 How do roots stop soil erosion?
6 Some plants grow very well in shady areas. What adaptations might these plants have?
7 Young trees in woods often grow extremely rapidly. Why do they do this?

KEY IDEAS

The stem holds leaves in the light.

The leaf makes food for the plant.

The root finds and absorbs water and anchors the plant in the soil.

8.2 The plant finds water

***Did you know that a lettuce leaf is 95% water?
Or that an oak tree can drink up to 200 litres in a single day?***

Like all living things, plants need water. They need it for at least three things:

- for chemical reactions inside cells, including photosynthesis
- for transporting minerals and sugar around the plant
- to help keep the stem and leaves stiff.

Extra water needed

Sometimes plants need extra water. They may need more water when they are growing or making fruit. Fruit itself contains a lot of water. And because they are growing, and have many leaves, trees drink more water in summer than in winter.

All plants, even desert plants, need water. Desert plants never waste water. Cacti manage to survive on very little. When it rains they take water in through the roots. Then they save it in their fat stems. A thick waxy skin stops water evaporating. There are no leaves, only spines. Spines have a smaller surface area than leaves. Hardly any water is lost through the spines.

The melon plant puts a lot of water in its fruit.

spines instead of leaves to reduce water loss

folds in the skin to allow cactus to expand when rain is plentiful

thick, waxy skin keeps water inside the plant

Cacti live for months without rain.

Water keeps plants rigid

Lack of water is making this plant droop. Without water it cannot hold itself so straight and rigid. Yet if the plant is given water it will quickly become rigid again.

The stem and leaves are made of cells. Inside each cell is a **vacuole** or water store. When there is plenty of water in the soil, each cell has a full vacuole. The vacuole presses against the cell wall and makes it rigid or **turgid**. When a plant does not get enough water, the vacuoles are not so full. Now the cells are less rigid. As a result the whole plant droops.

A wilting plant ...

... can recover very quickly.

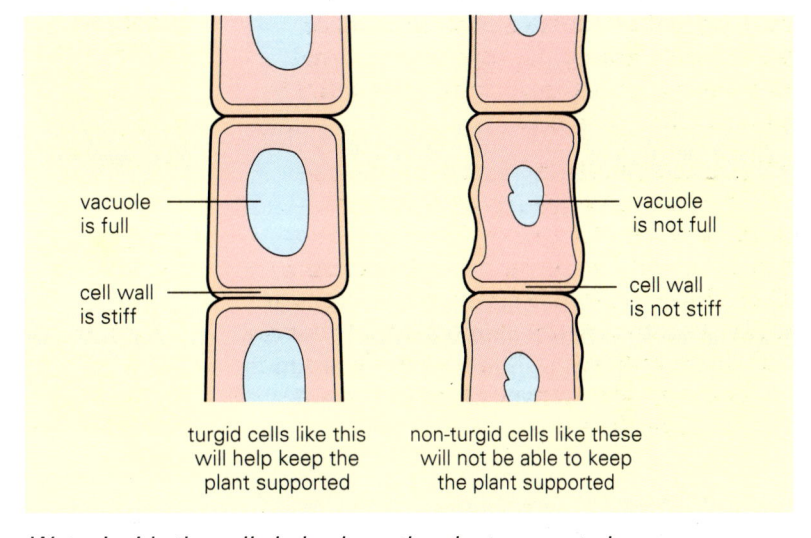

vacuole is full
cell wall is stiff

turgid cells like this will help keep the plant supported

vacuole is not full
cell wall is not stiff

non-turgid cells like these will not be able to keep the plant supported

Water inside the cells helps keep the plant supported.

QUESTIONS

1. Say which of the following need a lot of water, and which only need a little:
   a a cactus
   b a tree in summer
   c a growing melon plant
   d a tree in winter.

2. Describe how the following structures help a cactus keep its water:
   a a waxy skin
   b spines.

3. Explain how water can help keep plants standing straight.

KEY IDEAS

Plant cells need water for chemical reactions, including photosynthesis.

Water helps keep stems and leaves rigid.

8.3 Transpiration

If watered, a wilting plant can become rigid again after just a few minutes. But how does the plant suck the water up to the tips of its leaves?

Cut flowers in a vase carry on drinking water even though they have no roots. The stems are like straws, sucking up the water. They can do this because they contain xylem cells, which are like water pipes, connecting up the whole plant. It is the leaves and flowers at the top which are doing the sucking.

The **transpiration stream** is the name given to the upwards movement of water in a plant. The leaves are important for making water move up the plant. As water evaporates from the leaves it is replaced by water from the roots. If water stops evaporating from the leaves, then water enters the roots more slowly.

Flowers and leaves suck up water.

Transpiration: in the leaf

Plants must let gases like carbon dioxide and oxygen in and out of their leaves. To do this they have tiny holes called **stomata**. It is easy for water to pass out of the leaf through the stomata. So the leaf cells begin to dry out.

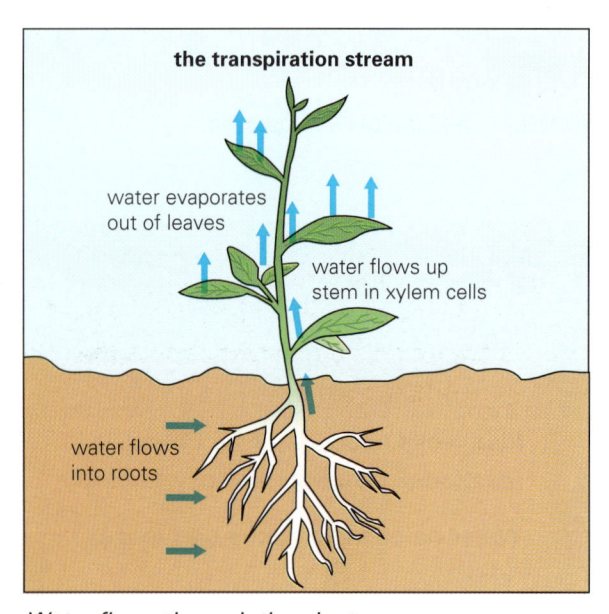

Water flows through the plant.

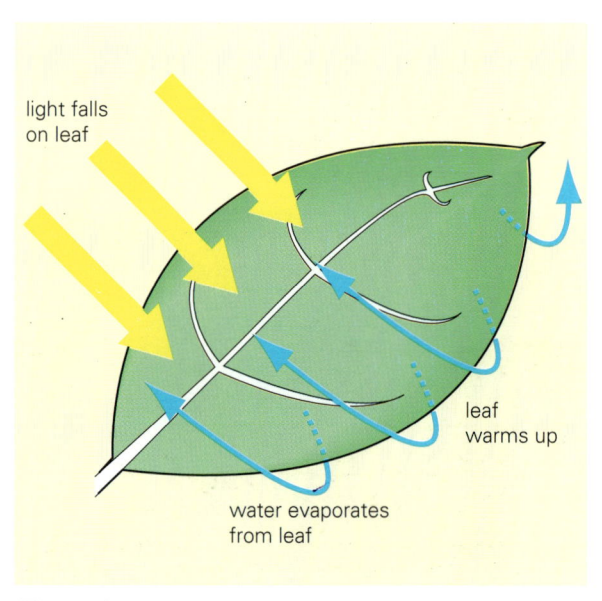

The leaf loses water by evaporation.

A lot of water in this photograph is coming from the trees. It is evaporating out of the leaves and going straight into the air to form clouds. Some of this water will then fall as rain.

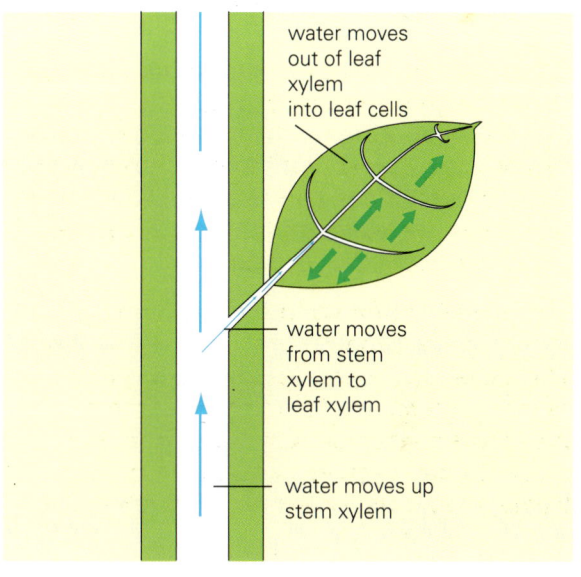

Water passes into the leaf from the stem.

Transpiration: in the stem

The leaf has xylem cells inside, full of water. They act like a straw. Water is sucked from the xylem cells into the leaf cells. In turn, water moves up the stem xylem.

Transpiration: in the roots

Because of transpiration, water passes up the stem xylem and into the leaves. New water must constantly pass into the stem. The stem gets its water by absorbing water from the roots.

QUESTIONS

1. Which substance travels in xylem cells?
2. What is the direction of water flow inside stem xylem?
3. The guard cells can close the stomata. When they do this the transpiration stream slows down. Why?
4. Explain how cutting down forests can affect the rainfall.

KEY IDEAS

Evaporation from leaves causes the transpiration stream.

Water vapour evaporates through the leaf stomata.

The xylem cells are the water pipes of a plant.

8.4 The plant finds minerals

Why do gardeners put horse manure on their roses?

Plants need more than water, air and light. They need minerals to grow and stay healthy. Their main source of minerals is the soil. Plants take in minerals through their roots.

Dead animals and plants decompose to release minerals into the soil.

Soil usually contains plenty of minerals such as **magnesium**, **nitrate** and **phosphate**. The minerals often come from rotting leaves and animals. When dead things rot or **decompose** the chemicals leak out of their body and nourish the soil.

The minerals are dissolved in the soil water. Soil is made up of small particles, each covered with a thin layer of water. When the plant absorbs this water, minerals in the soil pass into the plant too.

The diagram shows how roots run through the soil. The root hairs can burrow between the particles of soil.

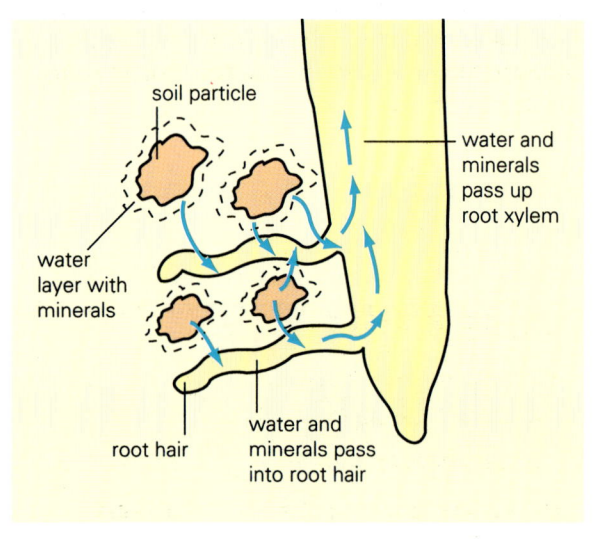

Root hairs reach into the soil.

Inside the plant

When the minerals get inside the plant they must be transported upwards. They are needed in the stem and the leaves. This is the job of the xylem cells (see 9.2). The minerals dissolved in water are transported upwards in the plant by the transpiration stream (see 8.3).

Some important plant minerals

Two important minerals are magnesium and nitrate.

- Magnesium is needed for making chlorophyll in the leaves.
- Nitrate is needed for making proteins and helping the plant grow.

The diagrams on the right show what happens when a plant doesn't get enough minerals.

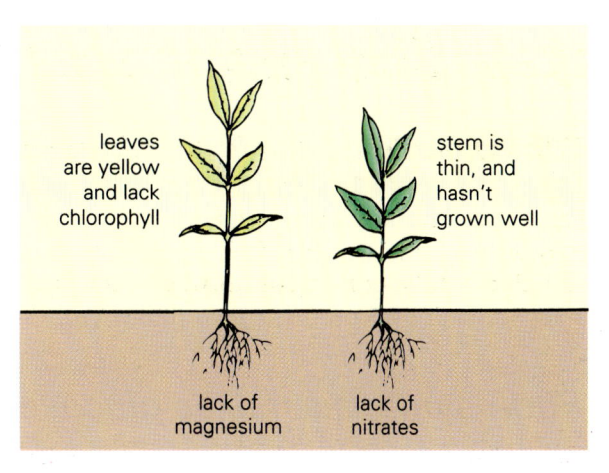

Plants grow badly without minerals.

Adding minerals

Not all soils contain enough minerals. If crops are being grown and harvested year after year, the minerals in the soil can be used up. So farmers often add minerals, or **fertiliser**, to their fields. Artificial fertiliser is a mixture of potassium, nitrate and phosphate.

Organic farming is when the fertiliser put on the fields is not artificial. Farm yard manure (a mixture of cattle faeces, urine and straw) may be used instead. By growing fewer crops, organic farmers prevent the soil from losing all its minerals.

Fertiliser is added to the soil to replace used up minerals.

QUESTIONS

1. Which part of a plant
   a absorbs minerals?
   b transports minerals upwards?
2. Where do the minerals in soil come from?
3. Explain the importance of
   a magnesium
   b nitrate
   to a growing plant.
4. Explain why farmers often add fertiliser to their fields.

KEY IDEAS

Minerals help plant growth.

Plants take in minerals through the roots.

Farmers add minerals to soil using fertiliser.

CHAPTER 9: HOW PLANTS FEED

9.1 Building food

Where does a strawberry get its sweet taste from? How can a plant turn sunlight into food?

Probably the most important difference between animals and plants is how they feed. We look for food; plants make it. They make it by a process called photosynthesis.

Photosynthesis makes glucose

Photosynthesis is the chemical reaction that happens inside leaves. The starting materials or **reactants** are carbon dioxide and water. The **products** (what gets made) are **glucose** and **oxygen**. For these reactions to work, energy is needed.

Plants make food for themselves – and for us.

Energy for photosynthesis

The energy for photosynthesis comes from the Sun. Plants do their food-making in the hours of daylight.

The test-tube in the diagram below contains pigment extracted from a plant. The colour is caused by **chlorophyll**. Chlorophyll is a green pigment able to trap the Sun's energy.

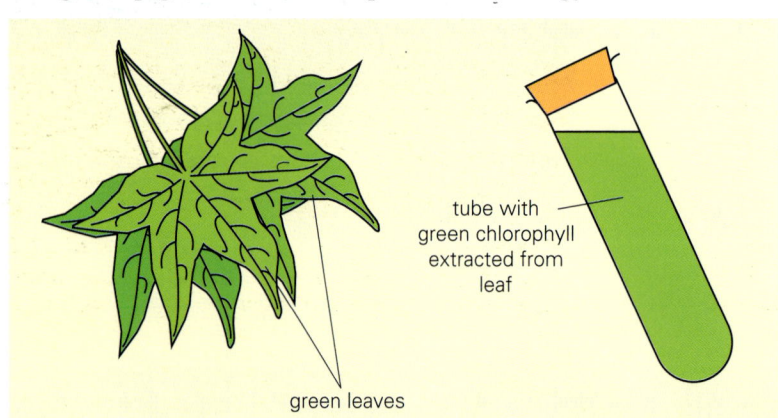

Green chlorophyll traps the light.

The nuclear reactions in the Sun provide our plants with energy.

The diagram on the page opposite shows the whole process of photosynthesis. Inside the leaf cell the chemical reactions begin. The energy has been trapped by the chlorophyll and can be used. Now carbon dioxide must be combined with water. The carbon dioxide comes mostly from the air. Water comes mostly from the soil. The equation summarises photosynthesis.

$$\text{carbon dioxide} + \text{water} \xrightarrow{\text{chlorophyll and sunlight}} \text{glucose} + \text{oxygen}$$

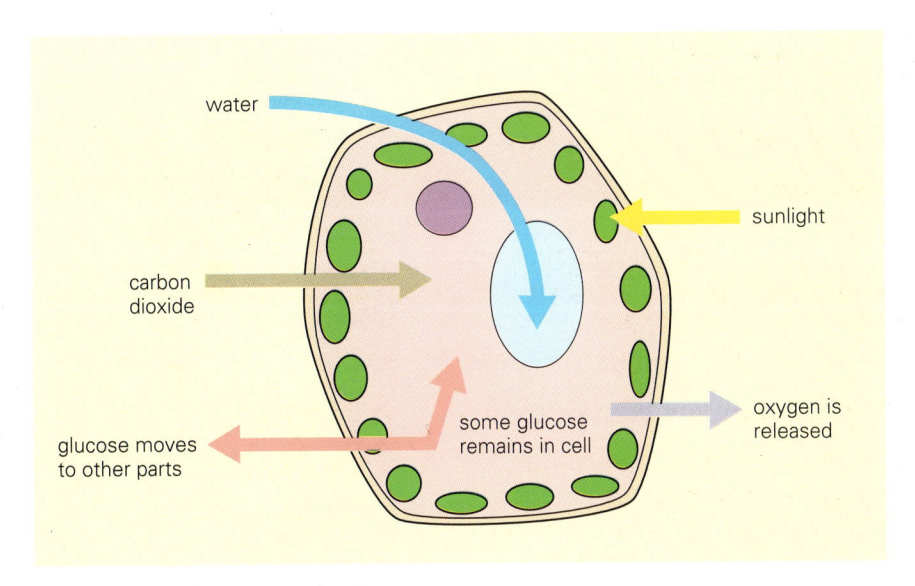

A summary of photosynthesis.

For plants, food is the important product of photosynthesis. Glucose is made, which is then stored as starch. But the waste gas of photosynthesis is oxygen. This is the gas which helps us all to live.

Our oxygen comes from plants

The oxygen we need comes from plants. When the planet formed, billions of years ago, there was no oxygen in the atmosphere. When the first green plants evolved, they began to make their food and release oxygen. Todays living things depend on the oxygen that plants have been releasing for so long.

The atmosphere is 20% oxygen – thanks to plants! The orange and blue layers of the lower and upper atmosphere of the Earth were photographed from space.

QUESTIONS

1. What colour is chlorophyll?
2. Describe the job of chlorophyll.
3. Which gas is needed for photosynthesis?
4. Which gas is produced by photosynthesis?
5. Give two ways in which animals depend on plants.

KEY IDEAS

Photosynthesis makes glucose for the plant.

Photosynthesis needs light, chlorophyll, carbon dioxide and water.

Photosynthesis also makes oxygen.

9.2 The leaf

What happens inside a leaf? Why are most leaves flat and thin?

The leaf is where photosynthesis takes place. A leaf is designed to make sure photosynthesis happens efficiently.

- Most of the chlorophyll is found in the palisade cells, near the top of the leaf and so closer to the sunlight.
- Xylem in the veins of the leaves give a good water supply.
- The spongy cells, or inner cells, have gaps between them to allow circulation and absorption of gases.
- The leaf is thin and flat, to give a large surface for absorbing light.

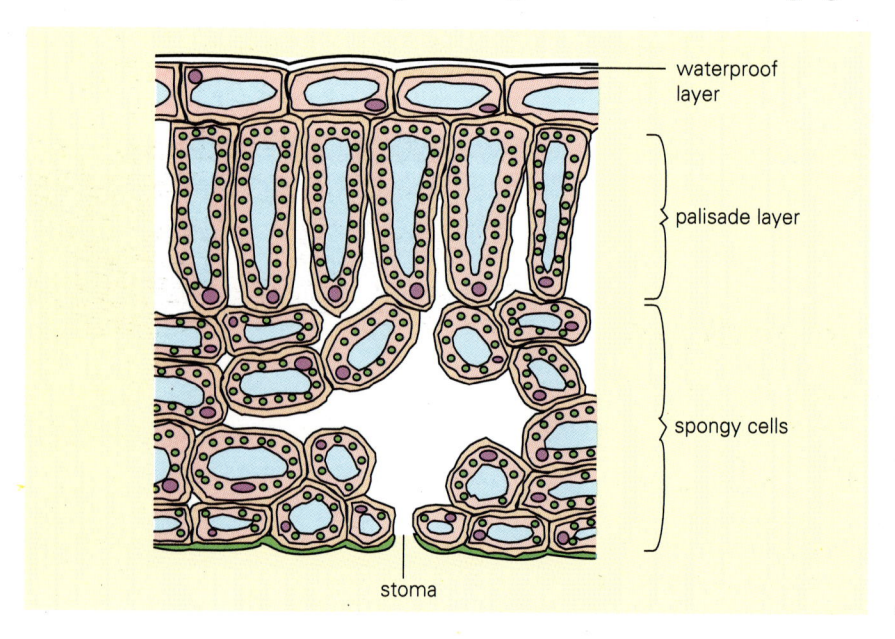

A leaf in cross section.

Chlorophyll traps the light

The leaf has to collect as much light as possible. So the leaf is usually flat and large, with most of the chlorophyll near the top surface, where the light is brightest. When light falls on a leaf it flows through the surface and hits small particles called **chloroplasts**. The chlorophyll is concentrated in the chloroplasts. It captures the energy of the Sun.

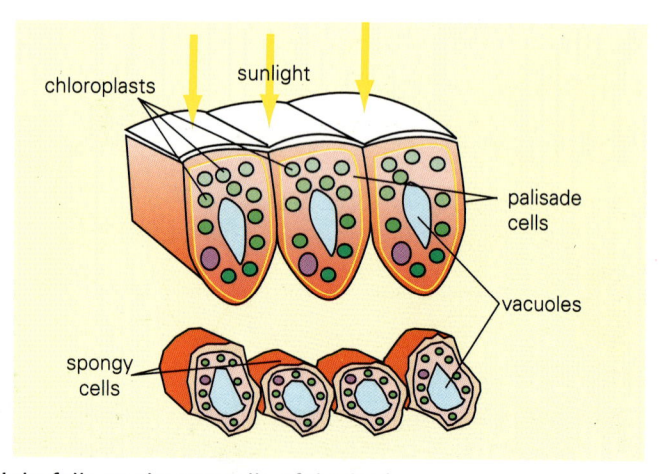

Light falls on the top cells of the leaf.

Leaves arrange themselves so as to get the maximum amount of light. They move and twist so as not to shade each other. For a leaf, getting light is the most important thing.

A good water supply

Running through the leaf are bundles of xylem. From the surface these bundles look like veins. One of the jobs of the xylem is to provide the leaves with water for photosynthesis.

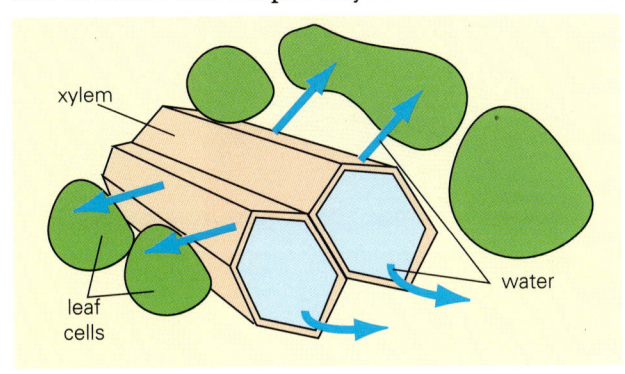

Xylem brings water to the cells.

Each leaf is arranged to absorb light and to avoid shading out other leaves.

Air for the cells.

A good supply of carbon dioxide

Leaves take in and give out gases. They need carbon dioxide for photosynthesis, and this mostly comes from the atmosphere. Small holes or **stomata** (singular, **stoma**) in the leaf surface allow air to circulate in and out of the leaf. Usually the stomata are in the bottom surface of the leaf. Sometimes stomata close, so as to prevent too much evaporation of water vapour.

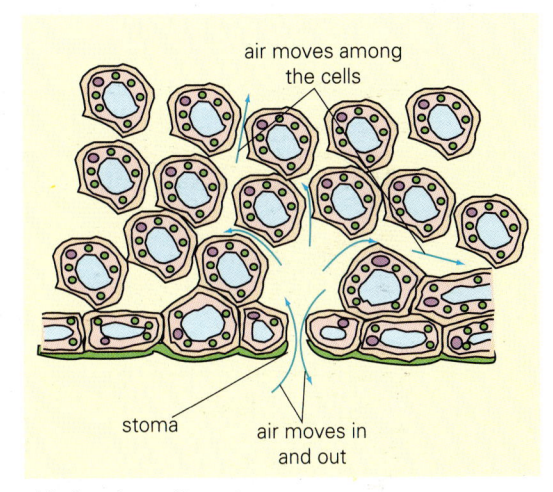

QUESTIONS

1. Efficient photosynthesis needs a good supply of which gas?
2. Why is most chlorophyll found in the upper half of a leaf?
3. Name the structures that carry water into the leaf.
4. Explain why stomata sometimes close.
5. Explain why photosynthesis may slow down when the stomata are closed.

KEY IDEAS

Leaves are flat and large for absorbing light.

Most chlorophyll is in the top of the leaf.

Stomata let gases in and out.

9.3 Limiting factors

Is life ever perfect for a plant? What happens if there isn't quite enough carbon dioxide? And why don't all the plants die when the Sun goes behind a cloud?

The greenhouse gives plants the living conditions they want; plenty of light, warmth and water. So in the greenhouse photosynthesis is going to work very well indeed.

But outside the greenhouse, photosynthesis doesn't always work well. Sometimes the conditions are not right. For example, it may be too dark. The amount of light can limit how fast the plant grows. Things which limit the speed of photosynthesis are called **limiting factors**.

Photosynthesis depends on

- availability of light
- availability of carbon dioxide
- availability of water.

More or less carbon dioxide

The graph shows that photosynthesis speeds up if you increase the amount of carbon dioxide. Greenhouse farmers can sometimes produce a crop more quickly if they slightly increase the amount of carbon dioxide in the air in the greenhouse.

The experiment in the diagram shows how to take away all the carbon dioxide from a plant's environment. In the diagram the plant is in a plastic bag, together with a little pot of the chemical **soda lime**. The soda lime absorbs all the carbon dioxide.

You can test a leaf to see if photosynthesis is working by boiling it and then adding iodine. Iodine reacts with starch, which is the stored product of photosynthesis. If a leaf turns black during the iodine test it is a sign that photosynthesis is happening.

A perfect life for plants.

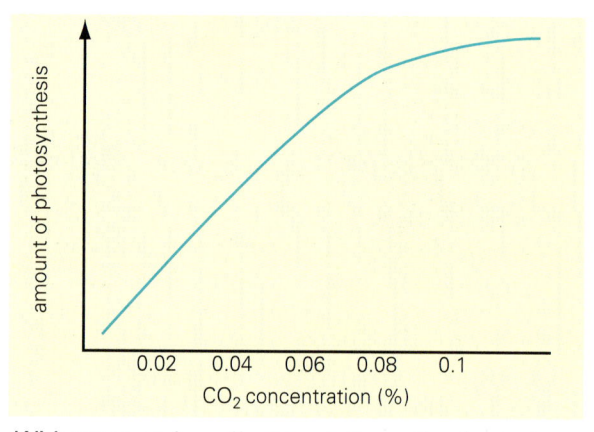

With more carbon dioxide photosynthesis works better.

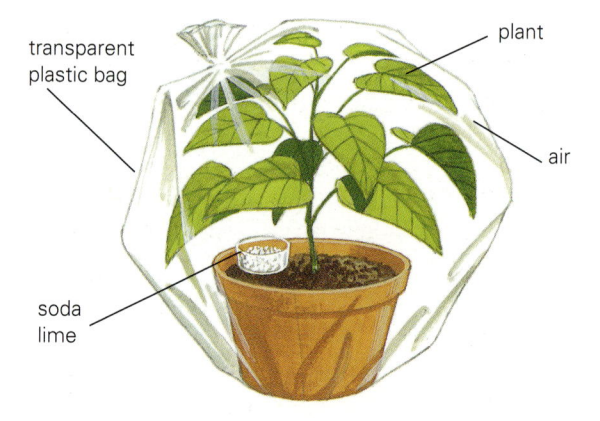

The soda lime removes all carbon dioxide.

This leaf has been living without carbon dioxide. It does not turn black with iodine because there is no starch present.

This leaf has been living in a normal environment. It turns black with iodine because it contains starch.

Temperature is a limiting factor

In this experiment, shown in the diagrams of plants A and B, photosynthesis is faster for plant B. Look at the thermometers to see why.

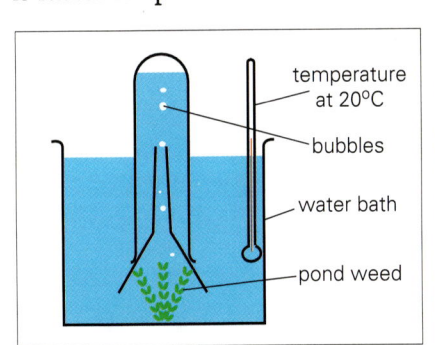

Plant A: slow photosynthesis.

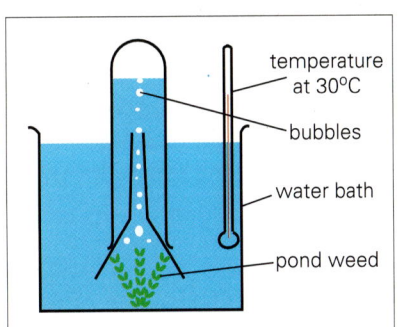

Plant B: faster photosynthesis.

QUESTIONS

1. Name the gas removed by soda lime.
2. How do each of the following conditions change the rate of photosynthesis:
   a. high carbon dioxide levels
   b. less light
   c. more light?
3. Which chemical do you use to test for starch in a leaf?
4. Which gas is being given off by plants A and B in the diagrams above?
5. Describe how you would design an experiment to test the effect of varying light intensity on photosynthesis.

KEY IDEAS

The main limiting factors for plants are light, water and carbon dioxide.

Photosynthesis increases with extra carbon dioxide.

Photosynthesis increases with extra warmth.

9.4 After photosynthesis, what next?

When plants make food, what do they do with it?
Where do plants store food, and why?

The most important product of photosynthesis is glucose. It may be needed anywhere in the plant, not just the leaves. So it must be able to travel. Glucose is transported around the plant in **phloem**. These are tubes running next to the xylem. Together the xylem and phloem are called a **vascular bundle**.

Glucose is burnt...

When glucose arrives where it is needed it is burnt or respired in order to release the energy. This process is called **respiration**. Exactly the same process happens in animals, and exactly the same gas is required – oxygen.

The sugar in cane is made by photosynthesis.

glucose + oxygen ⟶ carbon dioxide + water + energy

The energy released when the glucose is burnt keeps the plant alive. The waste products of respiration are water and carbon dioxide.

... or glucose is stored as starch

Plants must store foods too. They cannot photosynthesise all the time. They must have reserves for when temperatures are low or when there is not enough light or water. Some plants store glucose by transporting it below ground. Here the plant has its own storage areas, where glucose is turned into starch.

The vegetables shown in the photograph are all plant stores. The potato, the yam and the turnip are packed with starch. Starch molecules are thousands of glucose molecules linked together.

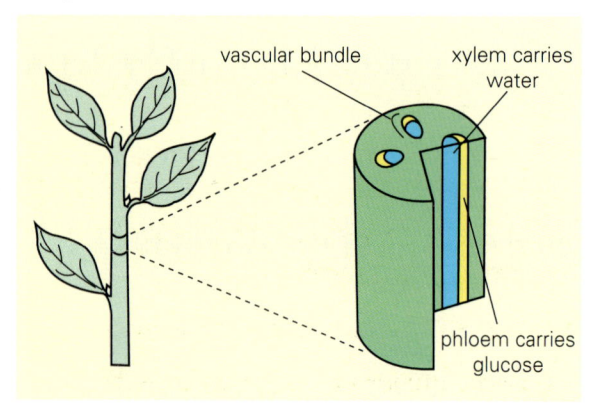

Glucose travels in the phloem.

Humans make good use of stored starch.

glucose is made in leaf

and travels underground

where the glucose molecules

combine to make starch

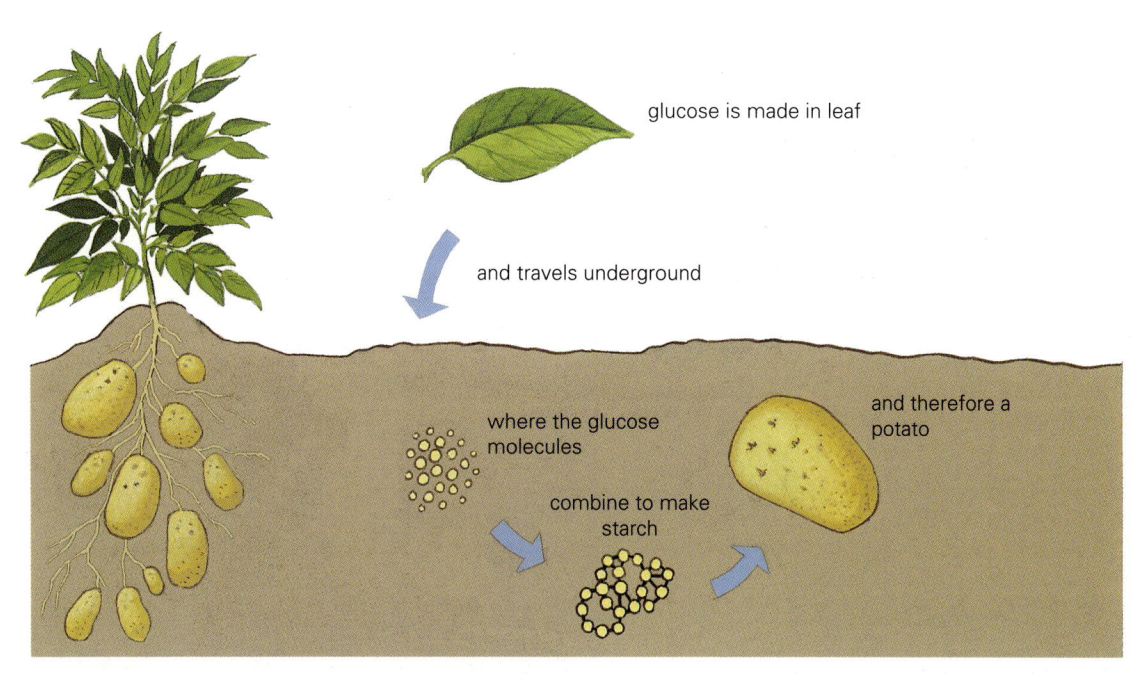

and therefore a potato

How a potato is made.

Nature's tempters.

Glucose tempts the birds

Many fruits contain glucose and another sugar called **sucrose** in order to tempt birds and other animals to eat them. Phloem carry large amounts of sugar to the developing fruit. The birds eat the sugary fruit containing the seeds. These seeds pass through the bird, are dropped in a distant place, and then begin to grow.

Plants make protein

Plants don't just make starch. They make fats, proteins and many other important substances needed for growth. They are transported by the phloem to where they are needed.

QUESTIONS

1. Which gas is needed to burn glucose?
2. What is transported in phloem?
3. List three plants which contain starch.
4. Explain why some plants make their fruits sweet.
5. Explain why starch is a rich source of glucose for animals.

KEY IDEAS

Glucose travels through the plant inside the phloem.

Some glucose is burnt for energy.

Some glucose is stored as starch.

CHAPTER 10: THE SENSITIVE PLANT

10.1 Knowing up from down

How does a root know which way to go? Why do shoots grow upwards? Plants don't think or make decisions – but they know which way to grow.

Plants have to know up and down. Roots must burrow in the soil to find water, shoots must rise up in the air to find the light. When the plant finds light and water it can photosynthesise and make its own food.

The race for light

When a buried seed begins to grow it is **germinating**. Under the ground there is no light for photosynthesis. The shoot's ability to dig upwards depends on food stores in the seed. The shoot must reach the light before the seed runs out of food. If the shoot takes too long to find the light it will die.

This plant knows where to grow.

The sensitive shoot

In the experiment shown in diagram **1** a bean was planted 2.5 cm under the soil. There is no light under the ground and yet the shoot knows which way is upwards. At this stage of its life, the shoot is responding to gravity.

In diagram **2** the shoot is lit from one side, and the soil is watered from the other side. Of course the shoot bends towards the light. It is sensitive to light. And the root bends towards the water. It is sensitive to moisture. Because of this sensitivity the plant survives.

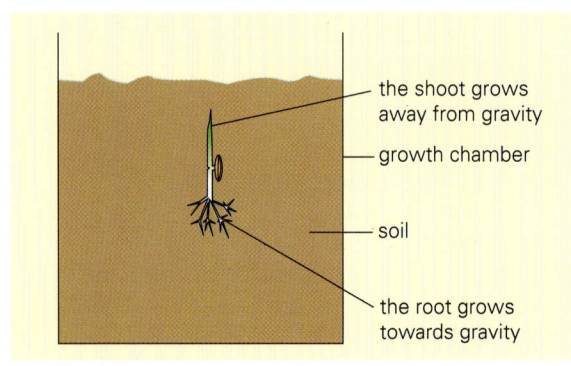

1 The bean detects gravity.

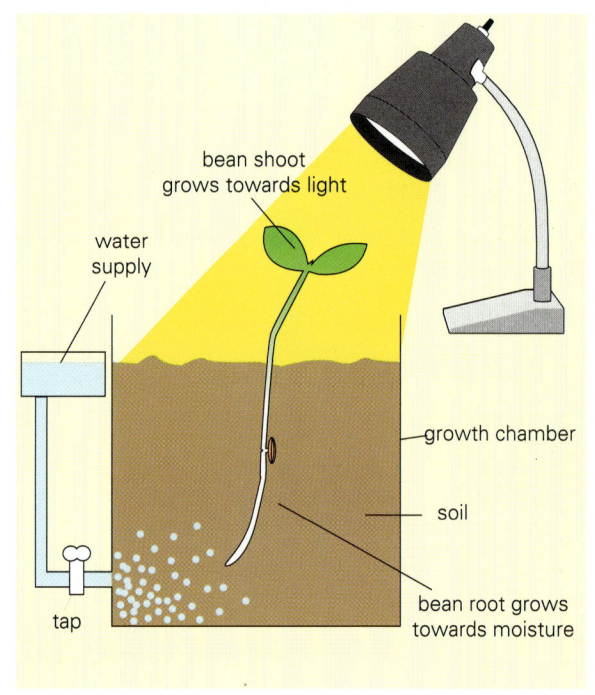

2 Now light and moisture are important.

Plant hormones

Plants don't have nerves or brains to send messages. Instead they have hormones. These are chemicals, and they can travel through the plant. Hormones make the plant grow in the right direction. When a plant bends towards the light plant hormones called **auxins** are at work.

Auxins make certain cells in the shoot grow fast. When a light shines on one side of a shoot, the auxins flow to the other side. That side then grows, and the shoot bends towards the light.

Plants will bend towards the light – wherever the light comes from.

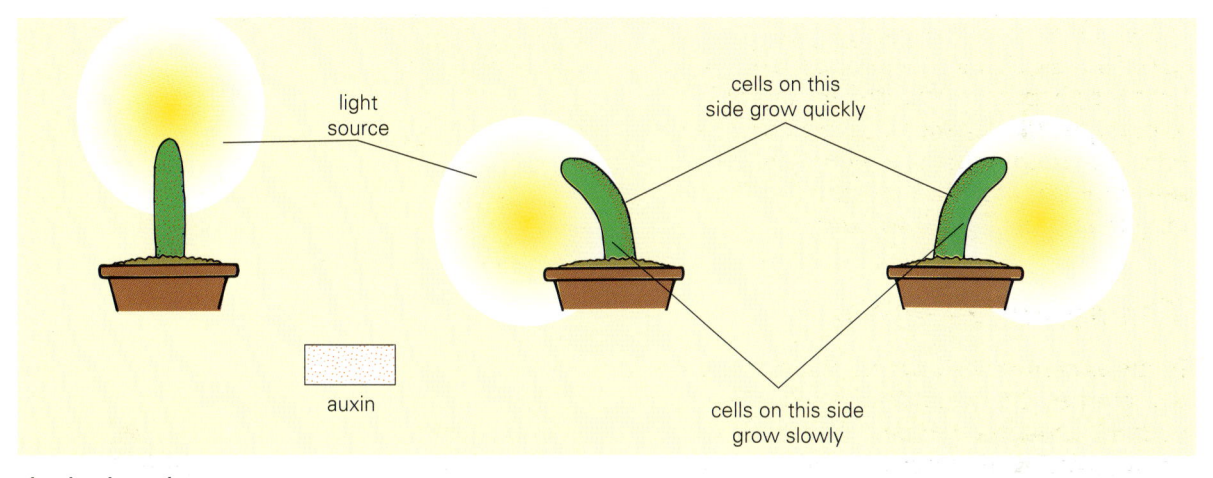

Auxins in action.

QUESTIONS

1. What is the scientific word for a buried seed beginning to grow?
2. How does gravity affect:
   a roots
   b shoots?
3. How does light affect:
   a shoots
   b roots?
4. Explain how auxin makes a shoot bend towards the light.
5. Scientists believe that only the tip of a shoot is sensitive to light. How would you investigate this idea?

KEY IDEAS

Shoots grow away from gravity and towards light.

Roots grow towards gravity and away from light.

Auxins make plants bend towards the light.

10.2 How to make plants behave

Why wait for a fruit to ripen? Why bother to dig out weeds? Scientists have found that plants will grow, make their fruit and even die – if they are artificially given auxins and other hormones.

Killing them

Auxins make excellent weedkillers. Auxins sprayed on lawns make the weeds grow wildly. But they are too thin and spindly and quickly die. The grass, surprisingly, is unaffected. This is because grass has very narrow leaves, and is a different kind of plant from most weeds. After a few days, with the weeds dead, the grass has more space, light and nutrients.

Killing the weeds.

Growing them

You can often make a new plant by taking a **cutting**. A cut stem, or even a leaf, can grow into a whole new plant if the stalk is left in water or poked into moist soil. Cuttings work well usually, but you can improve your success rate by using **rooting hormones**. These are plant hormones, such as auxins, available in powdered form in garden centres. When the powder is applied to the cutting, roots are more likely to grow.

roots growing out of stump

This cutting was dipped in rooting hormone.

Ripening them

Ripe fruits taste good but are hard to transport. Once a fruit is ripe, it is half way to rotten. For farmers and shops the easiest thing to do with fruit is to pick it unripe. Unripe fruits don't get crushed so easily and don't rot. They ripen in a warehouse and then get taken to the shops.

Bananas are picked green, and shipped when completely unripe. During the weeks on ship, plant hormones are used to make the bananas ripen slowly.

The tomatoes in the photograph are waiting to be sold. When they were picked they were still orange and hard. But now, a week later, they are almost ready to eat. In the warehouse they were treated with a plant hormone, to make sure they ripened just at the right time.

Fruit ripening is speeded up by hormones.

QUESTIONS

1. What foods can be picked unripe and then ripened later using plant hormones?
2. Why are plant hormones used on lawns?
3. When would a gardener use rooting hormone?
4. Explain how plant hormones can be used to make fruit farming more profitable.

KEY IDEAS

Hormones can be used as weedkillers.

Hormones can be used to help cuttings grow.

Hormones can be used to ripen fruit.

SECTION C: QUESTIONS

1. Which part of a plant:
   a. makes food
   b. takes in water
   c. carries water up the stem?

2. Explain the following:
   a. roots are never green
   b. plant cells are rigid when there is plenty of water
   c. plants help keep soil in place.

3. This is a diagram of the transpiration stream in a plant.

   a. Where is evaporation taking place?
   b. What is the name of the tubes carrying water up the stem?
   c. Plants sometimes close their stomata. How will this slow down transpiration?
   d. How does transpiration help plants take in minerals?

4. Sometimes rainfall changes when tropical rain forest is cut down. Why do you think this happens?

5. Explain how a cactus is adapted to reduce water loss.

6. Why is the mineral magnesium important to plants?

7. Use these words to complete the sentence.

   Sun   photosynthesis   water   chlorophyll   carbon dioxide

   Plants make their food by _____.
   This is a process requiring _____, _____
   _____ and a green pigment called
   _____. The energy for the process comes from the ___.

8. A class sets up a photosynthesis experiment using three plants A, B and C. Each plant is left for 24 hours and then tested for the presence of starch.

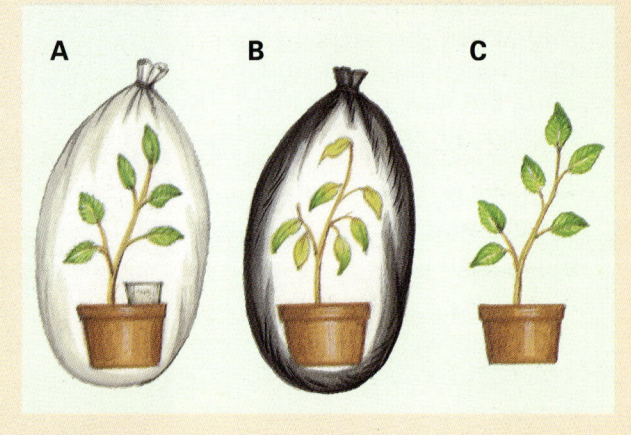

   a. How do conditions differ for the three plants?
   b. Which plants do not contain starch after 24 hours? Explain your answer.
   c. Which chemical would you use to test for starch?

9. A class used a water weed to investigate photosynthesis. They measured the number of bubbles given off per minute. They repeated the experiment at different temperatures. Their results are shown in the table below.

Temperature (°C)	No. of bubbles per minute
20	5
25	8
30	12
35	18
40	25
45	30
50	30
55	0

a Draw a graph of these results.
b At which temperature was photosynthesis fastest?
c Explain why there were no bubbles at 55°C.

10 Use these words to complete the sentence.

**storage organs   oxygen   starch
respiration   phloem   energy**

During photosynthesis the plant makes glucose and _____. Glucose travels through the plant inside _____.

The plant can release _____ from glucose by the process of _____ or store it as _____. Potatoes, carrots and other edible roots are all examples of plant _____ _____.

11 Photosynthesis can be increased by boosting levels of which gas?
  a Carbon dioxide.
  b Nitrogen.
  c Oxygen.
  d Methane.

12 What is the response of a shoot to:
  a gravity
  b light?

13 What is the response of a root to:
  a gravity
  b moisture?

14 Auxins make shoots bend towards the light. They do this by:
  a increasing cell growth on the light side
  b increasing cell growth on the dark side
  c moving into the roots
  d stopping the flow of water.

15 Explain the following:
  a Some weedkillers contain growth hormone.
  b Growth hormones are used in fruit farming.
  c Gardeners sometimes use growth hormone when they make cuttings.

16 In experiments A and B plant shoots were lit from one side.

These are the results:

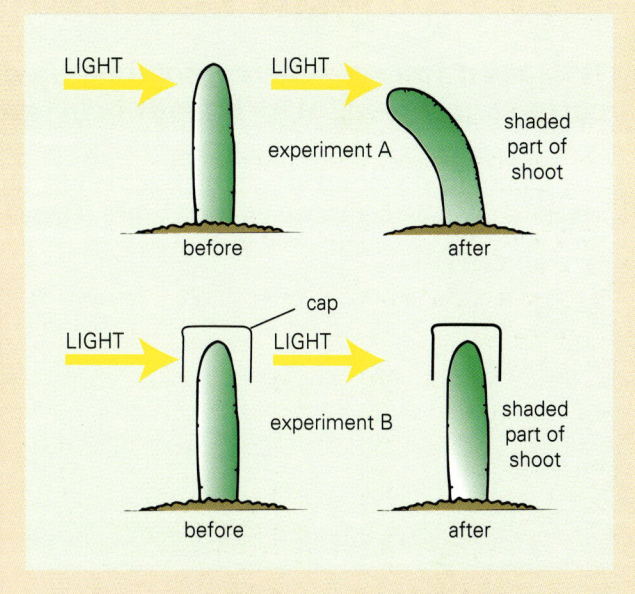

a What differences can you see between experiments A and B?
b Where in plant A would you find auxin?
c Which part of a plant shoot is sensitive to light?

17 A gardener plants some tomato seeds. When the tomato plants are grown, their heights are measured. These are the results:

Height (cm)	Number of plants
30–33	2
34–37	5
38–41	4
42–45	1
46–49	0
50–53	0
54–57	2
58–61	8
62–65	7
66–69	2

a How many varieties of tomato were there in the seeds?
b Each variety has a range of heights. Why is this?
c Describe an experiment investigating how the environment can cause variation in tomatoes.

CHAPTER 11: THE PATHWAY OF FOOD

11.1 Food for life

Why must you eat different foods every day? What is wrong with eating only bread? Which foods help you grow?

The mix of food you eat is your diet. A healthy diet must contain seven basic ingredients, called **food types**. These are:

- carbohydrates
- fats
- proteins
- vitamins
- minerals
- dietary fibre
- water.

Each food type gives you something you need. But no food gives you everything you need. If you eat fruit you may get plenty of vitamins, but hardly any fat. So you have to eat lots of different foods to make sure you get all your food types. A diet with the right mix of food types is called a **balanced diet**.

Enjoying a balanced diet.

Carbohydrate for energy

The body needs **carbohydrates** for energy. Sugar and starch are the two main kinds of carbohydrate. Biscuits, cakes, sweets and fruit contain plenty of sugar. Rice, bread, pasta, potatoes and other vegetables contain lots of starch. These foods are all said to be *rich* in carbohydrate.

These foods are rich in carbohydrate.

Fat for storing energy

Milk and cheese, fish and meat all contain a lot of **fat**. You use fats as a store of energy, and as a warm insulating layer under your skin to protect against heat loss.

You don't just *eat* fat, you make it too. If you eat more carbohydrate than you need, it may get turned into fat and stored.

The fat beneath this young seal's skin helps keep it warm.

Protein for growth

Protein is found in meat, beans and fish. Vegetables also contain protein, but in smaller quantities. When you grow your bones get longer and your muscles get bigger. Your skin area increases too. To do this body building you need protein.

Even when you stop growing you still need protein. Your cells must be replaced and repaired. Skin cells constantly flake off from your skin. To replace them you need to build new ones – using protein.

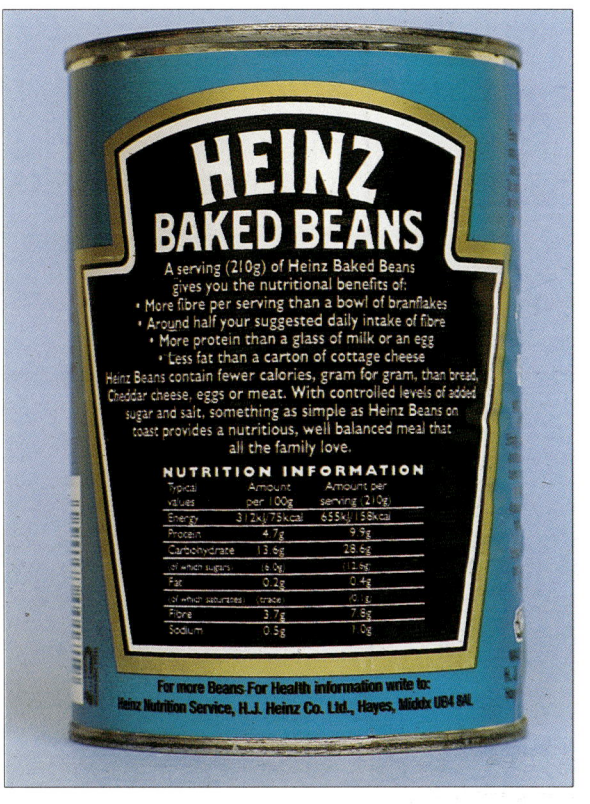

Baked beans are rich in protein and carbohydrate.

QUESTIONS

1. List the seven food types.
2. Which food type is starch?
3. List three foods containing starch.
4. Which food type is most important for growth?
5. Explain how fat is important in the life of a seal.

KEY IDEAS

A balanced diet is made up of seven food types.

The body uses carbohydrate and fat for energy.

The body uses protein for building.

11.2 Vitamins and minerals

Have you ever been told that milk is good for your teeth or that carrots help you see in the dark? Why are foods like these important?

A balanced diet includes a good supply of **vitamins** and **minerals**. The main vitamins are vitamins A, B, C and D. Minerals include iron, calcium and iodine. The health of your eyes, skin, bones and teeth depend on these two food types. For example vitamin A is important for good vision.

Vitamins in your diet

Vitamins are found in most fresh foods, such as fruit and vegetables, fish, milk and cheese. If you enjoy eating vegetables and fruit you are probably satisfying your body's needs. You need only small amounts. But many vitamins cannot be stored by the body so you need to eat some of these foods every day.

Vitamin	Food	How your body uses the vitamin
Vitamin **A**		helps skin and good vision
Vitamin **B**		is required by the nervous system
Vitamin **C**		helps keep skin and blood vessels healthy
Vitamin **D**		keeps bones and teeth strong

The common vitamins.

A cause of disease

Any disease caused by not enough vitamins is called a **vitamin deficiency disease**. An example is **scurvy**, caused by a lack of vitamin C. Hundreds of years ago scurvy was common among sailors. On long voyages they didn't have enough fresh fruit and vegetables in their diet. The symptoms of scurvy are aching limbs, bleeding gums and drying up of the hair and skin.

Two important minerals

Iron is found in meat, vegetables and fruit. The amount of iron in your body is about the same as you'd find in a two-inch nail. Iron is important for the health of your blood.

Without plenty of iron, you cannot make enough red blood cells, the part of the blood which carries oxygen. Having too few red blood cells is called **anaemia**.

Calcium is found in milk, cheese and other dairy products. It helps build strong bones and teeth, so it is important for growing children and for pregnant women. Mothers breastfeeding their children sometimes need extra calcium.

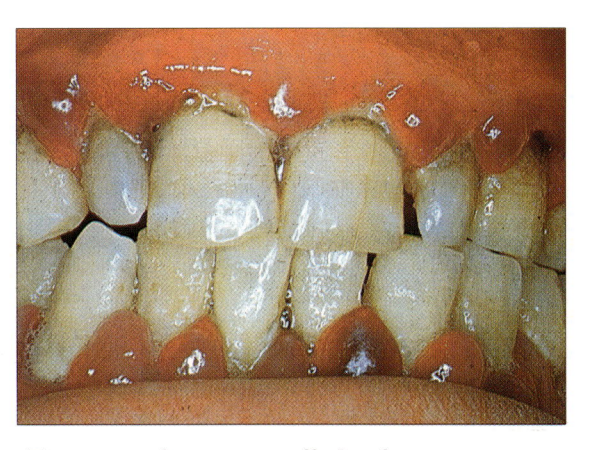

The gums of a person suffering from scurvy.

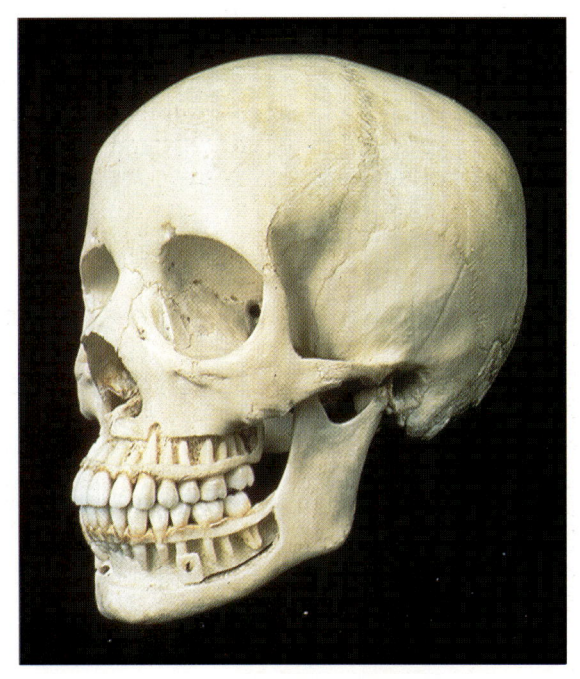

Calcium is used to make bones and teeth.

QUESTIONS

1. What are the main vitamins?
2. Name a food containing vitamin C.
3. Name a food containing vitamin D.
4. Which vitamin helps vision?
5. How is iron useful to the body?
6. Why might a pregnant women need extra calcium?

KEY IDEAS

Vitamins and minerals are needed in small amounts.

Lack of vitamin C causes the deficiency disease scurvy.

Lack of iron causes the deficiency disease anaemia.

11.3 Completing your diet

Why is brown bread good for you?
Why are some foods advertised as 'high in fibre'?

Fibre

Like every other part of your balanced diet, you need **dietary fibre** or roughage for your health. Dietary fibre is found in raw vegetables and fruit, wholemeal bread and muesli.

Wholemeal bread and cereals are rich in fibre.

Fresh fruit contains plenty of fibre.

Fibre consists of the cell walls and seed coatings of plants. This material is tough and indigestible. Instead of being broken down it stays in the gut, making the food more solid and bulky. Because fibre makes food more solid, the muscles in the wall of the intestine can easily grip the food and push it in the right direction. The way the intestines push the food along is called **peristalsis**. If there is not enough fibre in your diet it is harder for the intestines to keep the food moving. This may result in constipation.

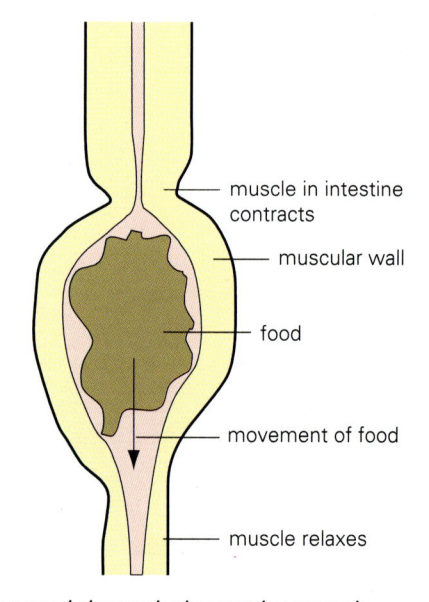

Food is moved through the gut by muscle contractions or peristalsis.

The body needs water

Water is the most common substance in your body. At least two-thirds of your body weight is made of water. Even your bones and teeth contain water. Each day you lose plenty of water in sweat, breathing, urine and faeces.

Water is lost in the breath.

You can replace water by eating and by drinking. Every food you eat contains some water. Ninety per cent of the weight of salad and fruit is water. You take in even more water when you drink tea, coffee and soft drinks.

The water in your diet must be clean and fresh. Some water does more harm than good. Salt water makes you more thirsty than before. Dirty water can cause diarrhoea, making the faeces watery and increasing the amount of water lost from the body.

QUESTIONS

1. List three foods which contain dietary fibre.
2. How much of your body weight comes from water?
3. Give three ways your body loses water.
4. How does your body replace water?
5. How can drinking dirty water increase water loss?

KEY IDEAS

Fibre is part of a balanced diet and helps to prevent constipation.

At least two-thirds of your body weight is water.

You must replace the water you lose in urine, sweat and faeces.

11.4 The human gut

When did you last eat? Where is that meal now? What happens in your stomach?

Most often a meal is forgotten straight after swallowing. Yet your digestive system gets into action as soon as your teeth begin to crush and you swallow the food.

Your food's journey

Breakfast and dinner are different to look at and taste. But to your digestive system every meal is much the same. Each meal must be *chopped* and *swallowed*. Then the meal is *digested* in the **gut**, *absorbed* into your bloodstream, and carried round your body. For this to happen, it must pass through the **oesophagus**, the **stomach**, the **small intestine** and the **large intestine**. Your pancreas and liver are involved too. Many organs are needed to keep your digestive system working.

First stop: your teeth

When you eat, food is taken into your mouth. For a few seconds only your mouth begins to process the food. Each mouthful is cut and ground by your teeth. The food is made wetter by saliva and your tongue mixes it together.

There are four types of teeth in your mouth, and each has its own job.

- Incisors are sharp. They grip and cut the food.
- Canines are pointed. They tear the food.
- Premolars and molars are flat and large. They crush and grind the food.

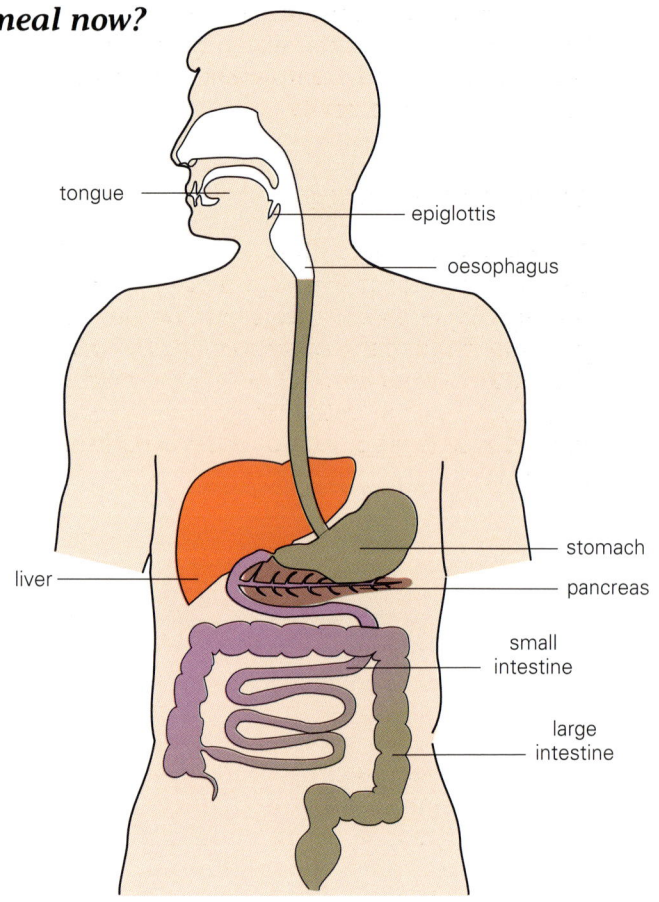

The main organs of the human digestive system.

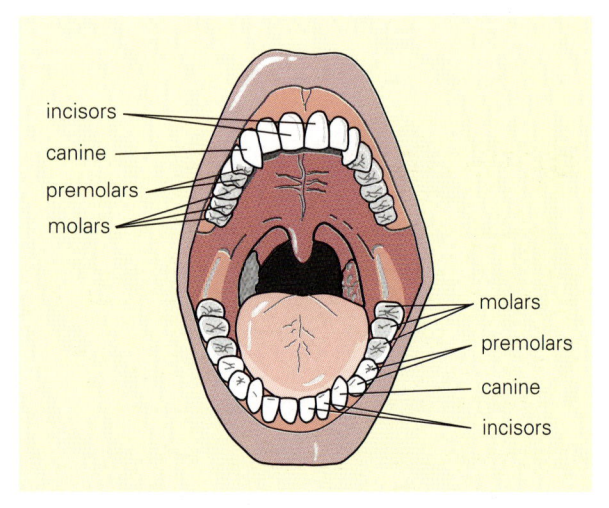

The position of teeth in the mouth.

All teeth must be strong and long-lasting. The enamel on the outside of a tooth is the hardest substance in the body. Beneath the enamel is a bony substance called dentine. Under the dentine is the soft pulp cavity. Teeth are alive and are nourished by blood vessels in the pulp cavity.

Why teeth decay

The main cause of tooth decay is sugar in the diet. When you eat sweets or a sugary meal, a syrupy layer covers each tooth. Bacteria in your mouth turn the sugar to acid. The acid then attacks your enamel, and may make a hole. Bacteria can enter the soft-part of the tooth through the hole and cause a painful infection.

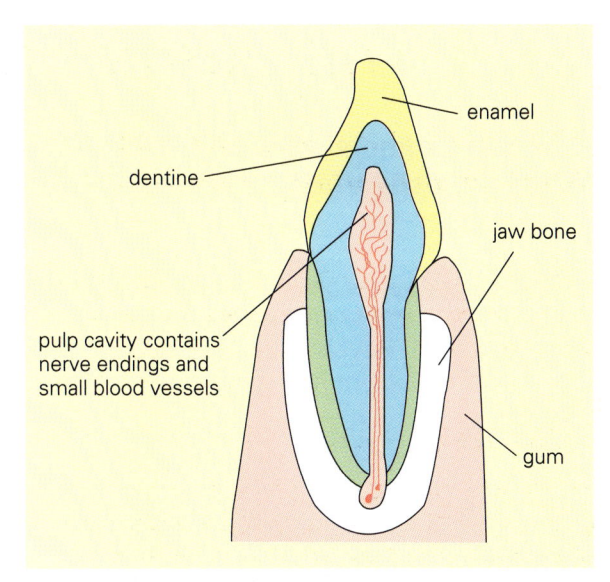

A section through a human tooth.

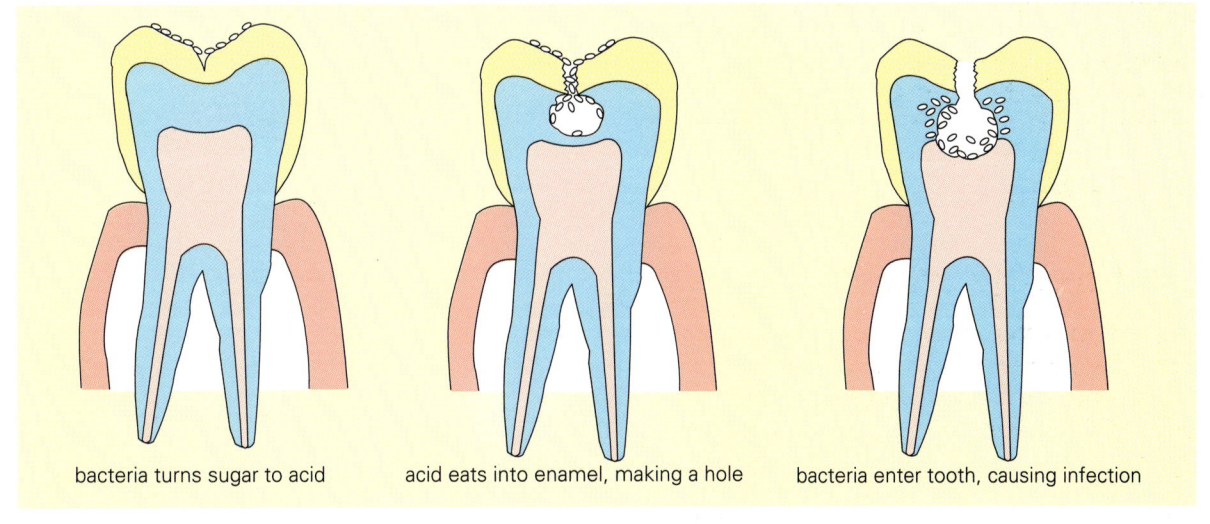

bacteria turns sugar to acid   acid eats into enamel, making a hole   bacteria enter tooth, causing infection

How infection starts.

QUESTIONS

1. List five of the organs in the digestive system.
2. What are premolars and molars used for?
3. What substance on the outside of your teeth helps to make them strong and long-lasting?
4. Explain how sugary foods can cause tooth decay.

KEY IDEAS

All meals must be chopped, swallowed, digested and absorbed.

Teeth cut and grind each mouthful of food.

Teeth are alive and contain blood vessels.

11.5 The food pipe and stomach

How do you know when to swallow?
What happens when you swallow the wrong way?

Swallowing

Once your teeth have crushed the food, your tongue pushes it to the back of your mouth, ready for swallowing.

Swallowing is usually automatic. You only sometimes think about it, perhaps when you swallow something the wrong way. Swallowing is triggered by food touching the back of the throat. First, muscles pull a flap called the **epiglottis** over your wind pipe or trachea, making sure the food goes into the food pipe or oesophagus. If you try to swallow too quickly the epiglottis may not have time to close properly. Some food gets into the trachea and you start to cough.

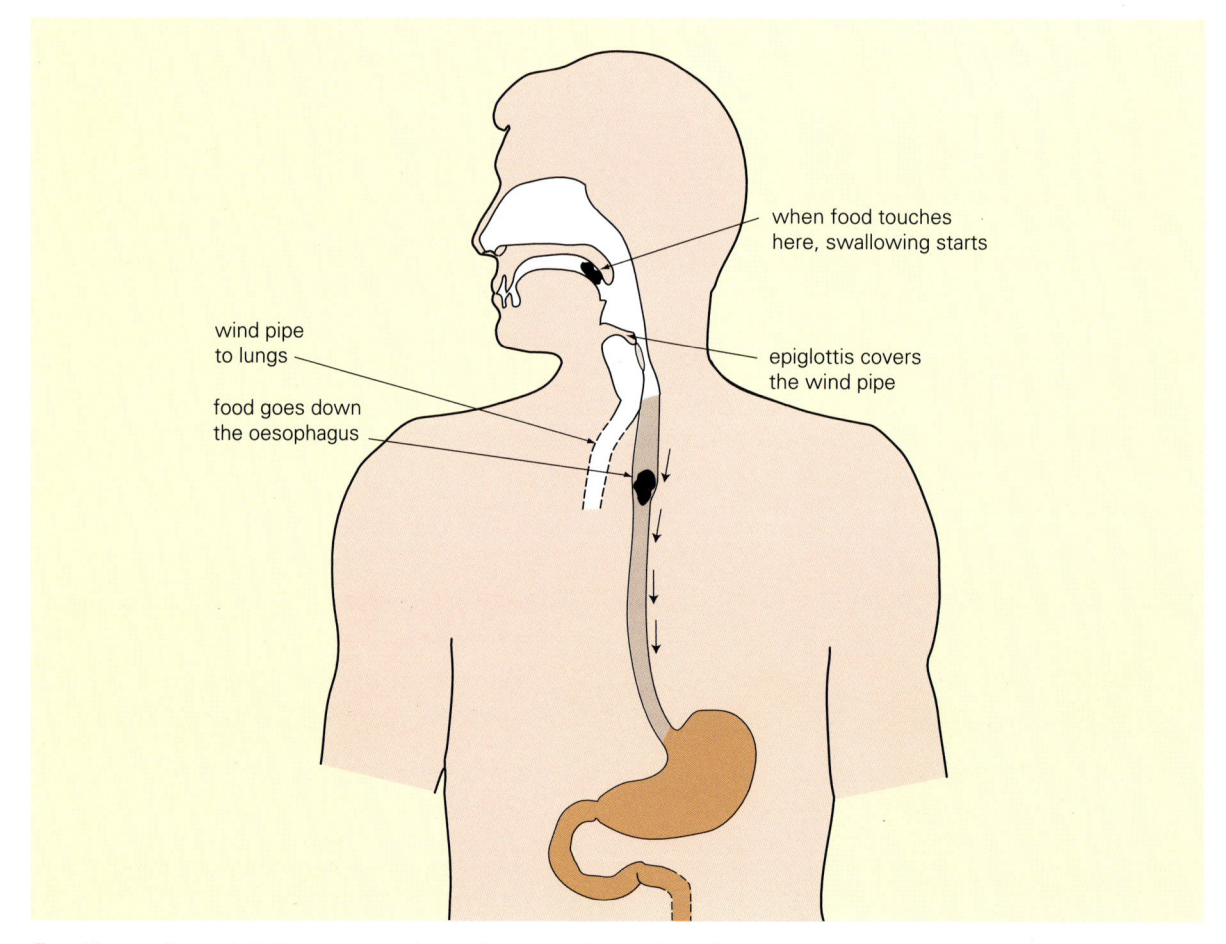

Food is swallowed. It then passes down the oesophagus into the stomach.

Down the food pipe

The food pipe or oesophagus is a muscular tube. As soon as you swallow, the oesophagus grips the food and forces it into the stomach. The food will go into your stomach even if you are lying down – or standing on your head.

Digestion in the stomach

The food you swallow is crushed and mushy, but it still consists mostly of large food molecules. The large molecules cannot be used by the body until they are broken down chemically. This is called **digestion** and happens inside your stomach and small intestine.

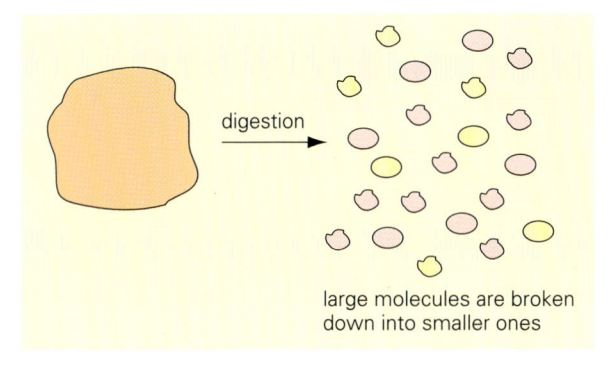

Food is digested into small molecules.

Digestive juices, including enzymes, are produced in glands in the stomach wall.

Digestion uses chemicals called **enzymes** to attack the molecules. The enzymes in the stomach digest only the larger protein molecules, breaking them down into smaller molecules.

The stomach is also a storage bag, mixing your meal and sending small quantities at a time into the small intestine.

QUESTIONS

1. What is another name for the chemicals used in digestion?
2. What are the two jobs of the stomach?
3. Explain how the epiglottis makes sure you swallow properly.

KEY IDEAS

Swallowing is triggered by food touching the back of the throat.

The oesophagus is a muscular tube taking food to the stomach.

Enzymes in the stomach break down the large protein molecules.

11.6 The small intestine

Is it your stomach that rumbles, or your small intestine? How important is your pancreas?

Noisy digestion is usually the fault of the small intestine. For this is where your food spends longest, and is changed most. The food is mixed and churned, pushed along and squeezed. Your meal becomes a watery soup which is absorbed through the wall of the small intestine and into the bloodstream.

The pancreas makes enzymes

The small intestine needs enzymes for digesting the food. Most of the enzymes are made by the **pancreas**, a small organ just beneath your stomach. When food passes from the stomach to the intestine, the pancreas pours out enzymes. They flow down into the intestine and are mixed in with the food.

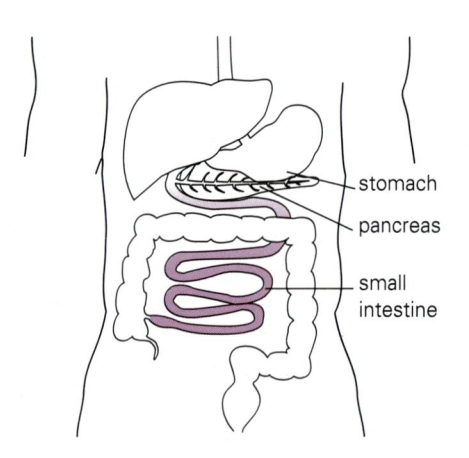

Digestion and absorption take place in the small intestine.

Digesting large starch molecules

Most meals contain the carbohydrate starch. Starch molecules are too large to pass through the wall of the small intestine into the blood. So an enzyme called **amylase** digests starch molecules into glucose molecules, which are small enough to be absorbed. The blood can then take the glucose molecules to the cells.

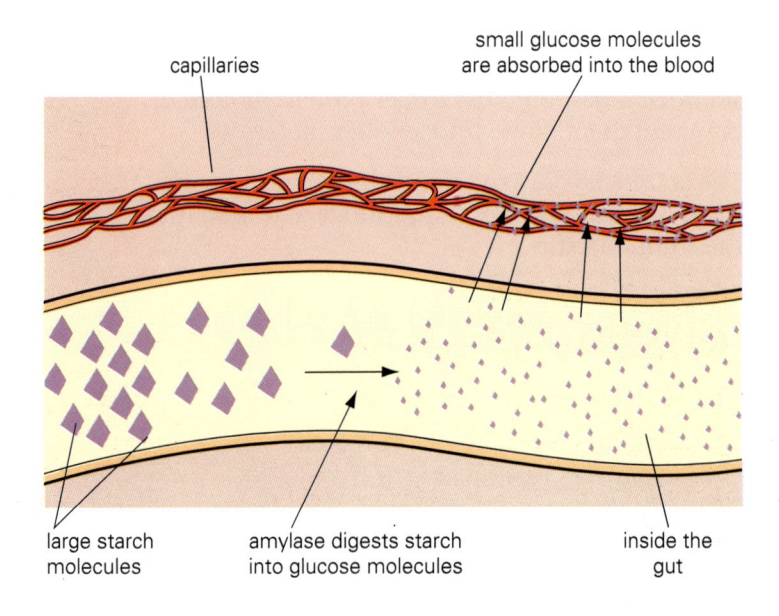

How digestion works.

A closer look

Digestion involves many chemical reactions. Each food type is digested by a different enzyme to make a different product useful for your body. The table shows which enzymes are used to digest your food.

Food	Enzyme	Product
carbohydrates	amylase	sugars
proteins	protease	amino acids
fats	lipase	fatty acids

The small intestine is designed to digest and absorb. Your body needs the food molecules that are circulating around the blood system for the cells. They must not remain too long in the intestine. So the intestine is designed to make sure absorption happens quickly. Folds in its walls make a larger surface area through which absorption can take place.

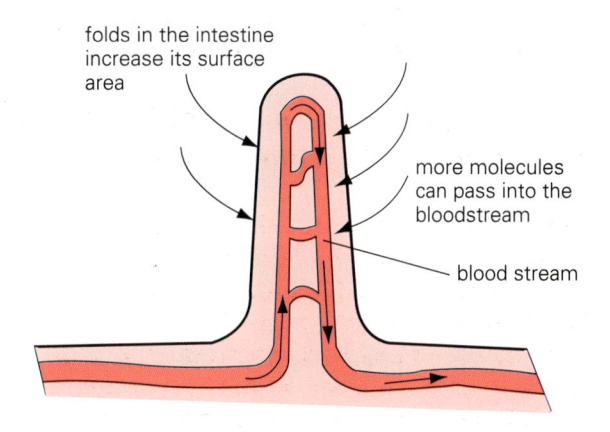

The wall of the intestine is folded to increase the amount of absorption.

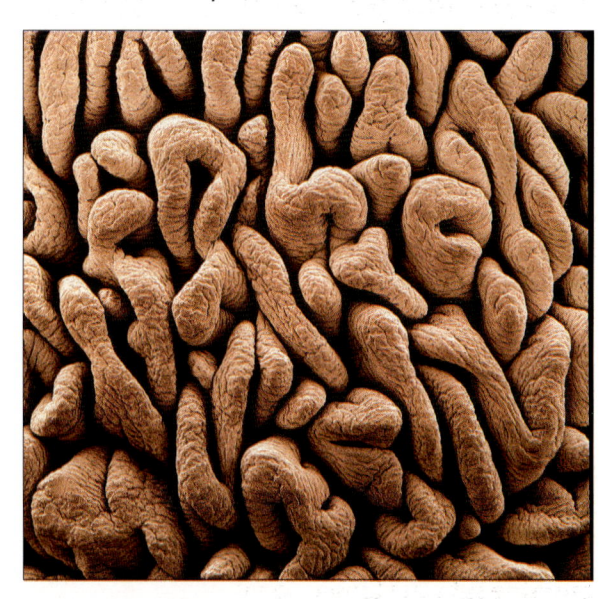

The inside of your small intestine looks like this.

QUESTIONS

1. Which organ makes many enzymes?
2. List three enzymes.
3. Which enzyme digests starch?
4. Explain how the small intestine is adapted for:
   a digestion
   b absorption.

KEY IDEAS

The small intestine is for digestion and absorption.

Amylase is the enzyme which digests large starch molecules into smaller sugar molecules.

The wall of the small intestine is folded to speed up absorption.

11.7 The large intestine

What is your faeces made of?
What makes you want to go to the toilet?

Your meal completes its journey by passing into the large intestine. By now the food molecules have been digested and absorbed. The nutrients in your meal are circulating in the blood. However, not everything you eat is digested and absorbed. The work of the intestine is not over. The last part of your food's journey is in the large intestine.

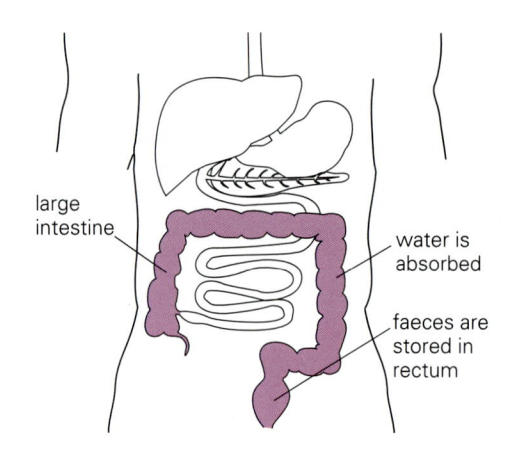

Absorbing water

The material arriving in the large intestine is very slushy. Not only have you taken in water with your food, your body adds extra water to the mix inside the intestine. The large intestine must take this water back by re-absorbing it. If the water left your body with your faeces you would quickly fall ill from lack of water. Lack of water in the body is called **dehydration**.

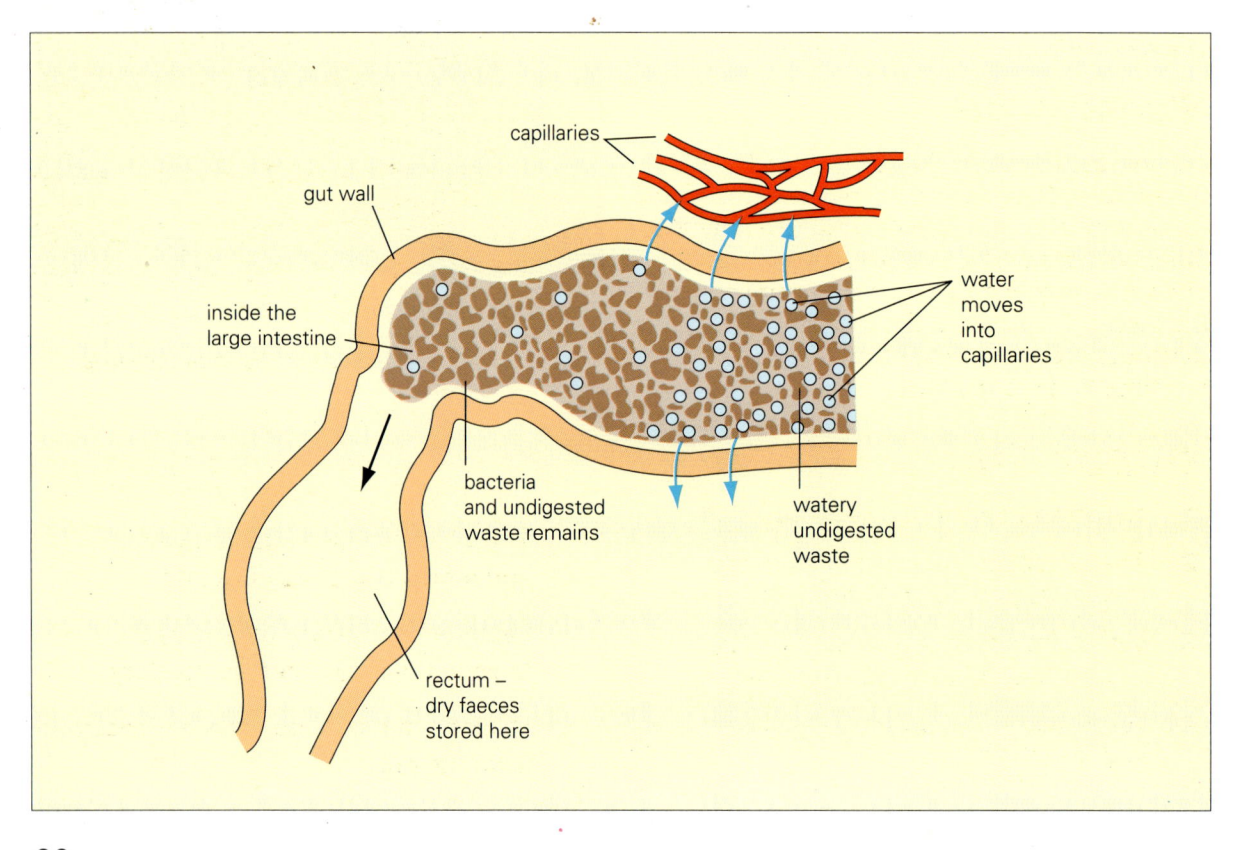

The large intestine.

Storing bacteria

Your large intestine is home to billions of bacteria. They feed on your undigested dietary fibre. They do you no harm – in fact doctors believe the bacteria are useful and may help in keeping your large intestine healthy.

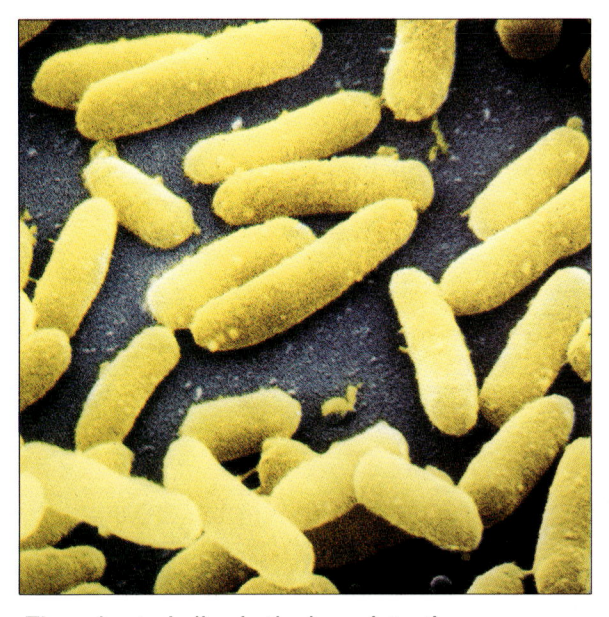

These bacteria live in the large intestine.

Storing waste

The last section of the large intestine is called the **rectum**. Here your meal reaches the end of its journey. It is now mostly undigested dietary fibre, bacteria and a *small* amount of water. The waste is called **faeces**. The rectum stores the faeces. Then, when the rectum is full, nerve messages are sent to the brain, reminding you it is time to go to the toilet.

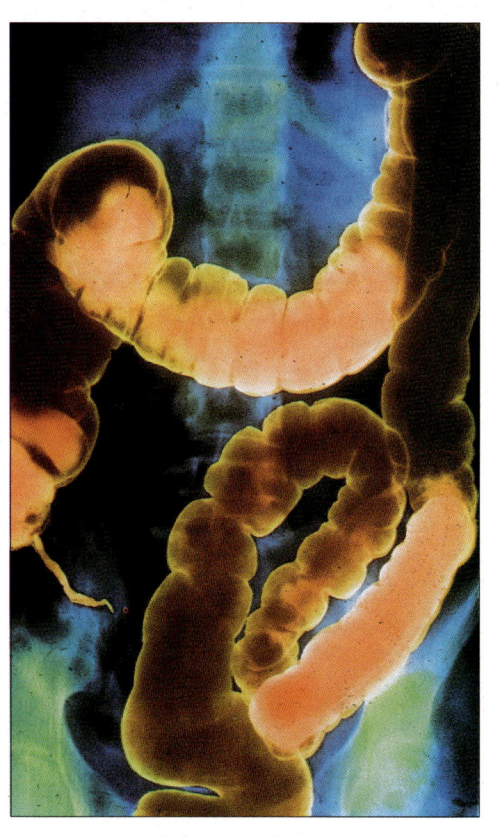

An X-ray shows the shape of the large intestine.

QUESTIONS

1. Name two jobs of the large intestine.
2. The intestines contain a lot of water. Where does it come from?
3. Which food type increases the growth of the bacteria in the large intestine?
4. Why must the large intestine absorb the water in the intestines?

KEY IDEAS

The large intestine absorbs water and stores bacteria and waste.

Bacteria and dietary fibre may help to keep the large intestine healthy.

Faeces is a mix of bacteria and waste from the gut.

CHAPTER 12: THE RESPIRATORY SYSTEM

12.1 Why we breathe

What happens to the air you breathe in? Where does it go?

You can remain alive without food and water for a few days but you need to breathe in and out every few seconds. Very few people have survived longer than five minutes without air.

You breathe in order to take in oxygen from the air and to get rid of waste gases. Your breathing, or **respiratory system** is designed to get oxygen into your body as quickly as possible. It is an efficient system, working even while you are asleep and making sure that you take in as much oxygen as you need.

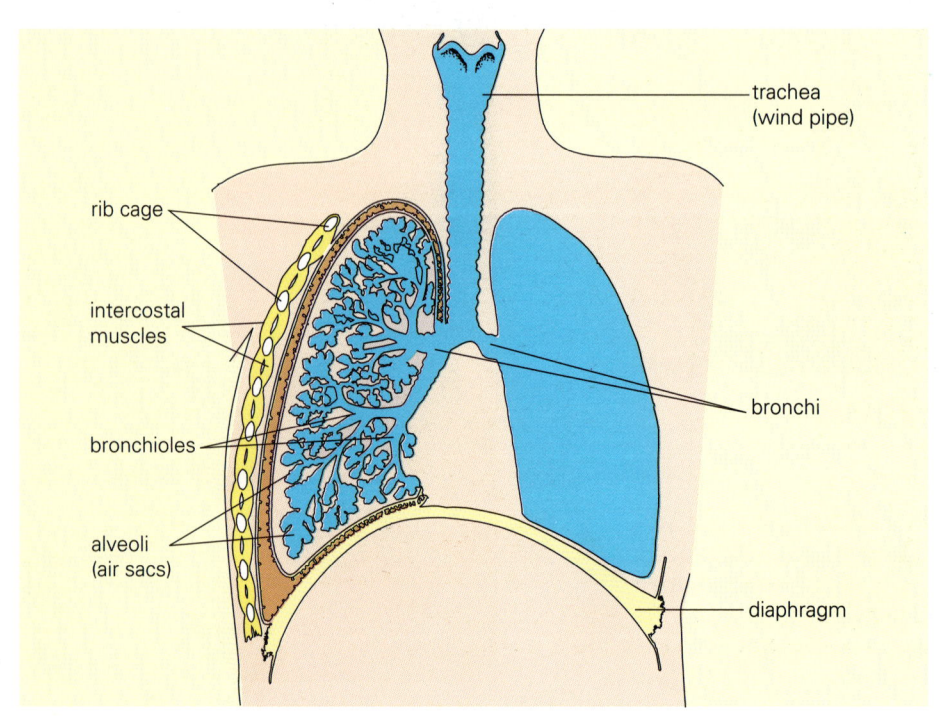

The breathing system.

Your breath's journey

Your respiratory system is made up of air passages, starting with your nose and mouth and ending in the millions of tiny air-filled sacs that form your lungs. The lungs are protected by the rib cage which surrounds them.

Your breath usually starts its journey in your **nose**. Your nose cleans the air as it enters the body, and warms it. Hairs inside the nose act as a filter. They remove some of the particles of dust and dirt that might otherwise clog up the air passages. You can also take in air through your mouth, though this air is not filtered.

Your wind pipe or **trachea** takes your breath from your mouth and nose, down towards your lungs. The trachea is strengthened by hard rings, which prevent the tube collapsing inwards. The photograph of the trachea was taken from inside the body and the rings are clearly visible.

Two large branches or **bronchi** come from the trachea and carry air into the lungs. The bronchi divide many times into smaller tubes called **bronchioles**.

At the end of each bronchiole is a group of tiny air-filled sacs, called **alveoli** (singular, **alveolus**). Each lung contains millions of alveoli.

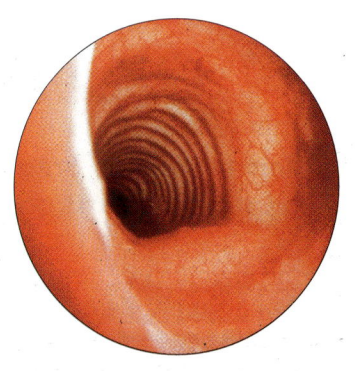

The trachea is strengthened by tough rings.

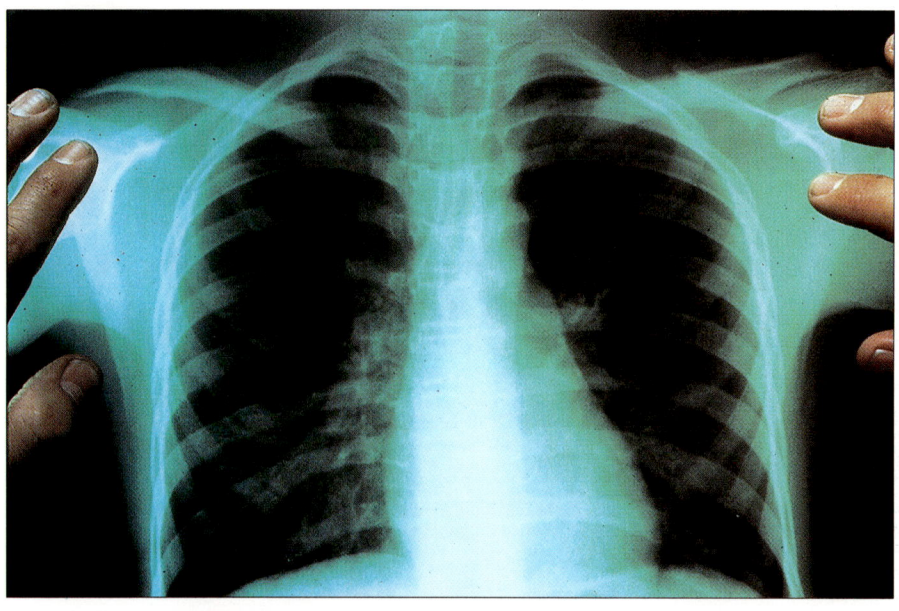

An X-ray shows the lungs beneath the rib cage. The lungs are the dark areas on the left and right and the white bulging area in the middle is the heart.

QUESTIONS

1. What is another name for your wind pipe?
2. What is the job of the bronchi?
3. What are alveoli?
4. How are the lungs protected?
5. Why is the wind pipe strengthened by hard rings of cartilage?

KEY IDEAS

You breathe in order to take in oxygen from the air, and get rid of waste gases into the air.

12.2 Gases in, gases out

Why do you need to breathe?
What is so important about breathing?

Every one of your cells needs oxygen. They die without it. They need a supply, 24 hours a day. The lungs are your way of getting oxygen to the cells.

The air sacs

Your lungs are not simple bags. They are red and spongy, formed from millions of tiny alveoli, or air sacs. Each alveolus has a very thin wall. On one side of the wall is the air you breathe in. On the other side is a network of small blood vessels. It is easy for gases to pass from one side to the other.

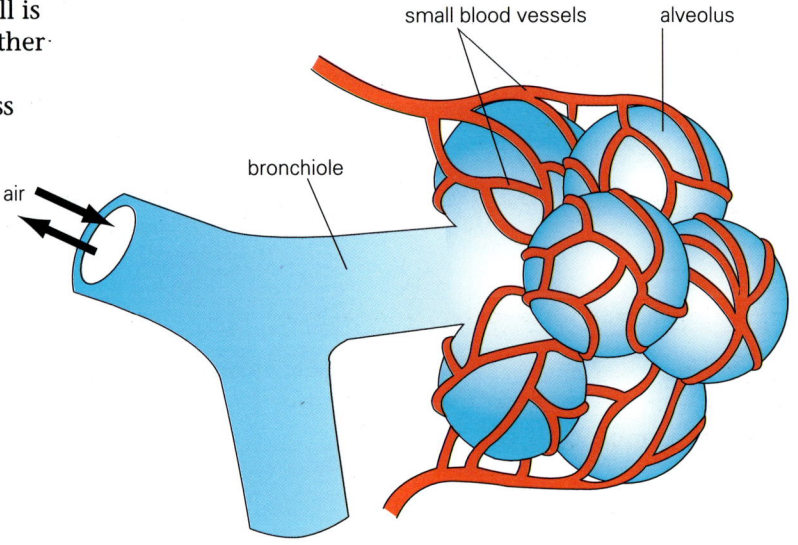

Small blood vessels run close to each air sac.

Your lungs do not remove all the oxygen from each breath. So the air you breathe out contains some oxygen. The table below shows how inhaled air is different from exhaled air.

Gas	Air going into the lungs (inspired air)	Air coming out of the lungs (expired air)
oxygen	21%	16%
Carbon dioxide	0.04%	4%
nitrogen	79%	79%
water vapour	a little	a lot

How your lungs change the air.

Oxygen passes across the wall of the air sac into the blood. At the same time, the waste gas carbon dioxide leaves the blood and passes into the air sacs. This movement of oxygen and carbon dioxide is **gas exchange**. Valuable oxygen moves into the blood stream and waste carbon dioxide moves out of the blood stream. They are *exchanged*.

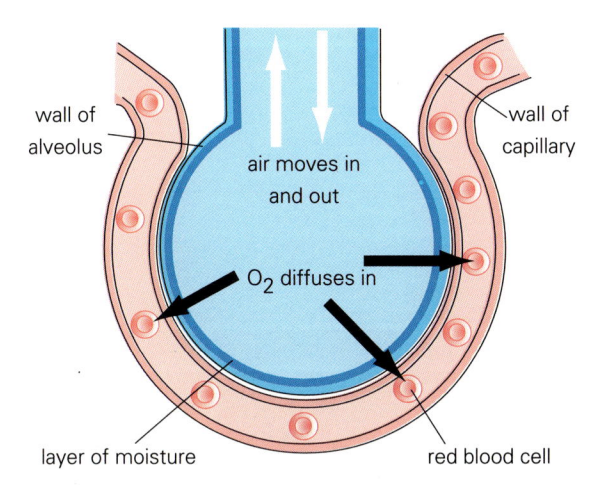

Oxygen passes out of the air sac into the blood.

Carbon dioxide passes out of the blood into the air sacs.

Increasing the surface area

Your lungs are efficient because they have a large surface area. Gas exchange can take place quickly and easily across the walls of so many millions of alveoli.

QUESTIONS

1. Which gas is needed by your cells?
2. Where are the alveoli or air sacs?
3. Which gases are exchanged in the lungs?
4. Give two differences between *inhaled* and *exhaled* air.
5. Why are there so many alveoli?

KEY IDEAS

Gas exchange takes place across the walls of the air sacs.

Oxygen passes into the bloodstream.

Carbon dioxide passes out of the bloodstream.

12.3 *Breathing in, breathing out*

What makes you yawn? Why don't you stop breathing when you are asleep?

When you breathe you fill your lungs with air, and then empty them. To make the lungs fill and empty you use a sheet of muscle attached to the bottom of your ribs, called your **diaphragm**.

Breathing is controlled by nerve centres in your brain. A message travels from the brain and makes the diaphragm contract and flatten. This gives your lungs more room, and so they get larger. As your lungs expand, air is sucked in. This is called **inhalation**.

After contracting, the diaphragm automatically relaxes. The relaxed muscle rises upwards, squeezing the lungs smaller. Air is pushed out. This is called **exhalation**.

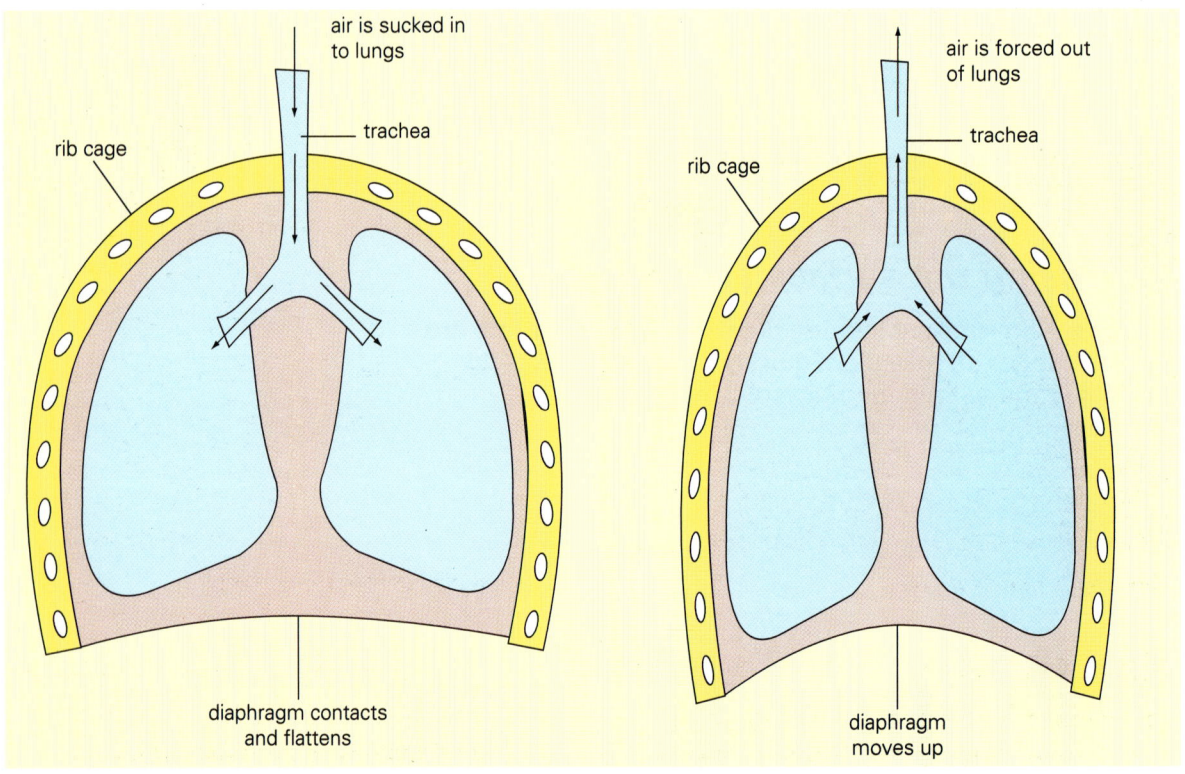

Inhalation.

Exhalation.

The **intercostal muscles** lie between each rib (see 12.1). When these muscles contract the ribs move up and out, making your chest larger. This expands the lungs and more air rushes in. When the intercostal muscles relax the rib cage falls. The lungs are squeezed and the air is forced out.

Controlling your breathing

Normally you take 15 breaths each minute. When you exercise the rate increases. When you sleep the rate decreases. The rate changes because your body's need for oxygen changes.

You don't usually think about your breathing. The brain automatically controls the diaphragm and rib cage. During exercise your brain senses that you need more oxygen for your muscles. Nerve messages are sent to the diaphragm and the rib cage. The messages increase your breathing rate.

A yawn is a big inhalation. You probably yawn sometimes during the day, not just when you are bored or sleepy. Yawning 'stretches' the lungs, and increases their efficiency. During yawning your rib cage expands and your diaphragm flattens.

Yawning is good for you.

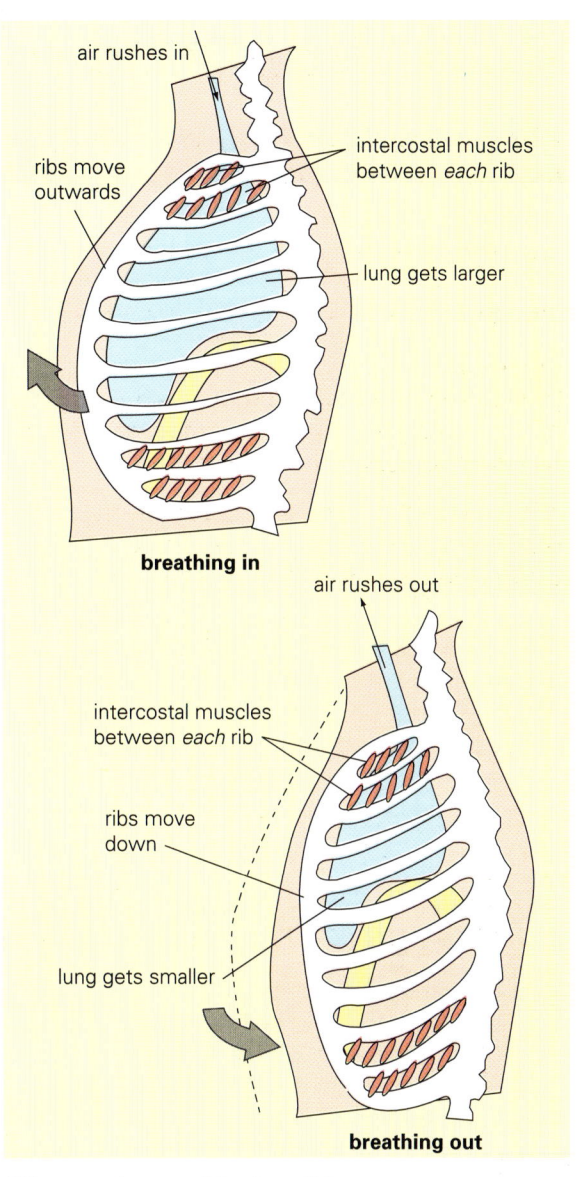

Ribs are also used for breathing.

QUESTIONS

1. How does the shape of the diaphragm change when you **a** inhale, **b** exhale?
2. Describe how the size of the lungs change during exhaling and inhaling.
3. When do you use the rib cage for breathing?
4. Explain how the intercostal muscles help in breathing.

KEY IDEAS

You inhale when the diaphragm flattens.

You exhale when the diaphragm rises.

You use your rib cage for heavy (deeper and faster) breathing.

12.4 Protecting your lungs

What kinds of 'dirty' air do you breathe in every day? Can you protect your lungs from pollution and disease?

Your body needs oxygen all the time, wherever you are. You cannot stop breathing just because the air is polluted. Unfortunately the bronchi and lungs are very sensitive to air pollution, and are easily damaged. But your body can protect itself against some dust and dirt.

The nose warms and cleans the air

Your nose *warms* and *cleans* the air you breathe, ready for the lungs. As air passes into your nose it flows near blood vessels, which warm it up. The hairs inside your nose are moist with mucus. They trap any dust and dirt you breathe in. Blowing your nose gets rid of the dirt.

Coughing can help to clean your lungs

Your nose may not catch all the dirt. If dust does travel down into the trachea, coughing may bring it back up again. When you cough you exhale violently. Dust in the trachea is blown out of you, together with saliva and germs.

When things go wrong

Sometimes viruses enter your breathing system and cause harm. A common cold is an infection of your lungs. The bronchi and lungs become irritated and you begin to cough. Each cough blows out millions of viruses, but plenty remain inside. Someone with **bronchitis** has a more serious infection of the bronchi.

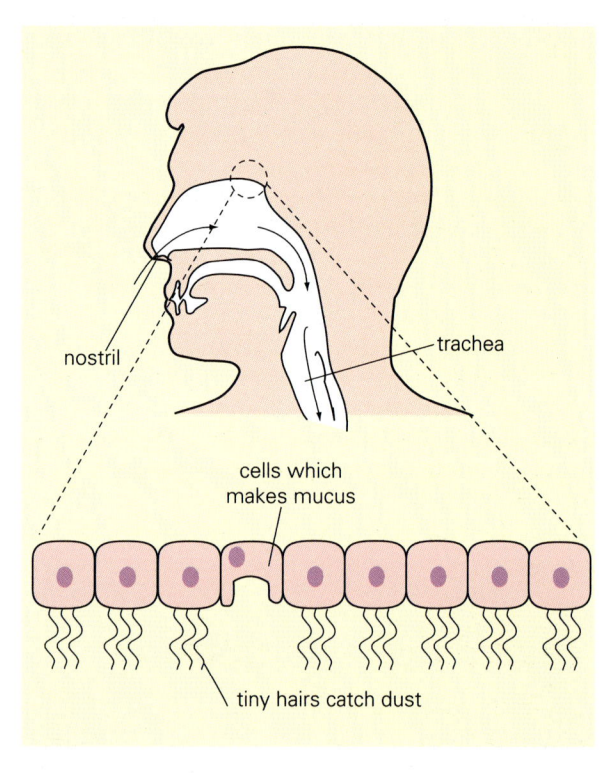

Your nose defends your lungs.

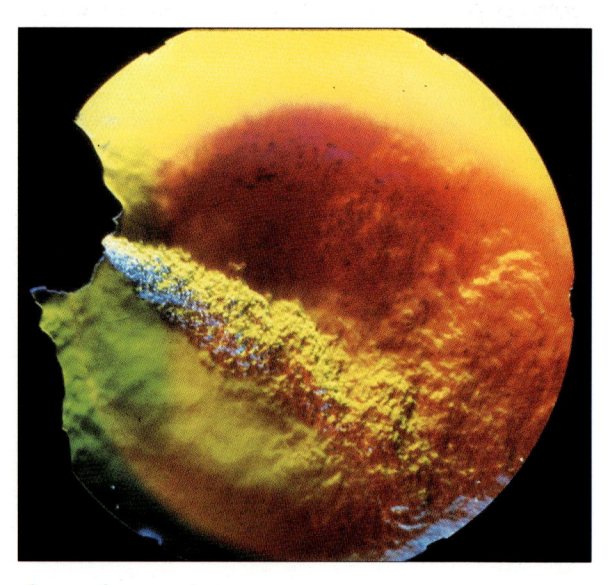

A cough may clean you up.

Air pollution

Most people have to breathe in polluted air. **Nitrogen oxides** are polluting gases released from cars. These gases irritate your nose, throat and lungs. People with breathing problems, such as asthma, may suffer more because their trachea and bronchi are especially sensitive.

Ozone pollution

Ozone is another gas which can harm your lungs. Most of the world's ozone is high up in the atmosphere. Up there, ozone is helpful for life because it filters out dangerous ultraviolet radiation But down at street level, ozone is a dangerous pollutant.

Street ozone only climbs to dangerous levels when there is a lot of traffic and the weather is sunny. The Sun's rays trigger chemical reactions among car exhaust gases, forming ozone. At times like these most people will find the air unpleasant to breathe. Then, when the sunny weather is over, ozone levels fall again.

The trouble with smoking

Cigarette smoke contains three poisons. Each harms you in a different way. Tar runs down inside your lungs and covers your alveoli with poisonous oil. Nicotine is addictive and causes heart disease. Carbon monoxide poisons your blood by making it less good at carrying oxygen.

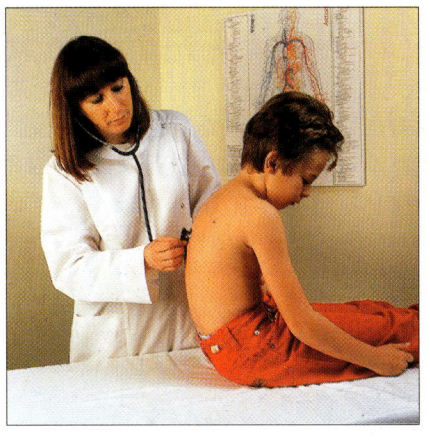

The doctor is listening for problems with breathing.

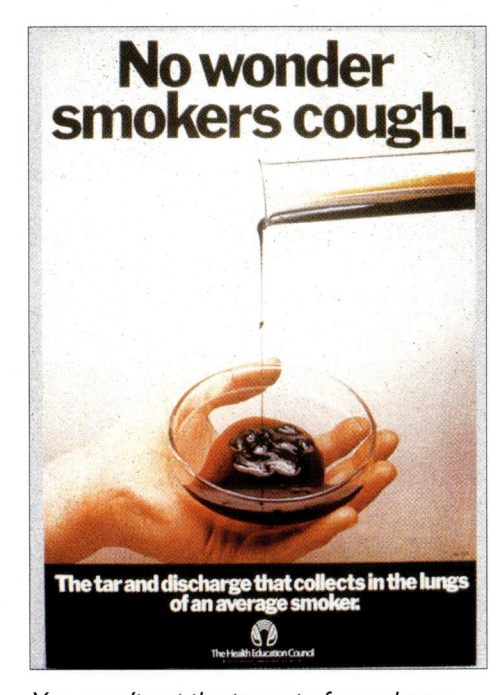

You won't get the tar out of your lungs.

QUESTIONS

1. Which illness affects the bronchi?
2. Explain what your nose does to the air you breathe.
3. Explain how smoking harms your health.
4. Why is ozone pollution most likely on sunny days?

KEY IDEAS

Your nose cleans and warms the air you breathe.

Air pollution harms the lungs.

Cigarette smoke contains three poisons – tar, nicotine and carbon monoxide.

CHAPTER 13: UNDERSTANDING BLOOD

13.1 A transport system

All the cells in your body need food, water and oxygen for energy and growth. How does the food in your gut reach a growing toenail? How does oxygen find its way from your lungs to your brain?

You need a system for *transporting* helpful substances around the body. Your blood is your transport system. Every cell in the body is connected to the blood system.

Lorries and roads are a transport system.

Blood circulates around the body

Your blood moves around the body inside tubes called **blood vessels**. These vessels reach every part of your body, including your nails, hair roots and teeth. The blood is pumped along the vessels by your heart. It always moves, or circulates, in the same direction.

Each time blood circulates round the body it picks up fresh supplies of oxygen from the lungs. When it visits the gut it picks up food molecules.

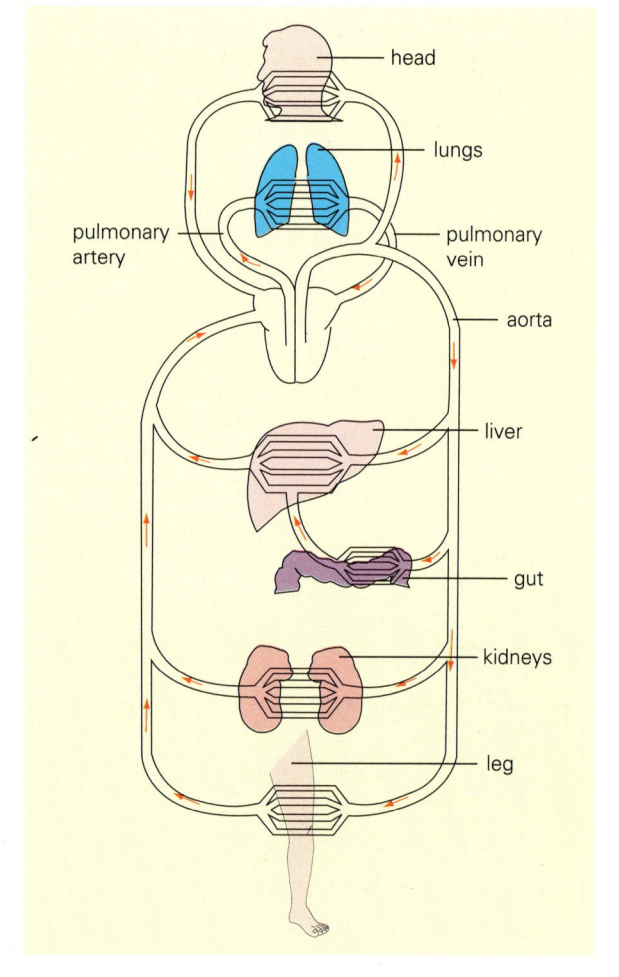

The human transport system.

What the blood carries

- Your cells need oxygen molecules. Your blood brings them from the lungs.
- Your cells must get rid of waste carbon dioxide. It is removed by the blood and taken to the lungs.
- Your cells need food molecules. Your blood brings them from the gut.

Changing the blood flow

Your body can control how much blood is sent to an organ. When you eat a meal, extra blood is sent to your gut, to help carry away digested food. After you have finished digesting your meal, blood is diverted away from the gut. Now extra blood is available for your muscles.

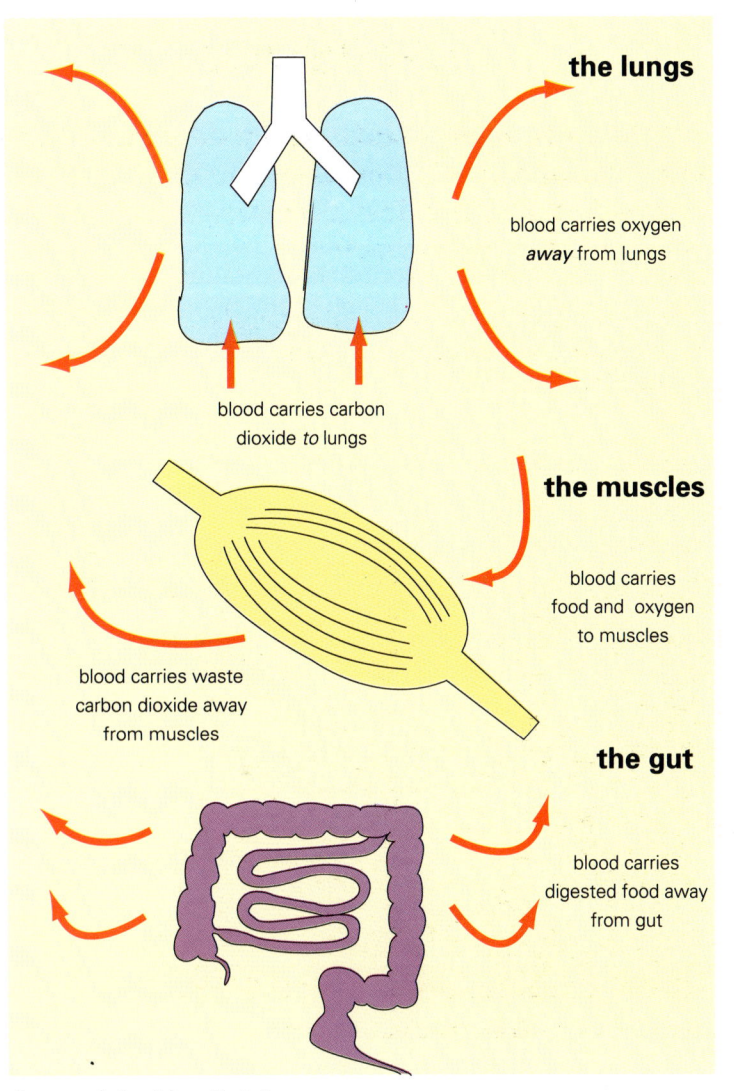

the lungs
blood carries oxygen *away* from lungs
blood carries carbon dioxide *to* lungs

the muscles
blood carries food and oxygen to muscles
blood carries waste carbon dioxide away from muscles

the gut
blood carries digested food away from gut

Some of the blood's jobs.

QUESTIONS

1. Name two substances transported by blood.
2. Where does the blood pick up food molecules?
3. Why does the blood take waste carbon dioxide to the lungs?
4. Why does the body sometimes send extra blood to the gut?

KEY IDEAS

Blood is the body's transport system.

Blood brings food from the gut to the cells.

Blood carries carbon dioxide from the cells to the lungs.

Blood carries oxygen from the lungs to the cells.

13.2 Your heart beat

Why does your heart beat? Why does your heart make a sound?

Your heart is made of strong muscle, called **cardiac muscle**. This type of muscle can contract many times a minute, day and night, without rest. The job of the heart is to force the blood through the blood vessels. When the heart stops pumping, the blood stops moving.

The double circulation

The heart is like two pumps, working side by side. The *right side* of the heart pumps blood only to the lungs. The blood returns from the lungs to the *left side* of the heart. This side of the heart pumps the blood to every other part of the body. The way the heart pumps blood first to the lungs, and then to the rest of the body, is called the **double circulation**.

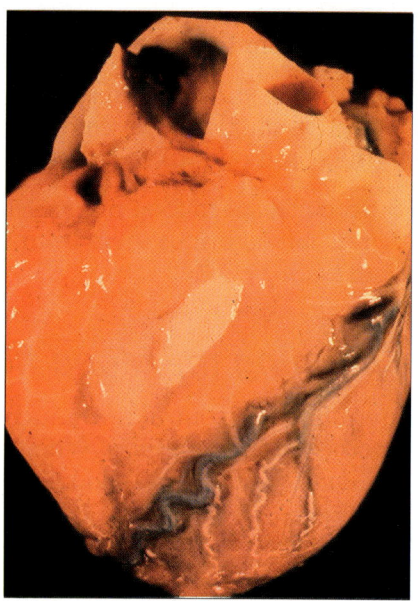

The heart is made of muscle.

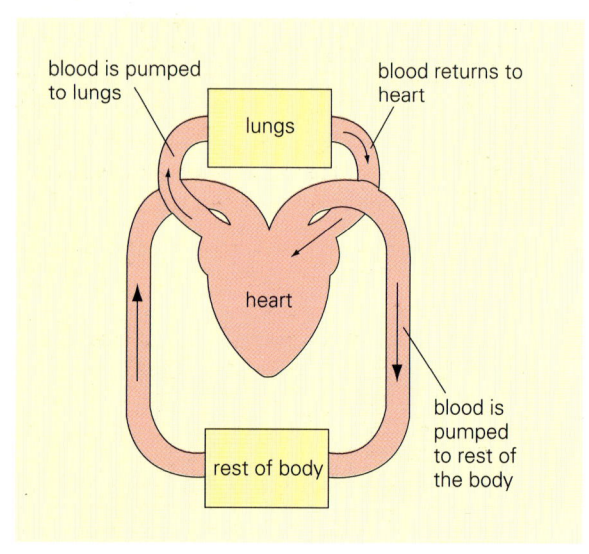

The double circulation.

In the diagram you can see the heart has four parts or chambers. The top two chambers or **atria** take in blood returning to the heart. The bottom two chambers or **ventricles** have the job of pumping the blood out of the heart.

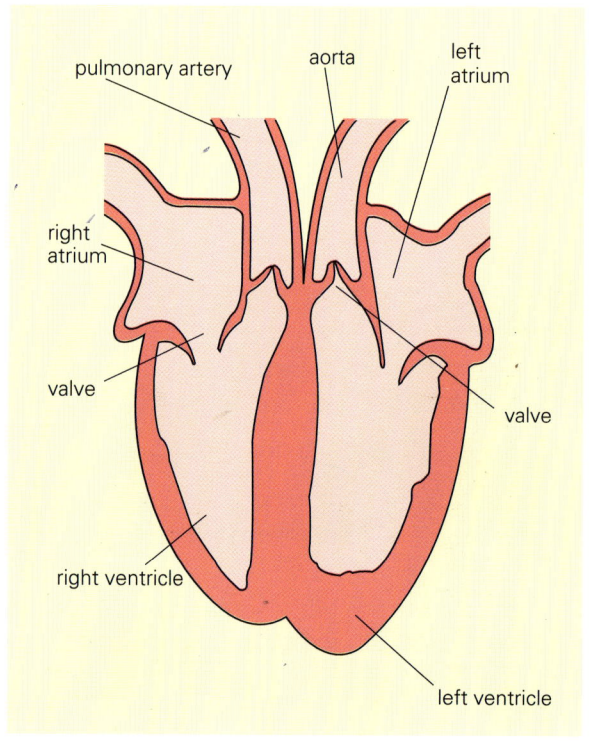

The human heart.

You can see that the muscles of the left ventricle are thicker than the muscles of the right. This is because the left ventricle has to pump blood right round the body. The right ventricle has less work to do. It has only to pump blood to the lungs and back.

Heart sounds

Heart sounds are made by **heart valves**. These are flaps which open and close, making sure the heart pumps blood in one direction. When the valves close, preventing backflow, they make a noise.

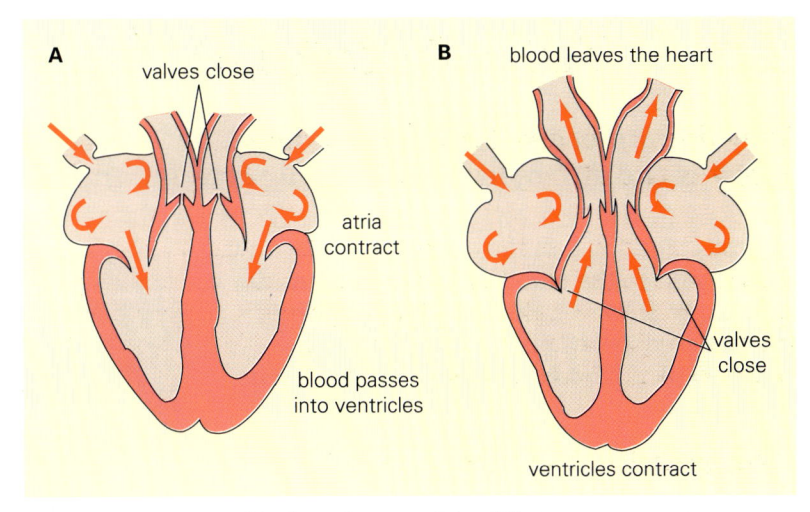

*The atria contract (**A**), then the ventricles (**B**).*

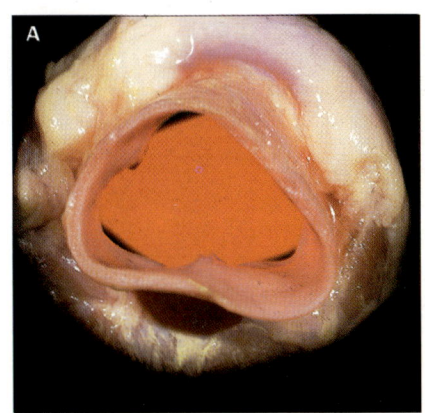

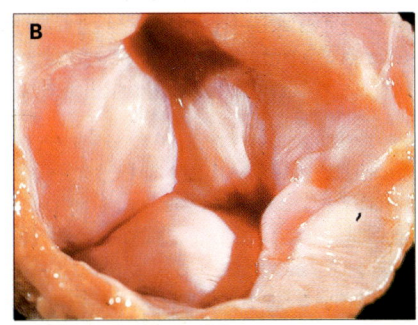

*Heart valves open and close to keep blood flowing in the right direction. **A** open valve, **B** closed valve.*

QUESTIONS

1. How many heart chambers are there?
2. Link these statements:
   a The left ventricle . . .
   b The right ventricle . . .
   c The left atrium . . .
   d The right atrium . . .
   e . . . receives blood from the lungs.
   f . . . pumps blood to the rest of the body.
   g . . . receives blood from the rest of the body.
   h . . . pumps blood to the lungs.
3. Explain why the left ventricle is more muscular than the right ventricle.
4. Explain why the human body has a double circulation.

KEY IDEAS

The heart pumps blood round the body.

The ventricles are the main pumping chambers.

Valves make sure blood flows in the right direction.

13.3 Blood vessels

Why do you have a pulse in your wrist?
What is the difference between your arteries and veins?

All your blood vessels have one main job, and that is to keep the blood moving safely inside your body. However, the size and strength of the vessels depends on whether they are carrying blood *towards* or *away* from the heart.

Arteries

Blood vessels leading away from the heart are called **arteries**. Arteries are tough and strongly built. They carry blood at *high pressure* away from the heart and towards the organs. Their thick walls are strengthened with stretchy muscle and elastic.

Sometimes arteries come close to the skin. The artery in your wrist comes so close to the surface that you can feel the **pulse**, or blood pressure wave. Each time your heart beats, high pressure blood surges out into the arteries. The high pressure causes the arterial walls to expand slightly. When you take your pulse you are feeling the expansion of the artery in your wrist.

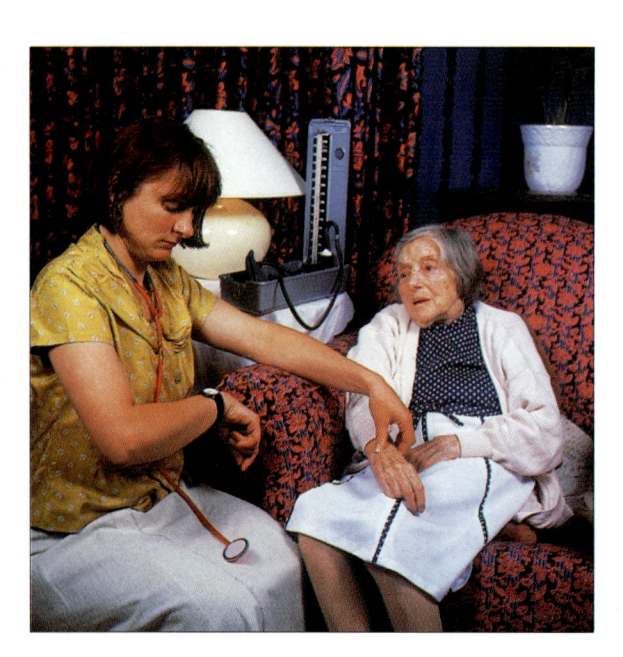

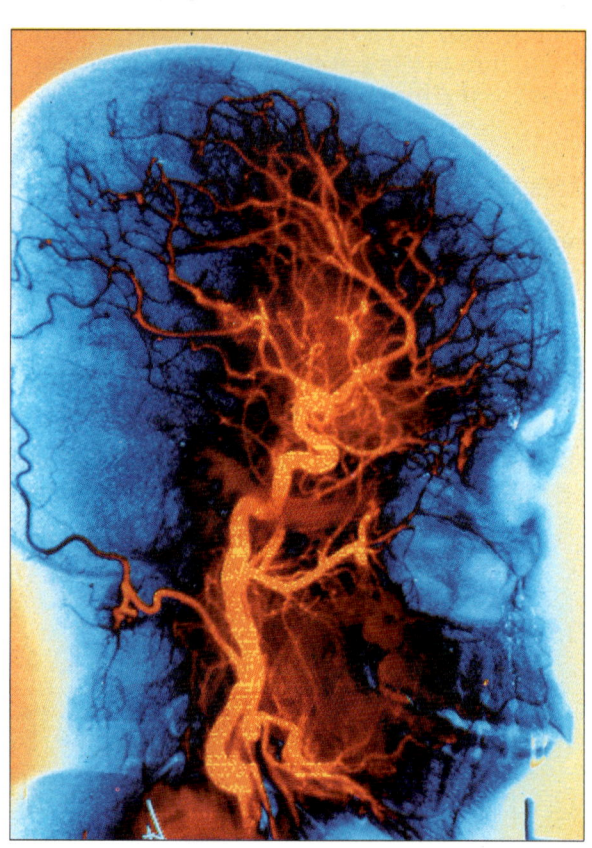

Many blood vessels lie just beneath the skin.

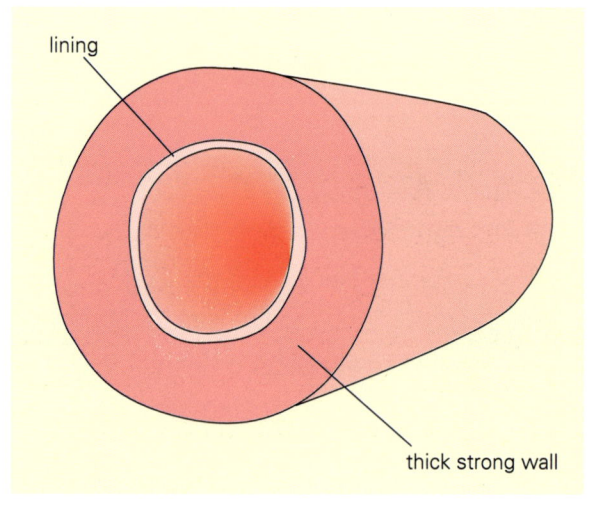

An artery has thick walls.

Veins

Blood vessels leading back to the heart are called **veins**. Veins bring blood back from the organs towards the heart. This blood has a *low pressure* and so veins do not need thick walls. Veins are not nearly as strong as arteries.

Capillaries

Capillaries are the smallest blood vessels. All your organs are criss-crossed with capillaries, which are small enough to run extremely close to the cells. Capillaries are fragile and have walls only one cell thick. It is easy for food, water and oxygen to cross through this wall.

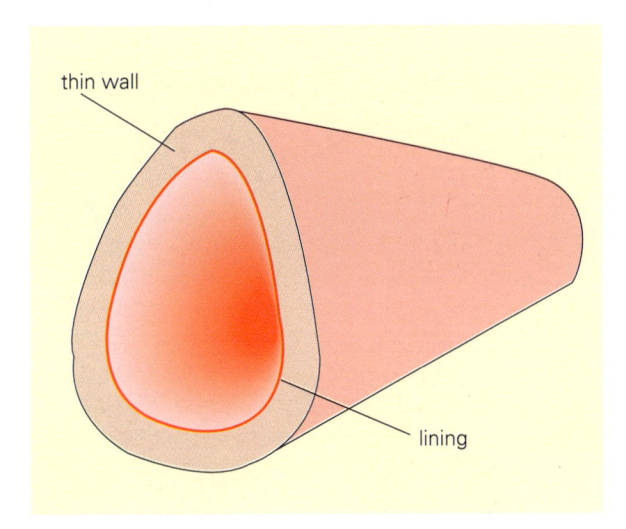

Veins have thin walls.

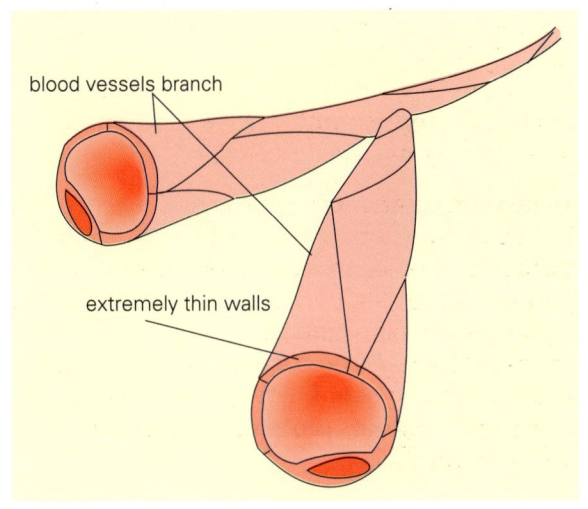

Capillaries are the smallest vessels.

QUESTIONS

1. What are the three kinds of blood vessel?
2. Where is the blood in veins carried to?
3. Why do veins only need quite thin walls?
4. Why do arteries have strong, thick walls?
5. Explain how capillaries do their job.

KEY IDEAS

Arteries carry blood away from the heart.

Veins carry blood back to the heart.

Capillaries are the smallest blood vessels, with walls only one cell thick.

13.4 Inside the blood

Why is your blood red? Is your blood alive? What is it made of?

Your blood has many different jobs to do. Each job is done by a different part or component. The diagram shows what blood looks like when the different components are separated.

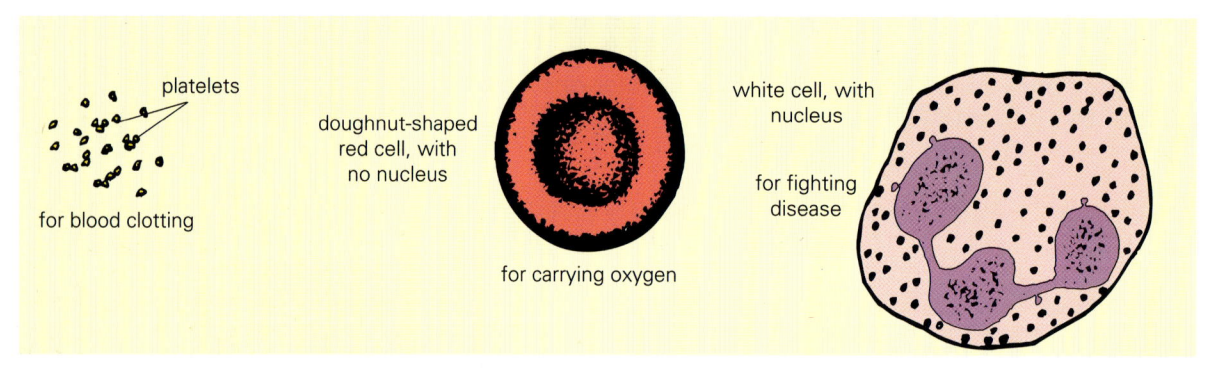

The cells of the blood.

Dividing up the blood

The **plasma** is the liquid part of the blood. Two kinds of cell are mixed in with the plasma. The colour of your blood is caused by **red blood cells**, which carry oxygen. There are fewer **white blood cells**. They fight disease. Blood also contains **platelets**, which help clotting.

Red blood cells

Red cells are filled with a chemical called haemoglobin, which is good at transporting oxygen. When the blood flows through the lungs the haemoglobin takes in oxygen from the air sacs (see 12.1). The haemoglobin inside the red cells is now called **oxyhaemoglobin**, to show that it is carrying oxygen. The blood then flows round the body, releasing oxygen to cells which need it.

Red blood cells have no nucleus, so they cannot reproduce themselves. Instead, they are made in the bone marrow. They are alive, but have a short life span of only four months. So the bone marrow must make new red cells constantly.

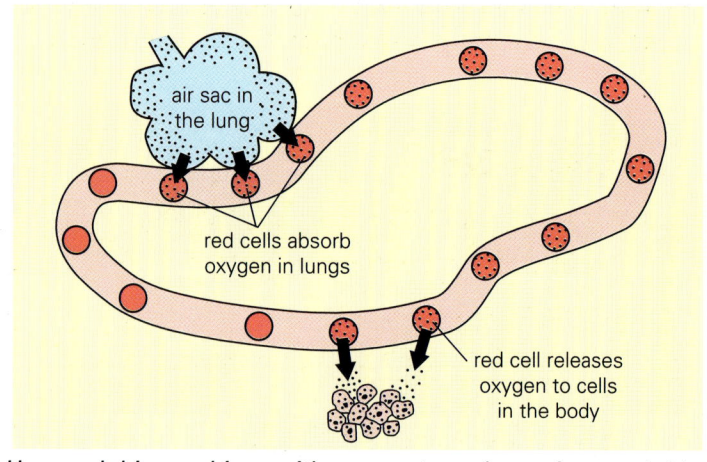

Haemoglobin combines with oxygen to make oxyhaemoglobin.

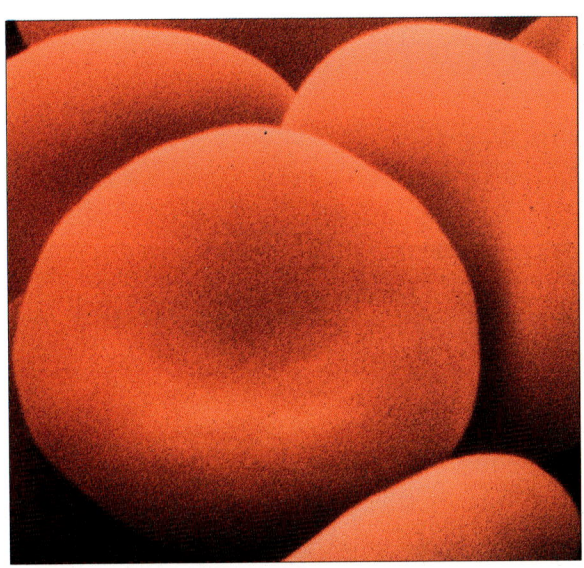

The flattened shape of red blood cells helps them to take in oxygen more easily.

Plasma

When your blood flows through the gut it absorbs **amino acids**, **sugars** and **fatty acids** broken down from proteins, carbohydrates and fats. These food molecules are carried by plasma. As the plasma flows past the body cells it releases food molecules.

Plasma also transports waste carbon dioxide from the cells to the lungs.

Emergency plasma

Plasma is often used during operations or for helping people get well. It contains minerals and sugars. If someone has lost blood, a plasma 'drip' will replace these vital nutrients.

Plasma contains minerals and sugars.

QUESTIONS

1. Which blood component carries oxygen?
2. Which blood component carries food?
3. Where are red blood cells made?
4. Where in the body is oxyhaemoglobin formed?
5. Why is plasma useful in hospitals?

KEY IDEAS

Blood contains several components.

Red blood cells carry oxygen.

Plasma carries food and carbon dioxide.

13.5 Your healthy blood

How does your blood fight disease? What makes a scab? What causes heart attacks?

Stopping infection and destroying harmful germs is one of the jobs of your blood. Your body's defence against infection depends on your white blood cells and your platelets.

White blood cells

When harmful microbes start to grow in your body you have an **infection**. The white blood cells collect in the area of infection and try to destroy the germs. When this happens you sometimes see a red **inflammation** in the skin near the area of infection caused by the extra blood flowing into the area.

Platelets

You cannot avoid cuts and bruises. But it is important you don't bleed for *too long*. Most small cuts stop bleeding quickly. This is because of your platelets.

When you cut yourself blood flows on to the skin. As platelets escape from the body they break up. This triggers a chemical reaction and a protein net forms over the cut. This net dries and hardens to form a scab.

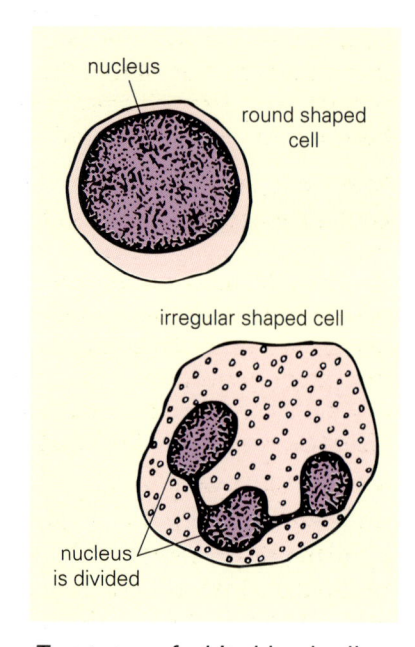

Two types of white blood cell.

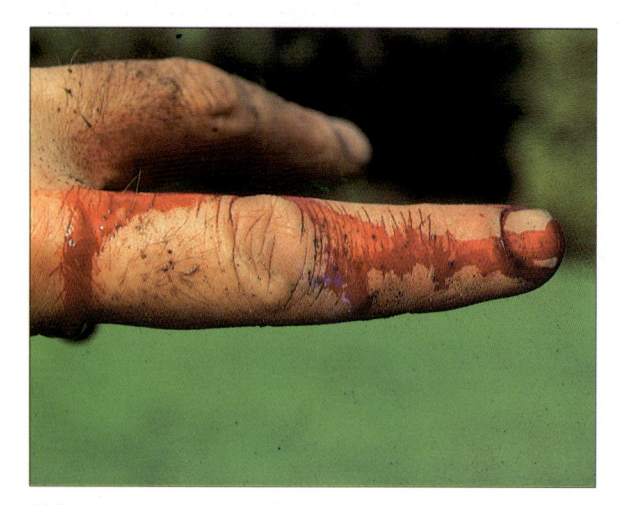

When you cut yourself . . .

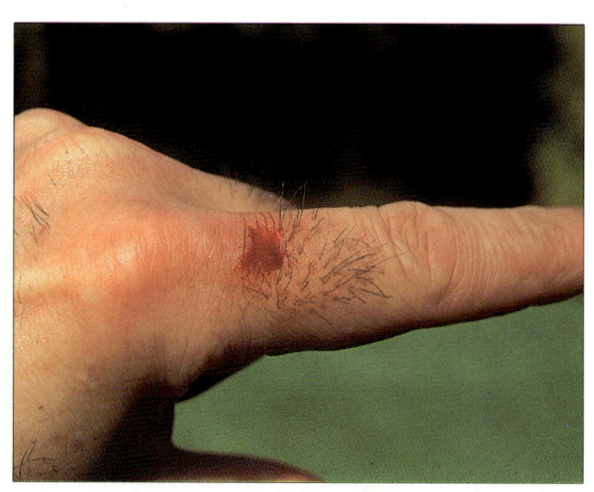

. . . your platelets will make a scab.

Arterial disease

Unfortunately the blood system itself can become diseased. The most common type of problem is **atherosclerosis**, or narrowing of the arteries. Diets high in fat, and smoking, may cause narrowing of the arteries.

Blood cannot pass easily through narrow arteries. This causes the blood pressure to rise above normal levels, which can be dangerous. Sometimes narrow arteries can lead to a thrombosis or clot. When this happens, blood cannot pass through the artery at all. Cells become starved of food and oxygen.

Many people die because their **coronary artery** – the artery feeding the heart muscle – becomes diseased. If the coronary artery becomes narrow, the cardiac muscle begins to starve. This may cause angina or heart pains. In the worst cases the coronary artery clots. Now there is a risk of a heart attack.

Anyone can reduce the risk of atherosclerosis and heart disease by reducing the amount of animal fat in the diet. Taking exercise also lowers the risk of heart disease. Smoking makes it more likely.

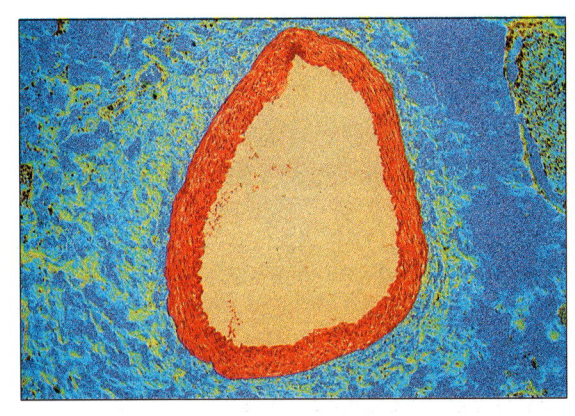

An artery cut through the middle.

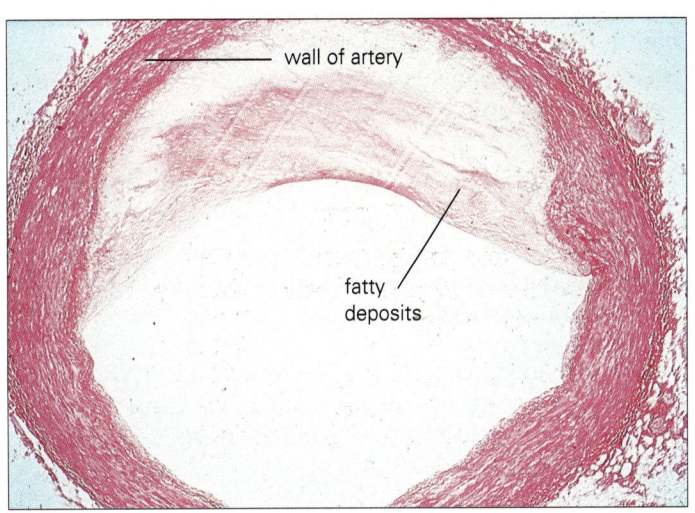

The wall of this artery is coated with fat.

QUESTIONS

1. Which blood components protect your body?
2. Describe how inflammation is caused.
3. Explain how a scab forms.
4. Explain why atherosclerosis can cause high blood pressure.
5. What happens if a clot forms in the coronary artery?

KEY IDEAS

White blood cells fight disease.

Platelets help in the clotting process.

Atherosclerosis is a dangerous disease of the arteries.

CHAPTER 14: GETTING ENERGY

14.1 The 'fire' in your cells

Why do long-distance cyclists eat pasta before a race?
Why might someone talk about 'burning off' a large meal?

Your cells need food and oxygen for energy. The type of food molecule needed for energy is glucose. You get most of your glucose by digesting the carbohydrate starch. Carbohydrates are called energy foods because they are broken down to glucose.

Glucose acts as fuel for your body. Breathing gives you oxygen to burn the fuel. Your blood carries glucose and oxygen to the cells. Here the fuel is burnt, releasing **chemical energy**. **Respiration** is the release of chemical energy from glucose.

The cell burns glucose in oxygen to get its energy.

Cells need glucose and oxygen for respiration.

Using chemical energy

Your cells need energy because they are active. Cells use energy in different ways. Ovary cells make the hormone oestrogen. Muscle cells contract to get smaller. Skin cells divide to replace others. All these activities need energy.

Chemical energy makes her muscles contract.

This animal uses chemical energy to make light.

Respiration produces waste

Waste gas and heat are produced by respiration. The waste gas is carbon dioxide. It passes into the blood, travels to the lungs and is breathed out. Heat can be used by the body to warm the tissues. But if too much heat is produced it can be released through the skin by sweating.

Respiration is slow burning

The burning or **combustion** of the fuel in your cells happens slowly. The energy must be released slowly and carefully. A cell needs a constant energy supply to stay alive, but only in small amounts. In a bonfire combustion is also happening – energy is being released from fuel. But in a bonfire this happens much more quickly. It releases light and a lot of heat.

During exercise extra heat is produced.

A bonfire burns fuel quickly.

QUESTIONS

1. What kind of energy is released by respiration?
2. Give two examples of cell activities that need energy.
3. What is the fuel for respiration?
4. Why do cells need oxygen?
5. Explain why carbohydrates are sometimes called *energy foods*.
6. What are the differences and similarities between a burning bonfire and a respiring cell?

KEY IDEAS

Your body gets energy by respiration.

The fuel for respiration is glucose.

14.2 The oxygen problem

Do you ever get cramp when you run fast?
Why do you pant when you have finished running?

During a fast sprint your body needs more oxygen than the lungs can deliver. When this happens the cells in your muscles must release energy from glucose without the help of oxygen. This process is called **anaerobic respiration**.

Aerobic respiration

When glucose is burnt in oxygen, respiration is aerobic. Your cells respire aerobically most of the time.

When you are sitting or walking, your lungs can easily supply your muscles with enough oxygen. Even when swimming or jogging, your muscles can keep respiring aerobically. Exercises which allow your muscles to respire normally are called **aerobic exercises**. This equation shows what happens during aerobic respiration.

glucose + oxygen ⟶ carbon dioxide + water + energy

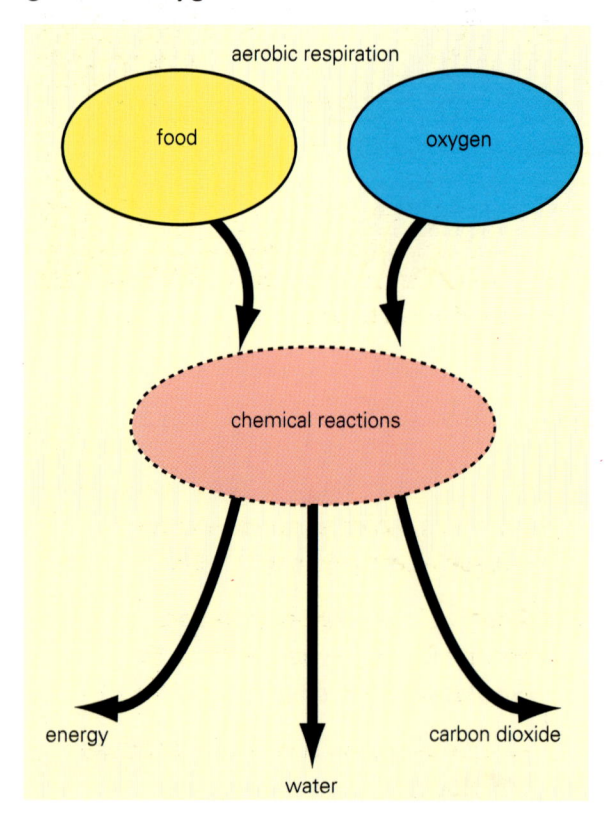

Oxygen is needed for aerobic respiration.

Oxygen is not needed for anaerobic respiration.

Anaerobic respiration

When glucose is burnt without oxygen, respiration is anaerobic. Your muscle cells respire anaerobically some of the time.

During sprints and other types of explosive exercise your muscles are working extremely hard. The heart beats faster and the lungs breathe deeper. But still there is not enough oxygen for the muscles. For a short while the muscles are able to continue their hard activity, by respiring anaerobically. But not for long: within a few seconds anaerobic respiration starts to poison the muscles. This is because the poisonous waste **lactic acid** builds up. Lactic acid causes pain and cramp in muscles. This is why sprinters run such short distances.

This equation shows what happens during anaerobic respiration.

glucose $\longrightarrow$ lactic acid + energy

After a sprint the muscles are full of lactic acid. The body gets rid of lactic acid by breathing hard. The extra oxygen burns it off as water and carbon dioxide. This is why, after a sprint athletes keep panting, even though they have stopped running.

In the final few metres their muscles are respiring anaerobically.

Getting rid of the lactic acid.

QUESTIONS

1. List three exercises which are aerobic.
2. Which kind of athlete might respire anaerobically?
3. Name the waste products of anaerobic respiration?
4. Why does a sprinter keep panting at the end of a race?
5. Why can no one respire anaerobically for a long time?

KEY IDEAS

Aerobic respiration uses oxygen to release energy from glucose.

Anaerobic respiration releases energy from glucose without the help of oxygen.

Anaerobic respiration also produces lactic acid.

CHAPTER 15: THE NERVOUS SYSTEM AND HORMONES

15.1 Making sense of things

The shoots of plants always grow upwards. But how do they know which way is up? How do you know when you are stung by a wasp, or the toast is burning? Why is it important to know these things?

What do organisms sense?

All organisms must be able to sense what is happening in their environment if they are to survive. Plants must know which way is up and which way down, so that they can find the sunlight. Animals need to be able to sense more things in their environment than plants, because they have to get their own food, move around and escape from predators. The things that humans can sense include sounds, light, taste, smell, the feel of things and which way up they are. All these things that living organisms can sense are called **stimuli**.

Why is it important to sense things?

Every moment of the day or night we are sensing, or detecting these stimuli and making use of them. If the temperature drops, we detect it and we put on a jumper or sit by a fire. If we see a car coming towards us we quickly jump out of the way. When people are looking for berries or mushrooms in forests, it is important that they can recognise the right food so that they don't become poisoned by it. Being able to detect stimuli in the environment is life saving.

Receptor	Stimulus
eye	light
ear	sound
skin	heat, pressure
nose	chemical (smell)
tongue	chemical (taste)

Receptors and stimuli in humans.

Detecting stimuli

We detect the stimuli in our environment using **receptors**. Some of the receptors are concentrated together to make an organ. Our receptors for detecting light are all in our eyes. Our receptors for detecting sound are all in our ears. We taste with our tongue and smell with our nose. The receptors which detect touch, hot and cold are spread all over our bodies, in our skin. Some areas of our skin have more of these receptors than other parts. Our finger tips have lots of touch receptors, so they are especially sensitive. This means that we can use our fingers for very delicate work, like sewing.

In our ears we have receptors which help us to keep our balance by telling us which way is up and which way is down. If these receptors get damaged, people find it very difficult to move about without falling over or swaying. Relying on their eyes alone is not enough. All our receptors are very important for us to be able to detect stimuli from our environment.

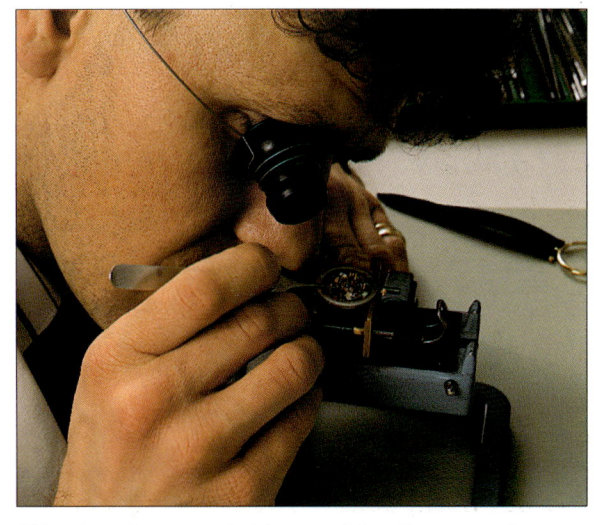

Watchmakers need very sensitive fingers to be able to work with tiny watch parts.

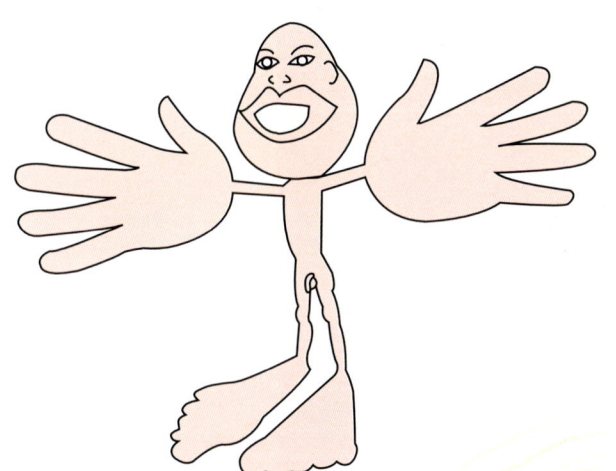

Some parts of the body are more sensitive than others

QUESTIONS

1. Write down three stimuli that humans can sense.
2. Which receptors can detect:
   a smell
   b light
   c taste?
3. Why are our finger tips especially sensitive to touch?
4. Write a paragraph to explain what you think it would be like if you didn't have the sense of touch.

KEY IDEAS

All organisms must be able to detect stimuli from their environment if they are to survive.

Receptors detect stimuli. Human receptors include the eye, ear, nose, tongue and skin.

15.2 The eye

You are looking at this page, seeing these words. But how does your eye make this happen?

Sight is one of our most important senses. You can try to imagine what it is like to be blind by blindfolding yourself and trying to get around a room.

Light is the stimulus for sight. Our eyes are the receptors which receive reflected light rays from things in the environment and make sense of them.

Focusing

Light rays enter the eye through the **pupil**, which is the black hole in the centre of the eye. The amount of light coming into the eye is controlled by the **iris**, the coloured ring of muscle around the pupil. The rays travel through the **cornea** and the **lens** first. These structures bend the light rays so that they all hit the back of the eye. This is called **focusing**. The lens changes shape to make sure the rays are focused by the right amount. The ciliary muscles and the suspensory ligaments allow the lens to change shape. When the lens is long and thin, the light doesn't bend very much. When the lens is short and fat, the light bends quite sharply.

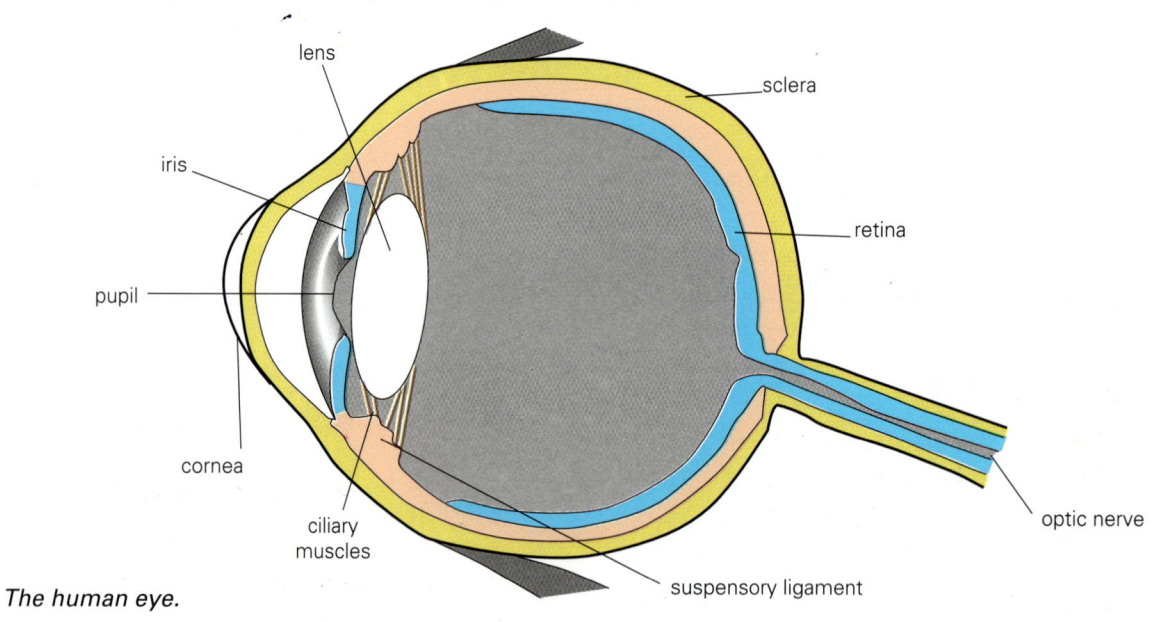

The human eye.

The rays of light are focused on a layer of light-sensitive cells at the back of the eyeball called the **retina**. When the light hits a light-sensitive cell, it sends a message which travels away from the eye to the brain along the **optic nerve**.

Message received and understood

The brain usually interprets the pattern of messages sent from the light-sensitive cells in the retina. In this way it can recognise the shape of the object the person is looking at.

But sometimes the optic nerve doesn't work, so the messages don't get to the brain. Or sometimes there is something wrong with the retina. These problems can cause blindness. Many people can see, but they can't focus properly because their lenses don't change shape enough. They may be 'long-sighted' and cannot focus on near objects well, or 'short-sighted' and unable to focus well on objects in the distance. These people wear glasses with lenses which do some of the focusing before the light even gets to the eye.

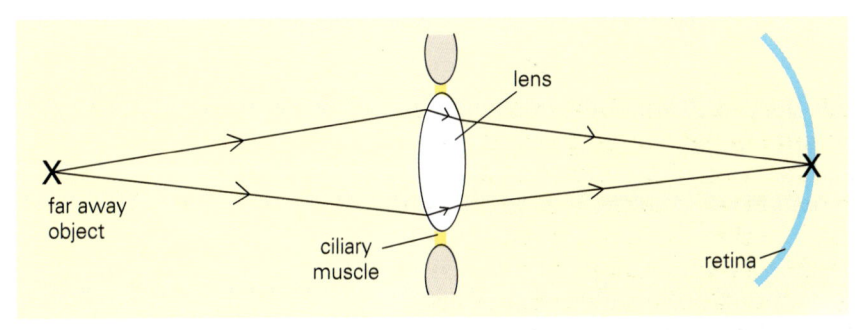

The lens is long and thin to focus light from a far away object.

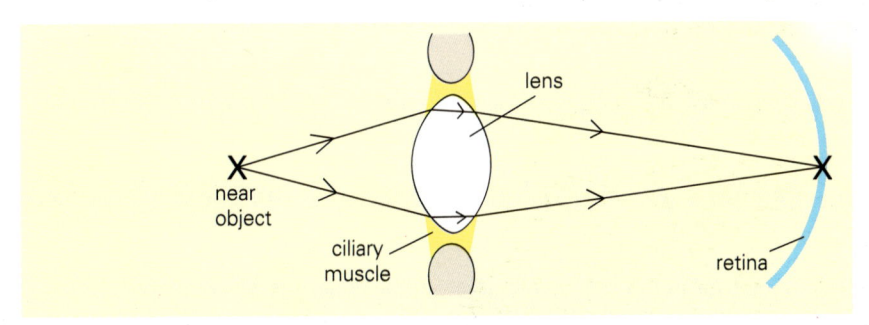

The lens is short and fat to focus light from a near object.

QUESTIONS

1. Which two structures in the eye do the light rays pass through first?
2. Name the layer of light-sensitive cells at the back of the eye.
3. Describe what happens when light hits a light-sensitive cell.
4. How does wearing glasses help someone who is short-sighted?

KEY IDEAS

The eye is our receptor for light stimuli.

The cornea and lens focus light on to the retina.

The optic nerve carries messages from the retina to the brain.

15.3 How the iris controls 'dazzle'

If someone suddenly shines a torch in your eyes, you are dazzled by the brightness. But most of the time your eyes are very good at controlling the amount of light coming in. How do they do this?

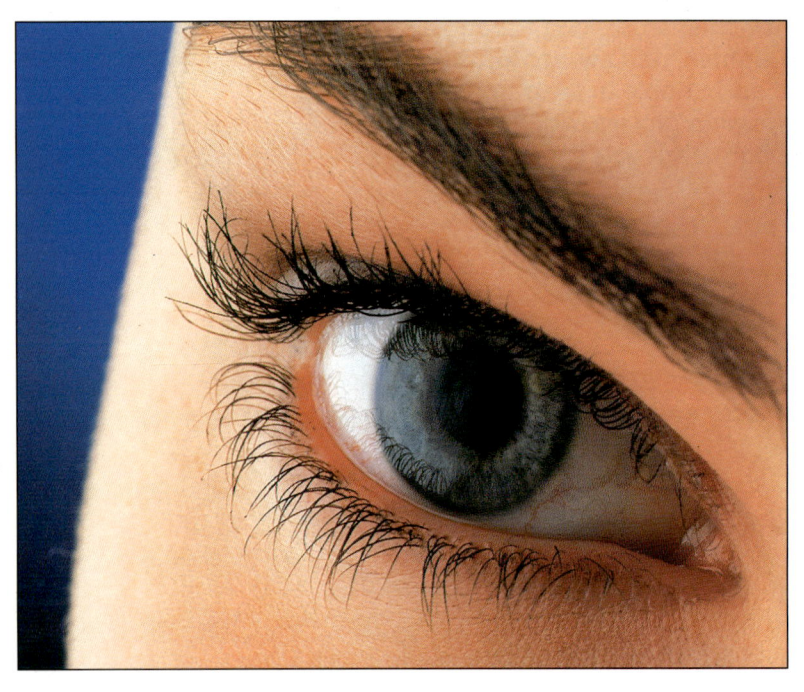

The human eye can control the amount of light coming in.

If you look at your eye in a mirror, you will see a black hole in the middle, surrounded by a coloured ring. The black hole is the pupil. Light comes into our eyes through the pupil. It looks very black because all the light is absorbed by the light-sensitive cells and none is reflected.

The coloured ring around the pupil is the iris. It is actually a ring of muscle which is very important for controlling the amount of light which enters the eye.

Imagine you are in a dark room, and you walk outside into bright sunlight. For a few seconds you find it hard to keep your eyes open as they get used to the Sun. When you were in the dark room, the iris muscles made a bigger pupil to let in as much light as possible. But outside the light is too bright, so the iris muscles change to make the pupil smaller. Less light is taken in and you are no longer dazzled.

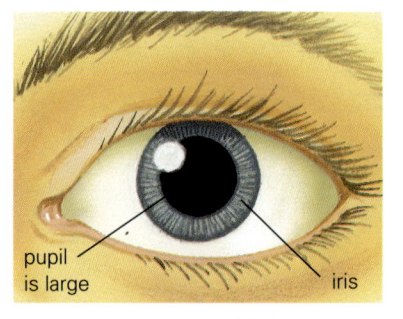

In the dark the pupil is bigger to let more light in.

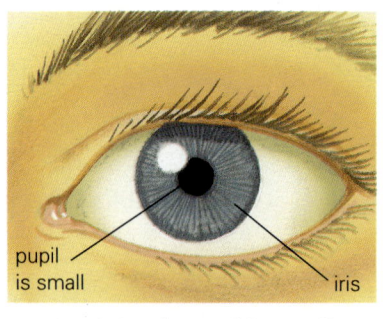

In the light the pupil is smaller to let less light in.

Can you control your iris?

The way your iris reacts when you walk out of a dark room into the light is called a **reflex action**. You can't stop it happening.

A reflex action is a very quick, automatic response to a stimulus. Nerve signals are sent by receptors through the nervous system to muscles called **effectors**. In this example, the stimulus is bright light. The receptors are the light-sensitive cells on the retina. They send messages to the iris, which is the effector.

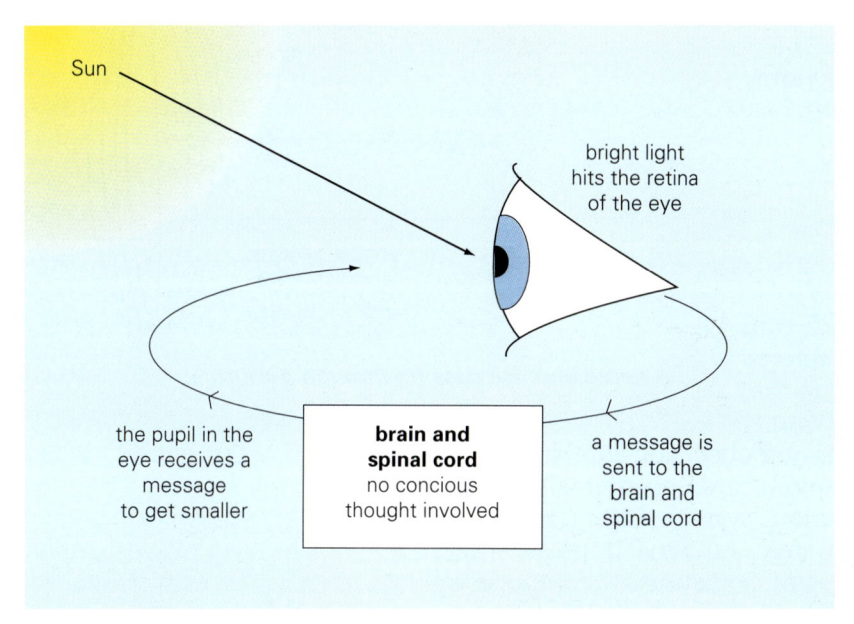

A reflex action.

Diagram labels:
- Sun
- bright light hits the retina of the eye
- a message is sent to the brain and spinal cord
- **brain and spinal cord** — no concious thought involved
- the pupil in the eye receives a message to get smaller

QUESTIONS

1. Name the following:
   a. the black hole in the middle of the eye
   b. the coloured ring around the hole.
2. Describe what happens to the eye when you suddenly step into bright sunlight.
3. What is a reflex action?

KEY IDEAS

The iris is a ring of muscles which reacts to the amount of light hitting the eye by altering the size of the pupil.

In dark conditions the pupil is big. In bright conditions the pupil is small.

The reaction of the iris to light is automatic and is called a reflex action.

15.4 The control centre

Receptors in the body are bombarded with information about the environment. But much of the information is not relevant or important. How does the body make sense of the information and respond to it?

You have seen that receptors such as the retina are sensitive to stimuli. These receptors send messages as electrical signals, called **nerve impulses**. The nerve impulses are sent along lengthy pathways made up of nerve cells, or **neurones**.

The central nervous system

Your backbone is the bone which runs up the centre of your back. It protects the **spinal cord**, which travels up the back to the brain. If you break your backbone and the spinal cord is damaged, you can become paralysed. This is because the spinal cord, together with the brain, make up the **central nervous system (CNS)**. This is the control centre for the nervous system. All nerve impulses travel through the central nervous system. Sometimes the impulse is sent straight to an effector muscle to produce a reflex action. In this case, the path travelled by the nerve impulse is called a **reflex arc**. The diagram shows a simple reflex arc.

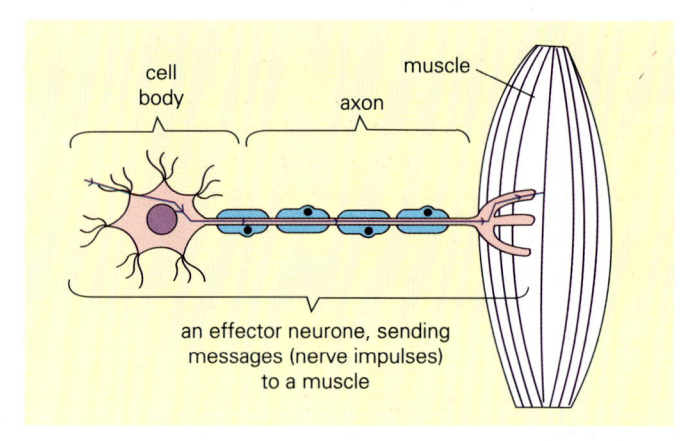

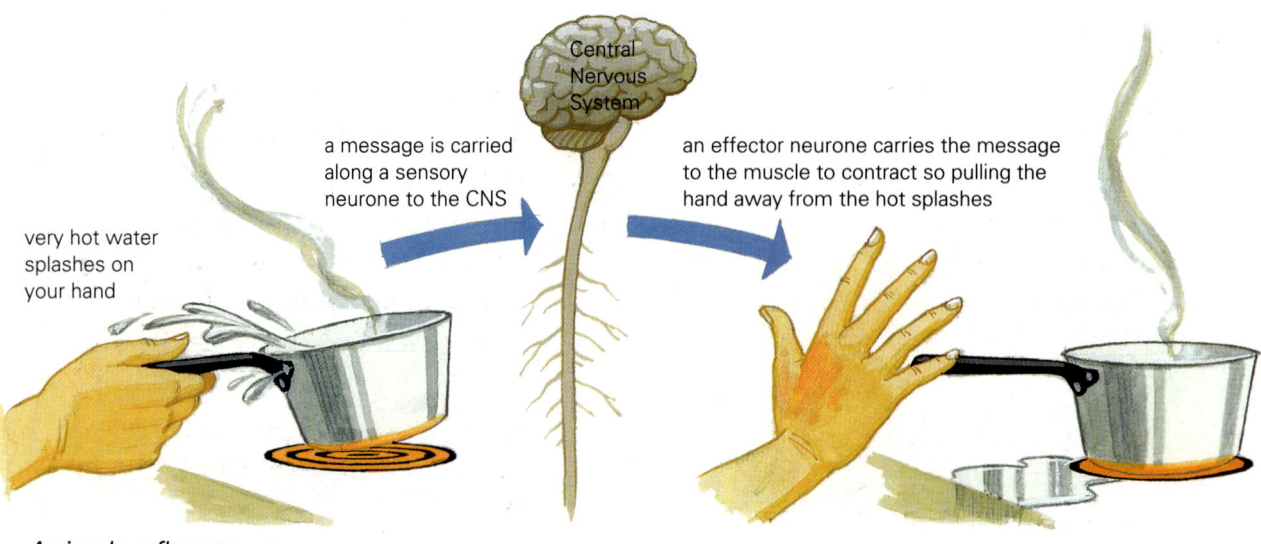

A nerve impulse passing through a neurone.

A simple reflex arc.

The reflex arc

Most people have had the experience of touching something very hot. You move your arm away very quickly, before you have even had time to think about it. This is what happens. A sensory neurone carries the message about touching something hot from the receptor to the spinal cord. A connector neurone carries the message through the spinal cord. An effector neurone carries a message to the effector, in this example a muscle in the arm, telling it to contract. The hand is moved away from the hot surface.

All this happens very quickly. At the same time, messages pass up the spinal cord to the brain, telling it what has happened. Once the brain has the information, you can make decisions about what to do next, if anything. Most people's brains would tell them to run the hand under a cold tap!

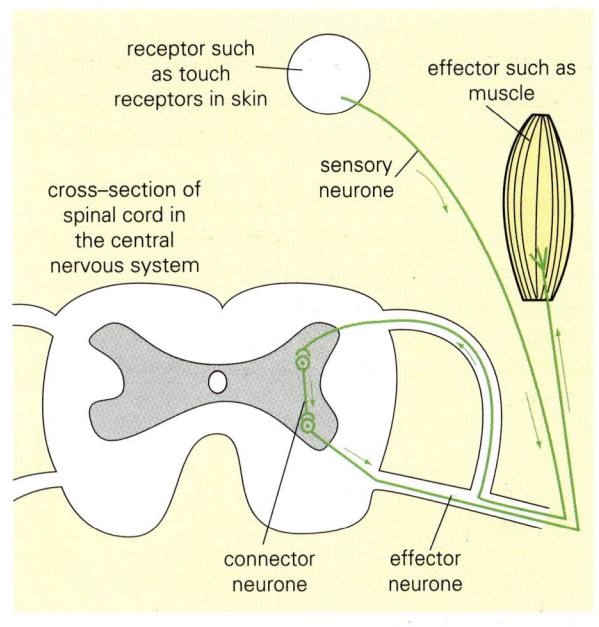

A nerve impulse travelling along a reflex arc.

Other sensations

Not all nerve impulses require a reflex action. If your nose senses that the toast is burning, the nerve impulses do not travel in a reflex arc but go straight to the brain. You become aware of the burning toast, and can decide how to respond.

QUESTIONS

1. What name do we give to nerve cells?
2. Name the system made up of the brain and the spinal cord.
3. Describe what happens in a reflex arc.
4. Various situations are described below. Say whether you think a reflex arc will be involved or not, and give the reason for your decision.
   a Walking in the garden barefoot in the summer, you step on an upturned drawing pin.
   b The doorbell rings.
   c You see the school bus arriving at the bus stop just down the road.
   d You get some dust in your eyes and your eyes water.

KEY IDEAS

The nervous system is made up of neurones, the brain and the spinal cord.

A stimulus may lead to a reflex arc, when a nerve impulse travels along a sensory neurone, a connector neurone and finally an effector neurone to carry out a response.

Messages which go to the brain let us make decisions about what to do next.

15.5 Chemical messages

Everyone has experienced 'butterflies' in the stomach. The feeling is the result of chemical messages released when we feel nervous. What do chemical messages do, and how are they different from nerve messages?

Messages are sent around the body quickly using the nervous system. But there is another system for sending messages. It is a system using chemicals called **hormones**. Hormones are made in glands. The glands release the hormones into the blood stream and they travel around the body until they reach the organ they affect. This organ is called the **target organ**.

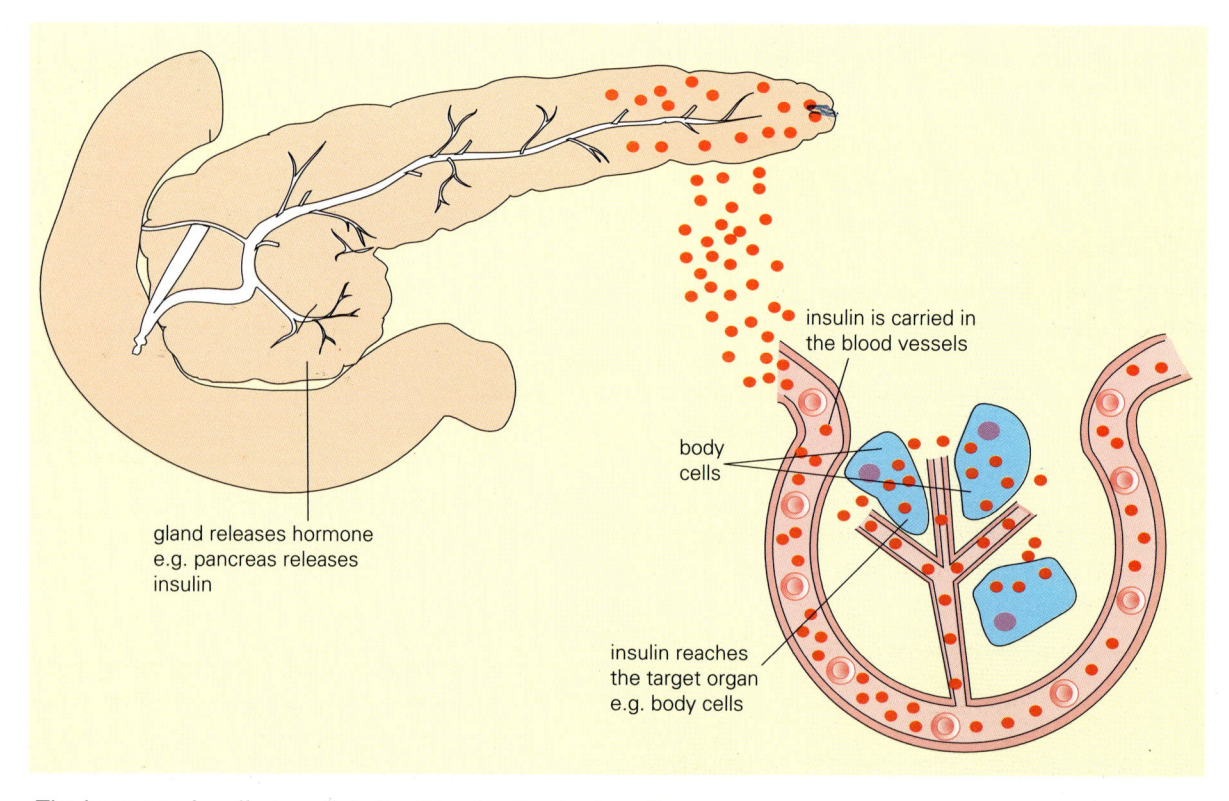

gland releases hormone e.g. pancreas releases insulin

insulin is carried in the blood vessels

body cells

insulin reaches the target organ e.g. body cells

The hormone insulin travels in the blood to the body cells.

Hormones are used for the control of many processes in the body. **Insulin** and **glucagon** are hormones which control the amount of sugar, or glucose, in the blood. Oestrogen and testosterone control the sexual development of adolescents (see 20.1 and 20.2).

Controlling glucose levels

It is very important to keep the levels of glucose in the blood constant.
If there is too much glucose, the kidneys may be damaged. If there is too little glucose, the person will become tired and faint.

Insulin and glucagon are both produced in the pancreas. If there is too much glucose in the blood, the hormone insulin is released into the blood stream. It acts on the body cells and decreases the amount of glucose in the blood. If there is too little glucose in the blood, glucagon is released. It acts on the liver and increases the amount of glucose in the blood.

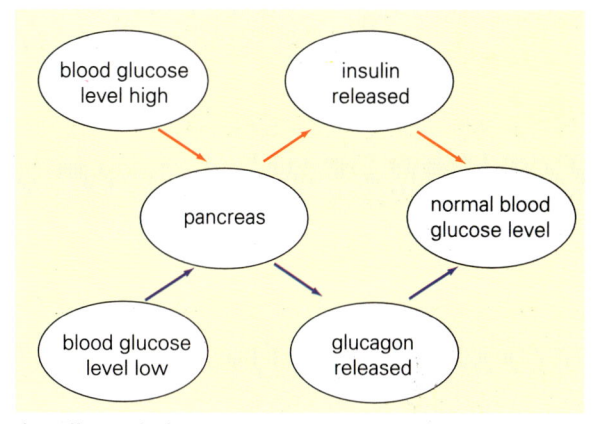

Insulin and glucagon control the amount of glucose in the blood.

Diabetes

In some people, the pancreas cannot produce insulin. The amount of glucose in the blood can get very high, and this can cause blindness or kidney failure. This condition is called **diabetes**. It can happen in young children who are born with a weak pancreas, or it can develop in older people.

Often, the diabetes can be controlled with a carefully balanced diet. Otherwise, the **diabetic** person must inject insulin regularly to lower the blood glucose levels. He or she will still have to have a well-balanced diet. If enough sugar has not been eaten the diabetic person will feel faint, and have to eat a glucose tablet.

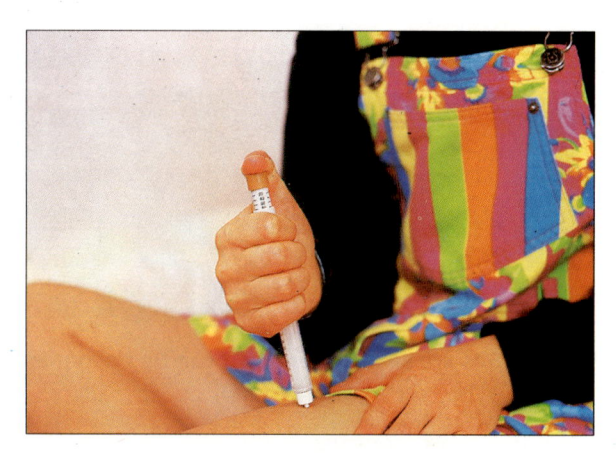

A diabetic person injecting insulin.

QUESTIONS

1. Where are hormones made?
2. What do oestrogen and testosterone control?
3. Name the hormone released from the pancreas if the blood sugar level is:
   a too high
   b too low.
4. Describe the condition diabetes, and explain how it can be controlled.

KEY IDEAS

Hormones are chemicals which control many processes in the body. They are made in glands.

Insulin and glucagon control the level of sugar in the blood.

Diabetes is a condition where the blood sugar level may rise dangerously high because not enough insulin is produced.

CHAPTER 16: DRUGS

16.1 Drugs which help sick people

What are drugs? How can they be used to stop a headache or fight a disease?

A **drug** is something which changes the way the body works. All drugs can be dangerous, but many are used by doctors to relieve pain and to treat diseases. These are called **medicines**. Some very widely used medicines include **painkillers** and **antibiotics**.

Painkillers

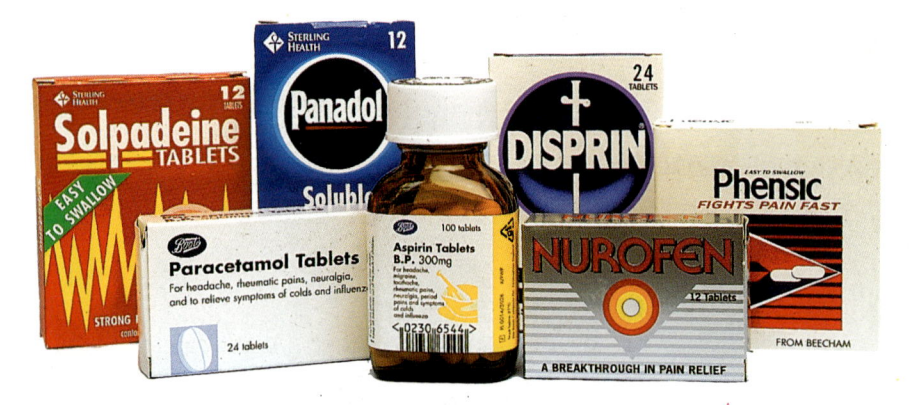

These drugs are all painkillers that can be bought at the chemist.

Painkillers are often used by people to relieve pain. They work by blanking out the part of the brain which makes you feel pain. You can buy many painkillers over the counter at the chemist. These are used to treat things like headaches and toothaches, and to relieve fever. But all painkillers can be dangerous to your health in various ways if you take more than the amount recommended on the packet. For example, large amounts of paracetamol can damage your liver so much that you may die.

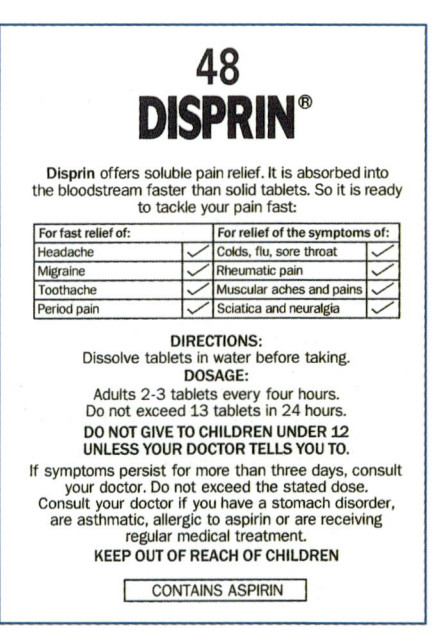

48 DISPRIN®

Disprin offers soluble pain relief. It is absorbed into the bloodstream faster than solid tablets. So it is ready to tackle your pain fast:

For fast relief of:		For relief of the symptoms of:	
Headache	✓	Colds, flu, sore throat	✓
Migraine	✓	Rheumatic pain	✓
Toothache	✓	Muscular aches and pains	✓
Period pain	✓	Sciatica and neuralgia	✓

DIRECTIONS:
Dissolve tablets in water before taking.
DOSAGE:
Adults 2-3 tablets every four hours.
Do not exceed 13 tablets in 24 hours.
DO NOT GIVE TO CHILDREN UNDER 12 UNLESS YOUR DOCTOR TELLS YOU TO.
If symptoms persist for more than three days, consult your doctor. Do not exceed the stated dose. Consult your doctor if you have a stomach disorder, are asthmatic, allergic to aspirin or are receiving regular medical treatment.
KEEP OUT OF REACH OF CHILDREN

CONTAINS ASPIRIN

Instructions for use are given on the packet of all medicines.

Antibiotics

Antibiotics are a very important group of medicines. They stop bacteria from growing. They were discovered in 1928 by Alexander Fleming. **Penicillin** was the first antibiotic to be discovered, and it helped to save many lives during the Second World War. Antibiotics are prescribed by doctors to people who have bacterial diseases like ear or chest infections.

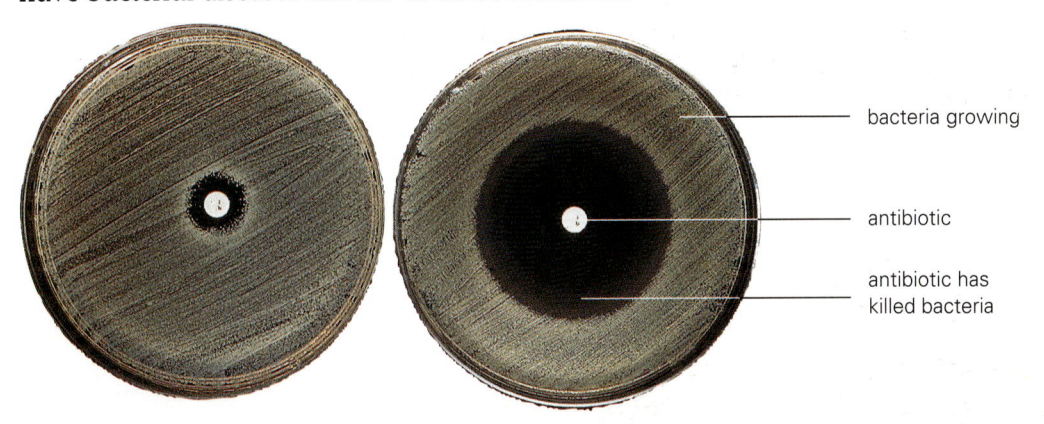

bacteria growing

antibiotic

antibiotic has killed bacteria

Some antibiotics were put on to the middle of the agar plate and the bacteria have stopped growing in this area.

But antibiotics are not the perfect drug. Some bacteria become resistant to antibiotics after a while. This means that the antibiotics no longer prevent some bacteria growing. So new kinds of antibiotics are constantly being developed. It is important that doctors don't prescribe antibiotics unless absolutely necessary so that bacteria don't become resistant to them as quickly. Antibiotics don't work against viruses, which cause diseases like colds and influenza, or 'flu.

Scientists are constantly researching to find new drugs to help cure diseases like cancer and AIDS.

QUESTIONS

1. What are drugs?
2. List the uses for painkillers.
3. Why do doctors only prescribe antibiotics when absolutely necessary?
4. Describe how to use Disprin safely.

KEY IDEAS

Drugs change the way the body works.

Medicines are drugs and include painkillers and antibiotics.

It is important to follow instructions about using medicines because they can be dangerous.

Antibiotics are a major group of drugs.

16.2 The misuse of drugs

Many drugs are helpful to the body, but if they are not used properly they can be extremely dangerous. How can drugs harm the body?

Some different kinds of drugs

The drugs talked about here are mainly drugs which are taken by people for the effect they have on their brain. They include nicotine (see 12.4) alcohol, caffeine, valium, cocaine and LSD.

Stimulants make the messages in the brain travel faster, and make you more alert. Nicotine, found in tobacco, and caffeine, found in tea and coffee, are mild stimulants. Cocaine is a very strong stimulant.

Sedatives, also called depressants, slow down the brain and make you feel sleepy. Tranquillisers such as valium, calm people down, and are prescribed by doctors for people who are very anxious. Alcohol slows down certain parts of the brain making people less inhibited. If a lot of alcohol is drunk, it will cause the person to fall asleep.

Hallucinogens are a particularly dangerous kind of drug because they make you feel, hear or see things which don't really exist. This is called having **hallucinations**. LSD is a powerful hallucinogen.

The dangers of misuse

Misusing drugs is very dangerous. Drugs affect the way the brain works and this can have fatal results. Many drugs, like alcohol, slow down your ability to react quickly so that you take longer to respond to a stimulus. This is especially dangerous if someone drives when they have been taking a drug like alcohol.

Drugs damage your body. They are poisonous and can kill cells. Alcohol kills cells in the brain and the liver. Sniffing solvents such as those given off from glue may also harm the liver, kidneys and brain. 'Ecstasy' is a relatively new drug which has unpredictable effects and can be fatal.

Alcohol is a sedative.

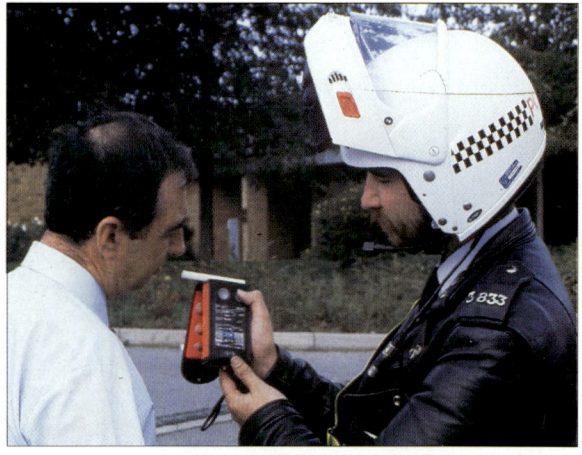

This driver is being tested with a Breathalyser for alcohol in his breath.

Daily Mail, Saturday, December 2 1995

FATHER'S EMOTIONAL TRIBUTE TO THE BIRTHDAY GIRL KILLED BY ECSTASY

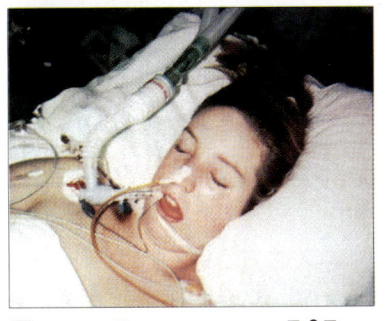

Leah lies in a coma after taking ecstasy.

Paul and Janet Betts arriving for the funeral.

Leah was like a little ship, dashed on the rocks of life

Leah Betts died after taking a single ecstasy tablet at her eighteenth birthday party.

Her grieving friends from college.

Drug dependency

You can become dependent on drugs. Even though people know smoking is harming their health, they can't give it up. They are **psychologically dependent** on it. The same thing can happen with cannabis.

Other drugs, like heroin and alcohol are even worse. Your body actually begins to need the drug, so if you don't get it, you experience **withdrawal symptoms**. These are very unpleasant and include dizziness, vomiting and muscle pains. We say that a person who is **physically dependent** on a drug is **addicted** to it. People who are addicted to drugs often resort to crime to fund their drug-taking.

QUESTIONS

1. Give two examples of stimulants.
2. What effect do hallucinogens have on the brain?
3. Describe what happens when a person who is physically dependent on a drug, can't get the drug.
4. How may sniffing solvents harm the body?

KEY IDEAS

Drugs are extremely dangerous if they are misused.

They change the way your brain functions and they harm your body.

You can become dependent on drugs.

CHAPTER 17: KEEPING THINGS STEADY

17.1 Control of body temperature

The human body temperature is usually constant at 37 degrees centigrade (37°C). What stops the body temperature rising on a hot day? Why is it important to keep temperature steady in the body?

Your body needs to keep certain things steady if its cells are to work properly. This is called maintaining constant conditions. The conditions include temperature, amount of water, glucose and salt concentration and acidity. If your body temperature increased on a hot day, the chemical reactions which take place in the cells would not work properly. This would probably kill you. Fortunately, your body manages to control the levels of body temperature, salt, glucose, water and acidity using a system that works rather like a **thermostat** in an oven.

In an oven, information about temperature is sensed by the thermostat. If the temperature is too high, the thermostat switches off the heater. If the temperature is too low, the thermostat switches on the heater. This is called a **feedback** system.

Feedback systems in the body

Your body uses a similar feedback system to control its temperature. If the body temperature rises slightly, this is sensed by the brain. The brain sends messages to the skin, telling it to start up its cooling mechanisms. If the body temperature drops, the opposite happens and the brain sends messages to the parts of the body which help to warm it up.

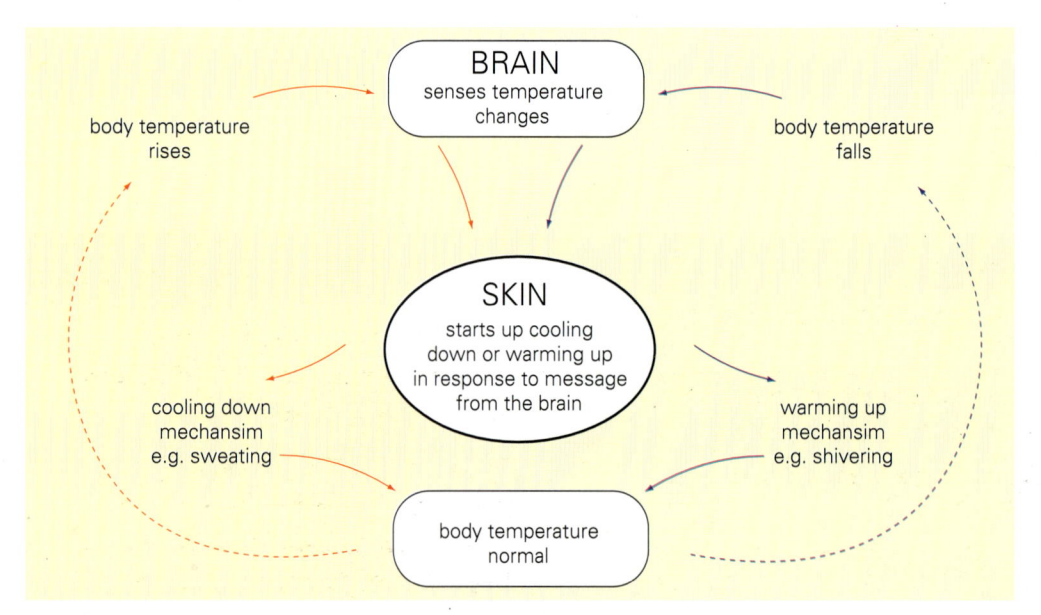

The feedback system is used to control body temperature.

A feedback system is also used by the body for keeping its salt and water levels constant. If you look back at the way blood glucose is controlled (see 15.5), you can see that this is a feedback system too. Keeping conditions in our bodies constant is called **homeostasis**.

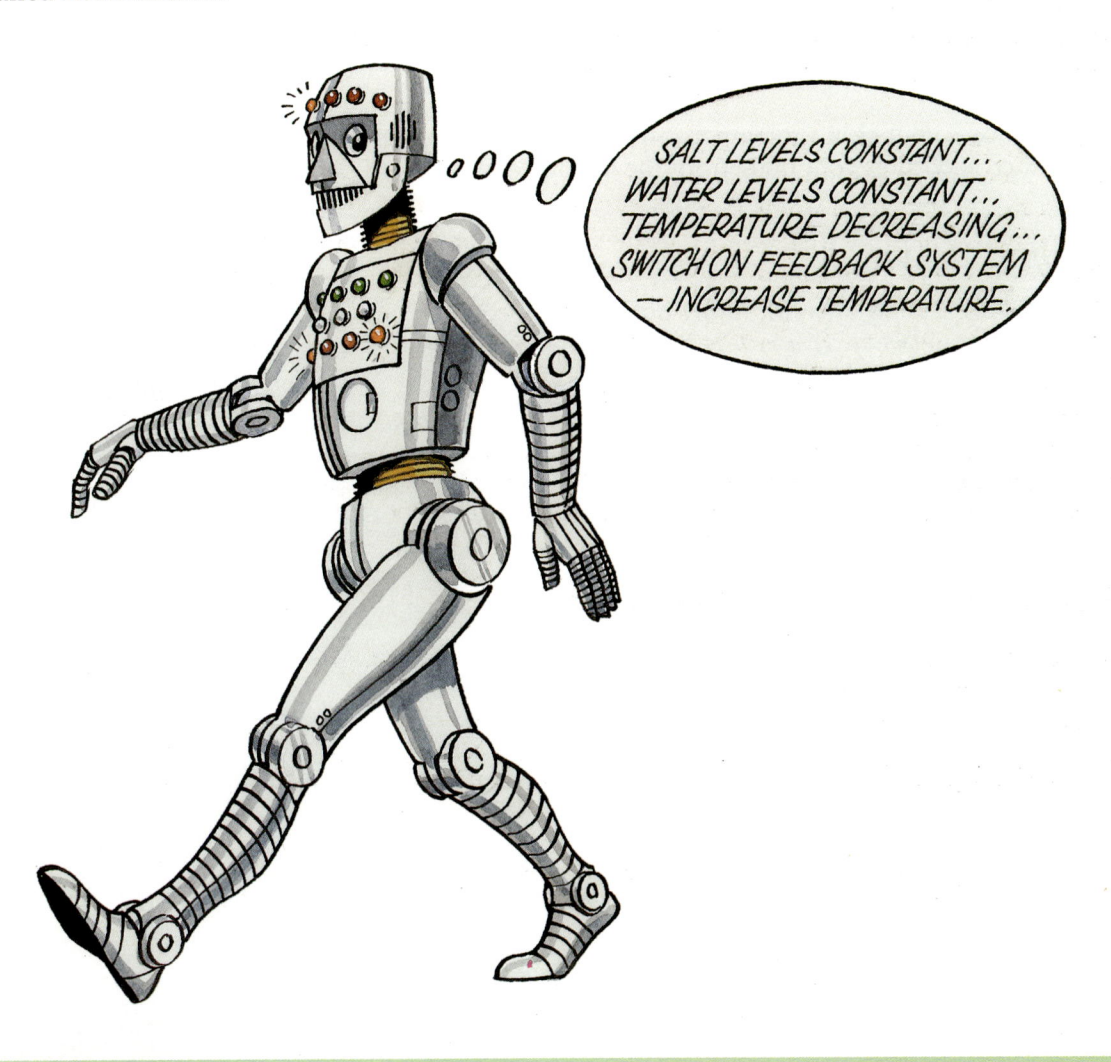

Speech bubble: SALT LEVELS CONSTANT... WATER LEVELS CONSTANT... TEMPERATURE DECREASING... SWITCH ON FEEDBACK SYSTEM — INCREASE TEMPERATURE.

QUESTIONS

1. Name three things which the body must keep constant.
2. What would happen if conditions were not kept constant in the body?
3. How does the body keep temperature constant?
4. Explain how thermostats and the body are similar.

KEY IDEAS

The body must keep its internal conditions quite constant if its cells are to work properly.

These internal conditions are controlled by feedback systems which detect changes and send messages to get the body back to normal.

17.2 How do we warm up and cool down?

On a hot day you can produce so much sweat that a T-shirt is soaked through! Why does the body produce sweat?

Your body uses your **skin** for temperature control. Skin is a waterproof layer which separates your body from the outside environment.

Cooling down

When you are feeling uncomfortably hot, you probably start to sweat. This is very important for temperature control because, as the sweat evaporates, it cools down the surface of your skin. The other thing that you might notice is that your skin looks redder. This is because more blood flows through the blood capillaries just below the surface of the skin. More blood can flow through them, and heat is lost to the environment as the blood passes near the surface of the skin.

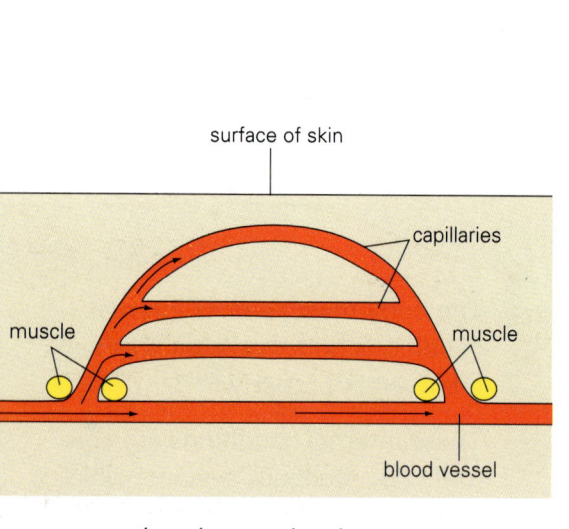

In warm weather, the muscle relaxes so more blood flows through the capillaries near the surface of the skin.

You can see the effect of the body heating up on this person, who has been running on a warm day.

Warming up

If you are feeling cold, the brain does not send messages to the sweat glands, so no sweat is produced. Messages are sent to the blood vessels so that less blood flows near the surface of the skin, and less heat is lost. You will probably look pale, or blue.

In very cold conditions, the body tries so hard to keep its central organs warm, and the surface capillaries get so small, that the nose, fingers and toes can be damaged through lack of oxygen. This is called **frostbite**.

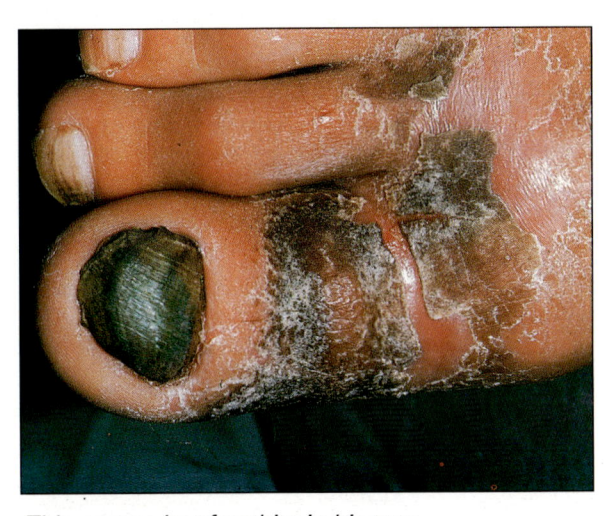

This person has frostbite in his toes.

QUESTIONS

1. Which part of the body is important for temperature control?
2. Describe how sweating helps to keep you cool.
3. What happens to the blood capillaries near the surface of the skin on a cold day?
4. Why do you think this reaction of the body could save someone's life?

KEY IDEAS

The skin is used for controlling your body temperature.

In warm conditions, you sweat and more blood flows through the skin capillaries. This cools you down.

In cool conditions, you don't sweat and less blood flows through the skin capillaries, so you save heat.

17.3 Control by the kidneys

*Do you, or does anyone you know, carry a donor card?
Why are your kidneys so important that you cannot live without them?*

The kidneys have two very important roles.

1. They keep certain conditions (salt and water concentration) constant. This is an example of homeostasis.
2. They get rid of **urea**, which is a poisonous waste product of the body.

The process of getting rid of urea is called **excretion**. So the system that carries out the process is called the **excretory system**.

Making urine

Salts, water and urea are transported around the body in the blood. The kidneys act as a filter. They filter all the poisonous urea out of the blood, and some of the water and salts, depending on how much water and salt is in the blood. The filtered water, salt and urea becomes **urine**.

The excretory system is an example of a feedback system. If you have drunk lots of water, the blood will contain a lot of water. The brain senses this, and sends messages (feedback) to the kidneys telling them to filter out lots of water into the urine. The urine will be weak, or dilute and a pale colour. The same happens with salt. If we have more salt in our blood, the kidneys filter more salt into the urine.

If you have little water in your blood, perhaps because you have been sweating, the kidneys will produce a very concentrated urine which is a deep yellow colour. If you have too much salt in your blood, the urine will contain lots of salt.

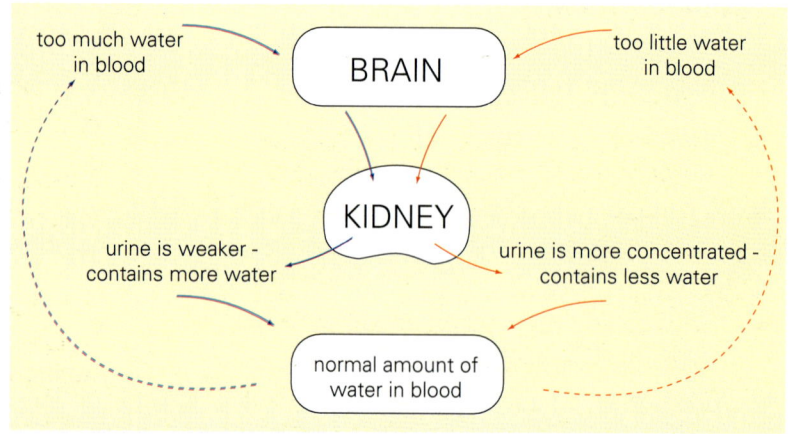

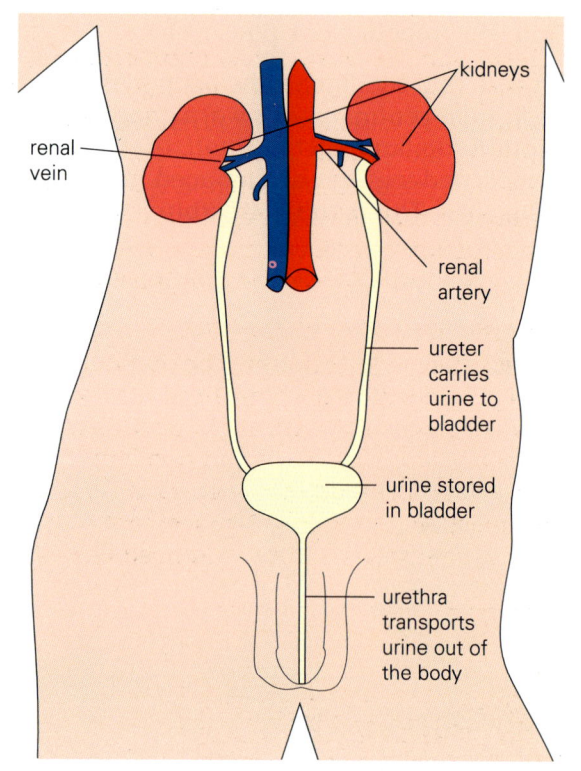

The excretory system.

The excretory system is a feedback system.

When the kidneys fail

Because you have two kidneys, it isn't too serious if one gets damaged. But sometimes, both kidneys are damaged in a person. If this person is left untreated, the build up of poisonous urea leads to death.

The person can be attached to an artificial kidney (a kidney dialysis machine) for several hours a day to remove the urea. This is called **dialysis**. Blood flows from the patient through a tube into the machine where it is filtered before it returns to the body. A person may have to undergo dialysis several times a week and it can be uncomfortable (see the graph below).

Another way of surviving kidney damage is to have a kidney transplant. The damaged kidney is replaced with a new one from a carefully matched **donor**, which might be a relative or someone who has died in an accident. Sometimes the kidney is rejected and there can be infection, but kidney replacement is the only permanent solution for a damaged kidney.

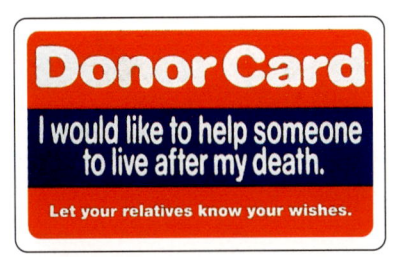

A kidney dialysis machine.

The kidney of a person who has died in an accident may be used if that person is carrying a donor card.

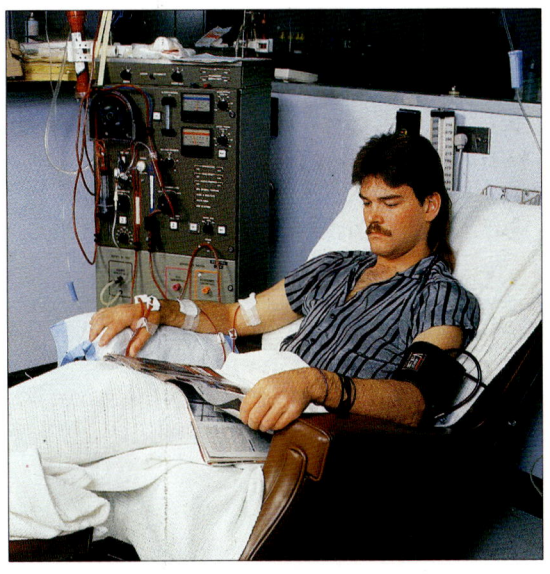

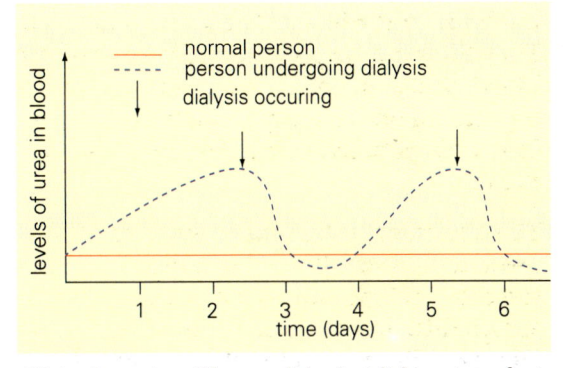

Dialysis makes life possible, but it is not perfect.

QUESTIONS

1. Name three substances that make up urine.
2. Describe how the kidney controls the amount of water and salt in the body.
3. How can a person survive if both their kidneys fail?
4. Why do you think patients who suffer from kidney failure often have to wait years before they can have a kidney transplant?

KEY IDEAS

The excretory system is an example of a feedback system.

It removes urea and controls the amount of water and salt in the body.

If kidneys fail, the person will die unless he or she has kidney dialysis or a kidney transplant.

CHAPTER 18: DISEASES

18.1 Avoiding disease

Some people tend to become ill quite often, while other people manage to avoid most diseases. But most people are ill at some point in their life. What are diseases, and what can we do to reduce the chance of catching them?

Most human diseases are caused by microbes like **bacteria** and **viruses**. These disease-causing microbes or germs can enter the body through openings like the mouth and nose. Once they are inside the body, the warm conditions and good food supply mean they can multiply very quickly indeed.

Bacteria

Disease-causing bacteria multiply in the body fluids like the blood and release poisons. These poisons make us feel ill. Bacteria called *Salmonella* give us food poisoning. Other kinds of bacteria live in the gut and give us diarrhoea. Bacteria which infect the lining of the brain cause meningitis. The person has a very bad headache, a high temperature, is sensitive to light and often has a small rash. If it is not treated, meningitis is fatal. Luckily, most bacteria stop growing when you use antibiotics, so bacterial diseases like meningitis can usually be controlled quickly.

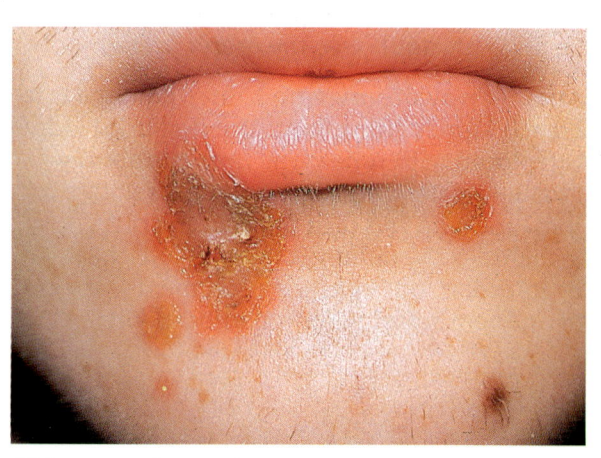

This person has an impetigo skin rash caused by bacterial infection.

Viruses

Viruses don't respond to antibiotics. This is because they get inside our cells and reproduce there, where nothing can attack them. They kill the cells where they reproduce, which is why we feel ill. Examples of viral diseases are the common cold, influenza and AIDS.

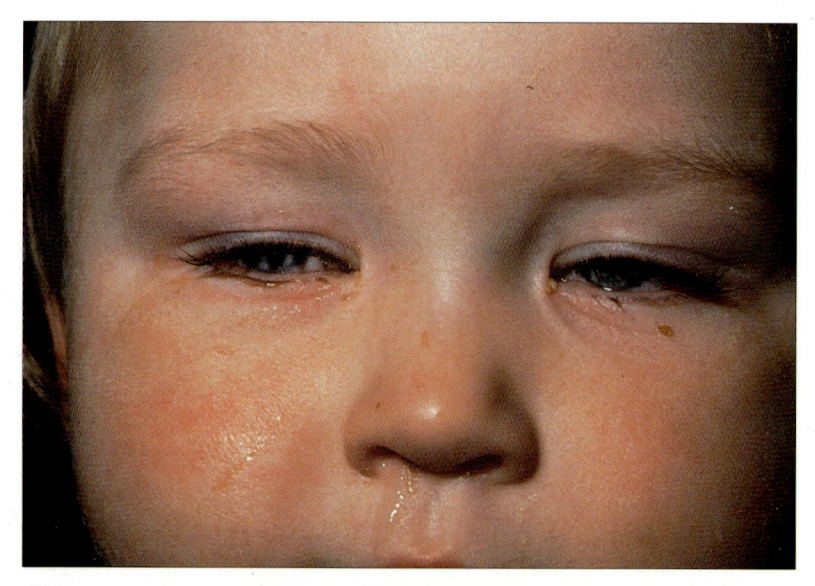

This person has caught the cold virus.

Spreading disease

People who have diseases are **infectious** for a period of time. Close contact with infectious people will increase your chances of catching a disease. Germs spread very easily in crowded conditions. If you have 'flu and you cough or sneeze, tiny droplets of water explode out of your nose and mouth. These are full of bacteria and viruses which other people around you can breathe in. This is why it is very important to hold your hand over your mouth and nose when you cough and sneeze.

Bacteria are easily spread by people who are suffering from diarrhoea if they don't wash their hands after going to the toilet. This is especially true if they are preparing food. When flies land on food they leave bacteria behind which multiply quickly so it is important to be **hygienic** when handling food.

Some people catch diseases more easily than others. You can make yourself less likely to catch diseases if you have a good diet, plenty of exercise and enough sleep.

Sneezing spreads diseases.

The fly's saliva contains bacteria. The bacteria are left behind when the fly leaves.

QUESTIONS

1. How do bacteria and viruses get into our body?
2. Describe the symptoms of meningitis.
3. Why don't viruses respond to antibiotics?
4. Write down five things you can do which will help to prevent you or other people catching diseases.

KEY IDEAS

Bacteria and viruses cause diseases.

You feel ill because of the poisons they produce and the damage they do to your cells.

You catch diseases in unhygienic conditions and after contact with infectious people.

18.2 Fighting disease

Every day you come into contact with millions of bacteria and viruses. Why don't you catch every disease? And once you have caught a disease, what stops the germs from multiplying until you die?

Before infection

Sometimes your body can prevent disease from taking hold, even if bacteria or viruses manage to get inside you. The skin is a very good protective barrier and it stops most germs from getting into the body. But if you cut yourself, germs could get in through the cut. When you cut yourself blood in the cut soon thickens to form a plug, or clot, which stops any more germs from entering your body. It is still important, though, to wash a bad cut and apply antiseptic.

Mucus

If you breathe bacteria and viruses into your lungs, many of them get stuck in a sticky substance called **mucus**. This is made by the **mucous membranes** in the lungs. The mucus is constantly being moved up the trachea to the mouth where it is swallowed into the stomach. Acid in the stomach harms the bacteria and viruses so they are not dangerous any more.

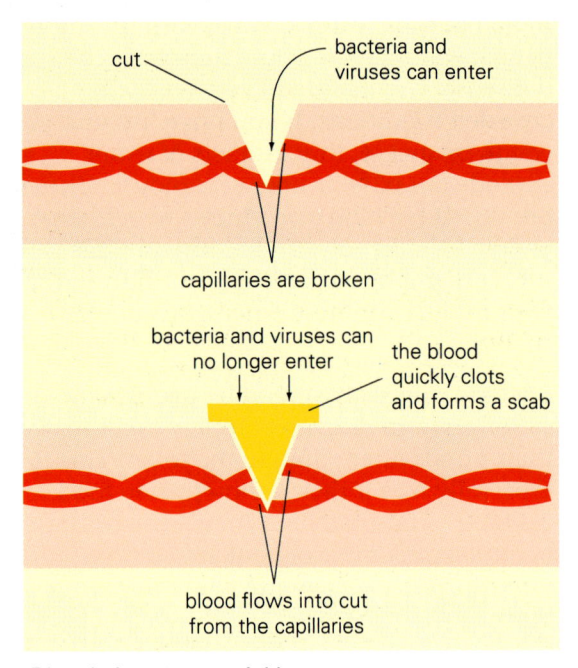

Blood clots very quickly.

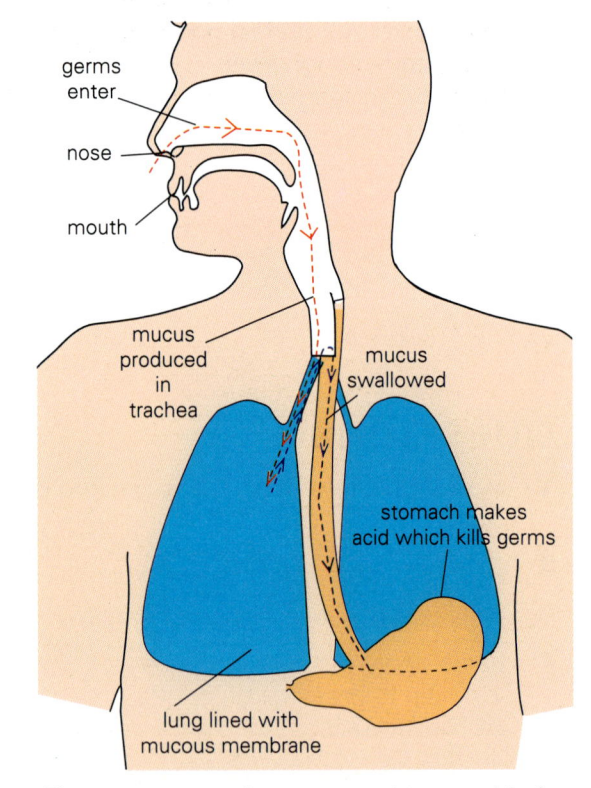

The mucus traps the germs and we get rid of them.

After infection

If you do become infected with a disease, your body's defence system begins to fight back. In your blood you have many white blood cells (see 13.5). These are vital in the fight against bacteria. Some of them engulf the bacteria and break them up.

Other white blood cells make two kinds of chemicals, **antibodies** and **antitoxins**. The antibodies stick to the bacteria and white blood cells then kill them. The antitoxins neutralise the toxins, or poisons, produced by the bacteria, so they stop you feeling ill. Once you have had a disease, the antibodies stay in your blood stream so you don't catch it again.

Immunisation

Scientists have found that if you put dead germs into the body, the white blood cells still produce antibodies against the germs. When you are **immunised** against a disease, like German measles, this is exactly what happens. The dead German measles germs are injected into you. They cannot harm you, but your white blood cells still make antibodies to fight the German measles. You are then protected against the disease.

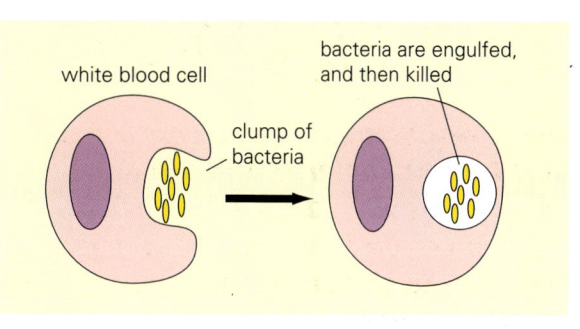

Bacteria are engulfed by white blood cells.

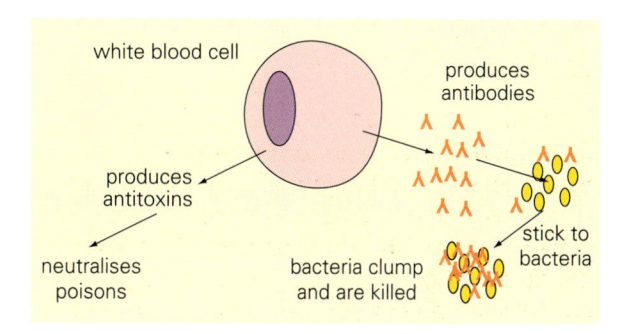

The action of antibodies and antitoxins.

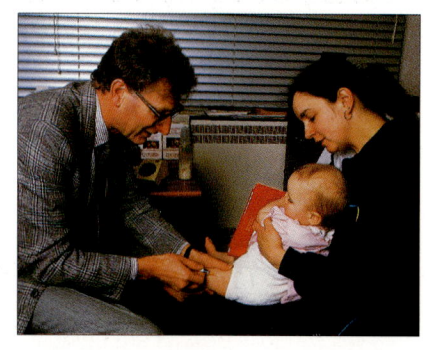

Children are immunised against many diseases now.

QUESTIONS

1. In what three ways does your body defend you against being infected with a disease?
2. How do white blood cells kill bacteria?
3. How does immunisation stop you from getting a disease?

KEY IDEAS

The body's defence against infection by disease includes a tough skin, mucus in the lungs and stomach acid.

If you are infected, white blood cells can fight back by engulfing the germ, and producing antibodies and antitoxins.

You can be immunised against some diseases.

SECTION D: QUESTIONS

1. Use the diagram to identify the parts A–E of the human digestive system.

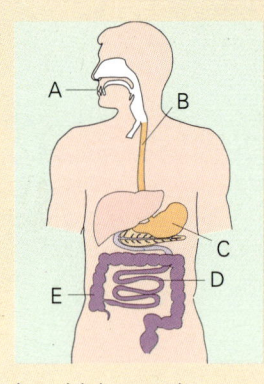

2. Explain why a balanced diet must contain:
   a. carbohydrate
   b. dietary fibre
   c. protein.

3. An experiment was done in which starch was digested by amylase. This is a graph of the results.
   a. When (time **X**, **Y** or **Z**) was amylase added?
   b. Why does the body digest starch?
   c. This experiment was done at 37°C. Why?
   d. Name two other digestive enzymes.

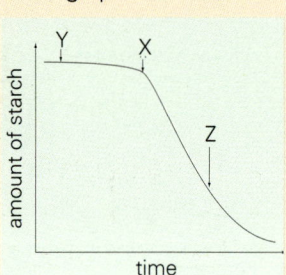

4. This is a diagram of an air sac in the lung.
   a. Which gas is moving in direction **A**?
   b. Which gas is moving in direction **B**?
   c. Why does the capillary have a thin wall?
   d. What is the scientific name for air sac? 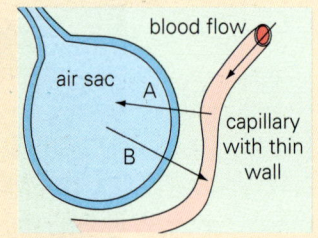

5. Two school students are doing an experiment which involves finding their heart rate by measuring the pulse. Their results are shown in the table.

Before exercise (beats per min.)	No. of minutes after exercise				
	1	2	4	6	8
Tom 75	110	93	90	86	80
Ashwyn 65	90	80	70	67	65

   a. Draw a line graph showing these results.
   b. Explain why the heart rate increases when exercise is taken.
   c. Whose heart rate returns to normal fastest?
   d. Explain how you would investigate the effect of coffee on the heart rate of a group of students.

6. Which of the following are true?
   a. When the rib cage rises, air is inhaled.
   b. When the diaphragm flattens, air is exhaled.
   c. Ribs move because of intercostal muscles.
   d. When the diaphragm rises, air is inhaled.

7. Look at this labelled diagram of the human heart.

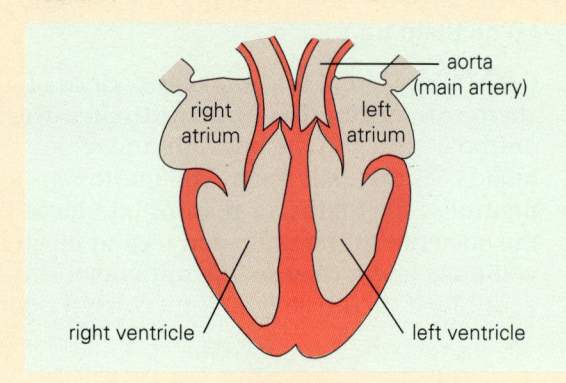

   Explain the following:
   a. hearts have valves
   b. the left ventricle has a very thick wall
   c. atria have thinner walls than ventricles
   d. the aorta is the biggest artery in the body.

8. The diagram shows the structures in a human eye.

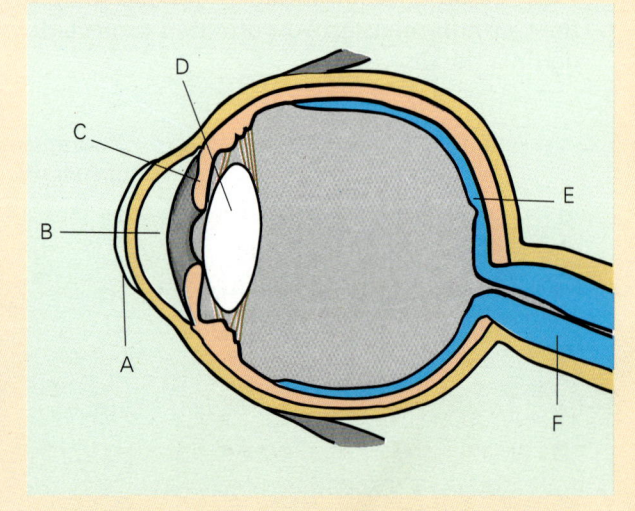

   a. Write down the names of the structures **A** to **F**.
   b. What is the function of structure **D**? Explain how it does this job, using diagrams to help you.
   c. Explain how structure **C** controls the amount of light entering the eye.

144

9 Which vitamins might be given to cure:
  a scurvy
  b night blindness?

10 Look at the diagram of a reflex arc.

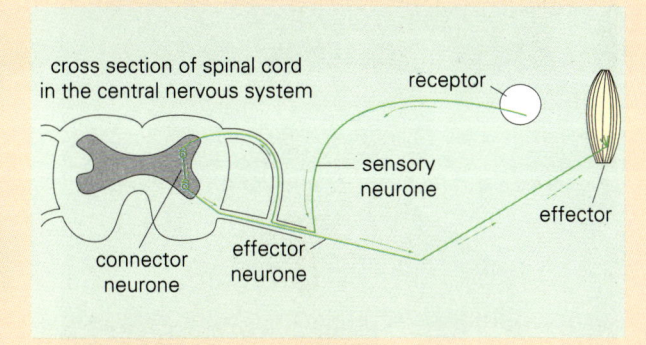

  a Give another name for a nerve cell.
  b What do we call the messages that are sent through the nervous system?
  c Give an example of a stimulus that might start off this reflex arc.
  d What sort of receptor would sense this stimulus?
  e What response would the effector carry out? How is this response helpful to the person?

11 The skin is responsible for controlling body temperature.
  a Give two ways in which the skin can cool us down.
  b How does the skin help us to stay warm?

12 Complete the passage below about hormones using the words that follow. You can use these words once, more than once or not at all.

  bloodstream target organ glands hormones insulin glucose much little decreases increases.

  _____ are chemical messengers which are released by _____ into the _____. They travel around the body until they reach the organ they affect. This is called the _____ _____. An example of a hormone is _____. It is used to control the level of _____ in the blood. If there is too _____ _____ in the blood, _____ is released. This _____ the blood _____ level.

13 The diagram shows the human excretory system.

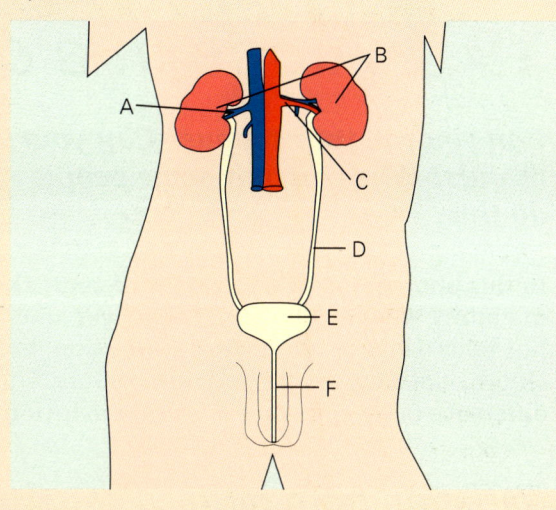

  a Name the parts labelled **A** to **F**.
  b Which part makes the urine?
  c Where is the urine stored before it is released?
  d Briefly explain why the urine is likely to be more concentrated on a hot day than on a cold day.
  e What is dialysis and why do some people need it?

14 Many people who had eaten at one restaurant complained that they were ill with diarrhoea after eating there. A health inspector went to the restaurant. This is what she found out.

  1 One of the cooks had had diarrhoea two days before.
  2 The cooks did not use antibacterial fluid to wipe down the kitchen surfaces.
  3 Food was left uncovered at room temperature before serving.

  a How could the cook who had diarrhoea have transferred the bacteria to the kitchen?
  b How might using antiseptics have helped prevent the customers from getting diarrhoea?
  c Why was it bad that the food was left uncovered before serving?
  d Why do we put food into fridges?
  e Once bacteria have infected us, and are in our bloodstream, there are three ways that our blood can fight them. Describe these three ways, using diagrams if it helps you.

145

CHAPTER 19: GENETICS AND INHERITANCE

19.1 Alone in a crowd

Can you roll your tongue? Can your friends? Why can only some people do this?

In this photograph everybody is different. There are many ways to tell them apart. Everyone has their own eye colour, face expression, hair length, clothing, height and skin colours. The difference between people is called **variation**.

Variation from birth

Some things about you were there from birth. Your skin colour won't change during your life. Your hair colour may, but much later. Hair or eye colour is passed down the generations. This is called **inheritance**. The kind of variation that can be inherited is called **genetic variation**.

Variation among a group of people.

Different environments

Not all variation is inherited from birth. Some variation among people is caused by their surroundings or environment. If you spend some time in the Sun your skin may darken. If you spend a lot of time in a gym, you'll probably get larger muscles. You make this variation happen, you do not inherit it.

These beech trees vary because of their environments.

Plant A: This plant has a poor environment.

Plant B: This plant has a good environment.

Plants A and B show how the environment can cause variation. Plant A was planted in poor soil, and wasn't given much sunlight. Plant B was given plenty of sunlight and all the proper nutrients.

Continuous and discontinuous variation

The photograph shows how height varies in people. You can see that some people are taller than others. There is a range of heights, with most people somewhere in the middle. Height is an example of **continuous variation**.

Tongue rolling, however, is an example of **discontinuous variation**. This is the kind of variation where you don't have people somewhere in the middle. Some people can roll their tongue, others cannot. What about you?

Height varies continuously.

QUESTIONS

1. List five ways in which people differ from each other.
2. Name three characteristics passed down the generations.
3. How can the environment cause variation in plants?
4. Give three examples of variation in humans caused by the environment.
5. Some people say personality is inherited. What do you think?

KEY IDEAS

Living things vary.

Some variation is inherited.

Some variation is caused by the environment.

147

19.2 Passing the message

How different are you from other people? What makes you different?

You may be similar in some ways to the person next to you. But no two people are exactly alike. So what makes you unique? How is it possible there is only one 'you'?

In this photograph of a family everyone looks different. But there are similarities too. For example, you can see that the children and the parents have similar hair. The most likely explanation is that the children have inherited their hair colour from their parents. They have inherited their parents' **genes**.

Instructions for the body

Genes are instructions. They provide the information needed for making different parts of your body. Some genes affect visible parts of you, like height, hair colour and eye colour. Other genes are instructions for things you are almost never aware of, such as the enzymes in your stomach.

Your own genes are stored inside your cells. Each cell carries a full set of genes. They are grouped together on long strands called **chromosomes**. The chromosomes carry thousands of genes.

Chromosomes are in the cell nucleus; they can be stained and examined using a microscope and can be seen under the microscope. Most of your cells contain 46 chromosomes.

Differences and similarities.

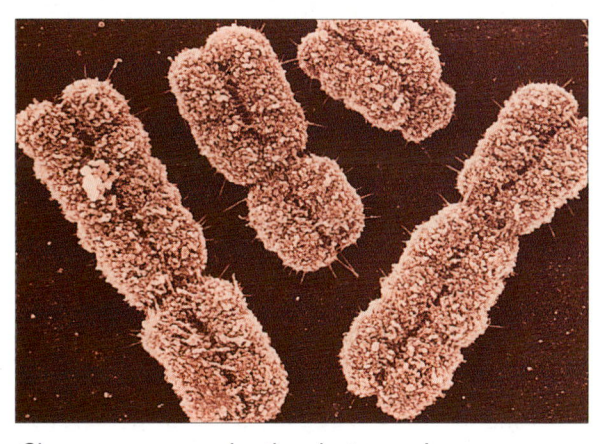

Chromosomes under the electron microscope.

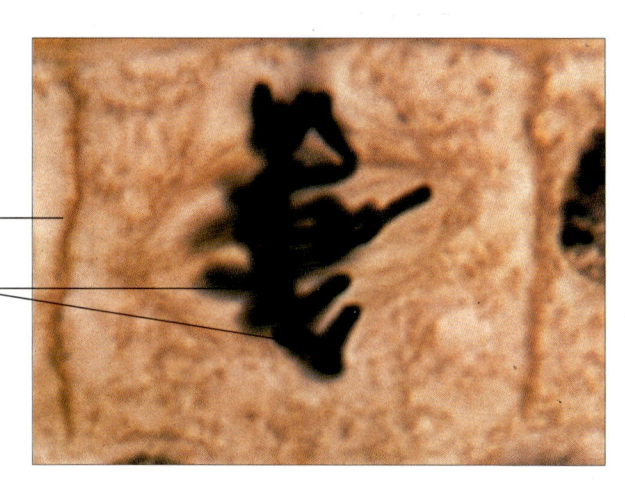

cell wall

chromosomes are dark structures inside the cell

You can see the chromosomes inside the cells of this onion root.

You look a bit different...

Every sperm made by the father has a slightly different set of instructions. And no two eggs are the same, either. This is because, when these cells are made, the genes in the chromosomes are rearranged. Each sperm cell made in the father, and each egg cell made in the mother, comes with a unique combination of genes. No two eggs and no two sperm have the same genetic message.

When **fertilisation** happens, a unique egg combines with a unique sperm. It is not surprising brothers and sisters look a little different from each other.

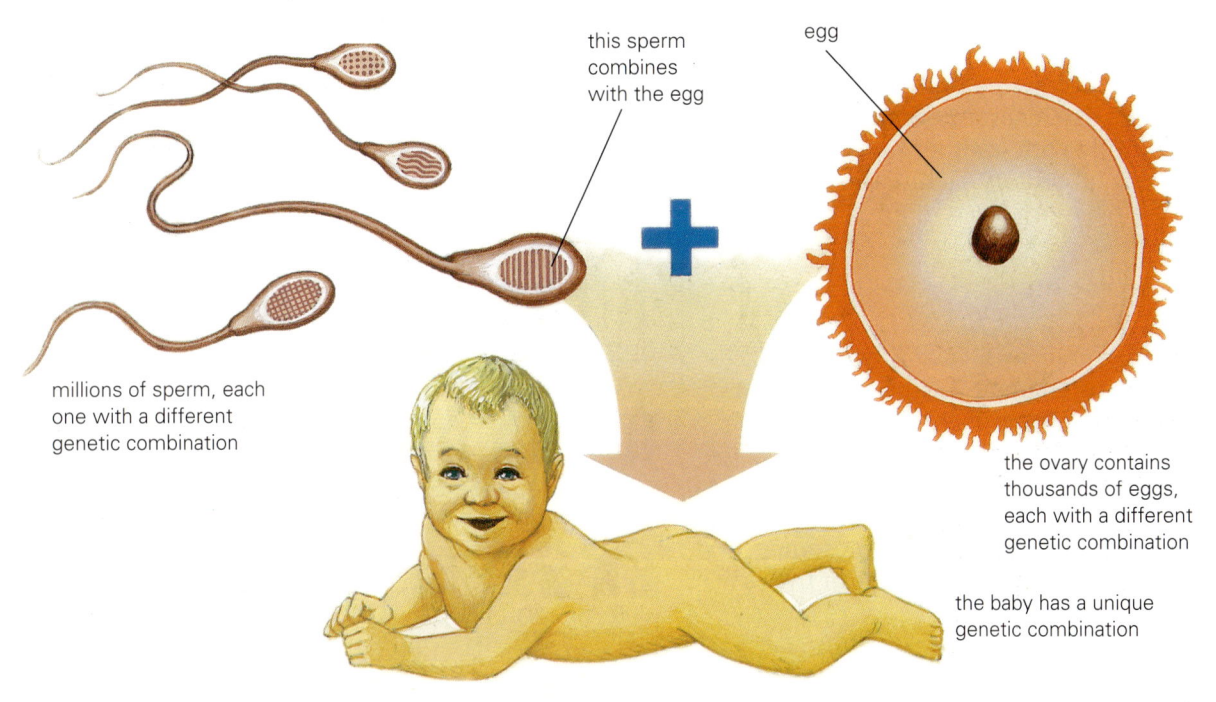

millions of sperm, each one with a different genetic combination

this sperm combines with the egg

egg

the ovary contains thousands of eggs, each with a different genetic combination

the baby has a unique genetic combination

Each sperm and each egg has a unique genetic combination – and so does the baby.

QUESTIONS

1. Where in the cell are the chromosomes?
2. How many chromosomes are there in a human cell?
3. Which cells transport the father's genes to the egg?
4. Explain why family members:
   a look a bit similar
   b look a bit different.

KEY IDEAS

Genes are instructions for the body.

Genes are stored inside cells.

Chromosomes carry thousands of genes.

19.3 Boy or girl?

What was the first question anyone ever asked about you? It was probably a question about gender. Is it a boy or a girl?

Boys have a slightly different set of chromosomes from girls. The sex of a baby in the womb can be discovered by looking at its chromosomes.

Chromosome pairs

This picture shows how your 46 chromosomes are arranged in pairs. Chromosomes are different sizes and shapes. Each chromosome pairs up naturally with another similar one. In this laboratory picture the 23 pairs have been arranged in lines, and labelled.

The sex pair

Chromosome pair 23 has its own name. This pair of chromosomes is called the **sex pair**. The sex pair has the job of giving you your gender. A male sex pair consists of an X chromosome and a Y chromosome. The female sex pair consists of two X chromosomes.

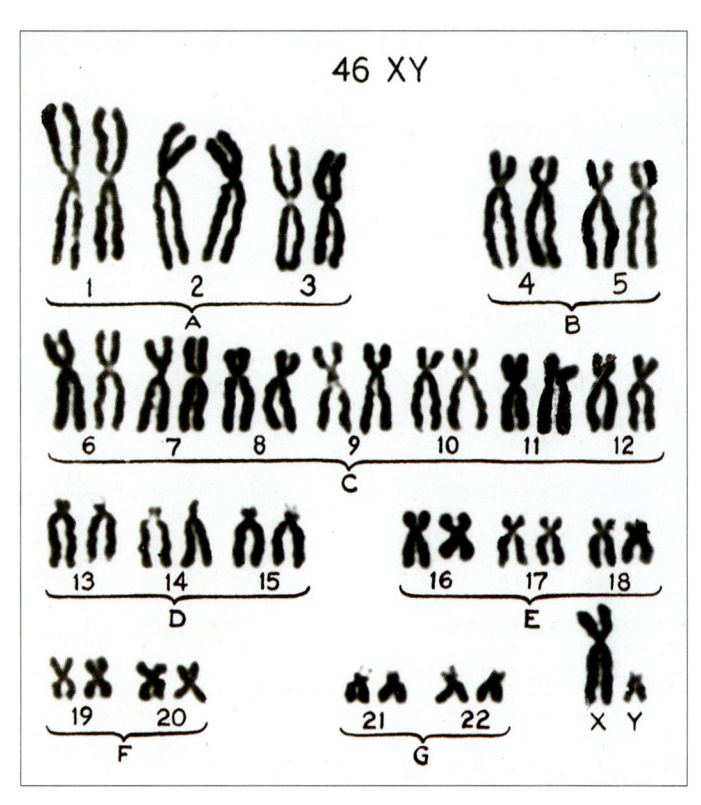

A laboratory photograph of the human chromosomes in a male.

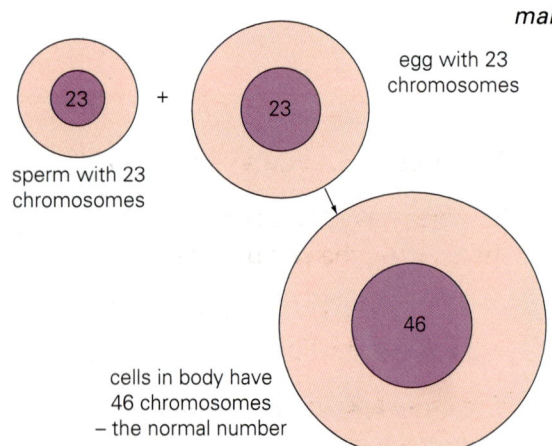

The sex cells: sperm and egg

Sperm and **eggs** are unusual because they contain 23 chromosomes instead of the normal 46. When sperm and eggs are made, they are given single chromosomes, not pairs. One result of this is that sex cells contain only half of a sex pair: either X or Y.

Sperm and eggs have only half the normal number of chromosomes.

Every human egg has one X chromosome. But a sperm may be X or Y. This is because a man's sex pair is XY. The diagram below shows that when an egg is fertilised by a Y sperm, then a baby boy will be born. If an egg is fertilised by an X sperm, then a baby girl will be born.

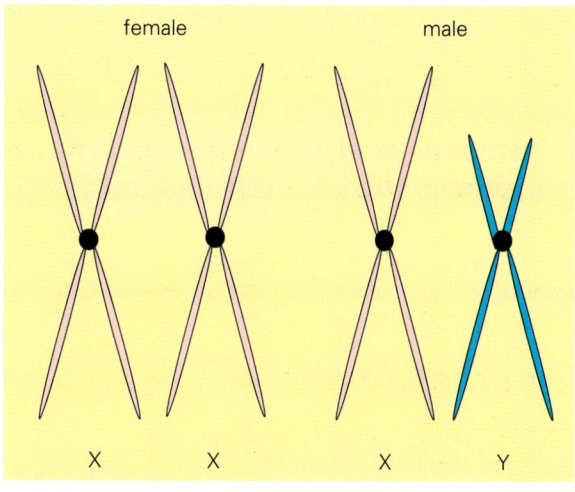

A diagram of the sex chromosomes.

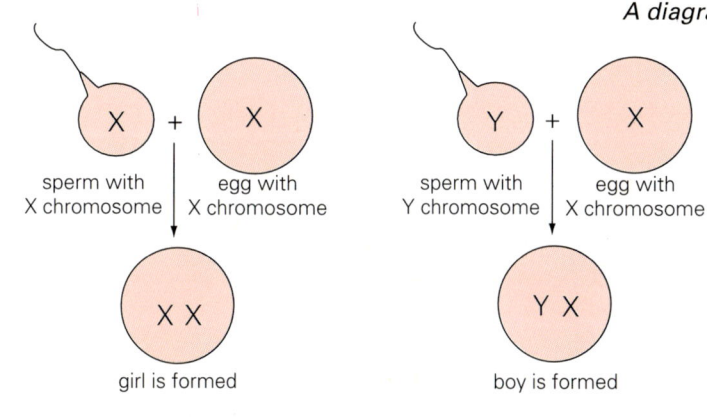

How the sex chromosomes are inherited.

QUESTIONS

1. How many pairs of chromosomes are there in a human cell?
2. Which sex pair do boys have?
3. Which sex pair do girls have?
4. In the following diagram, will the baby be a boy or a girl? 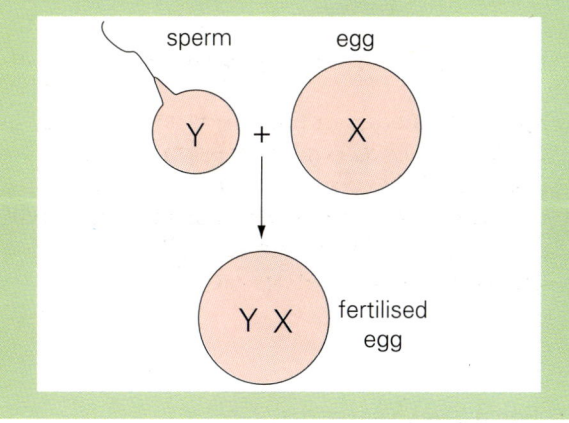
5. How many chromosomes are there in sperm and eggs?
6. Explain the following:
   a Sperm cells are either X or Y.
   b All human eggs are X.

KEY IDEAS

Chromosomes are paired.

Females have the sex pair XX, males have the sex pair XY.

Eggs are female sex cells, sperm are male sex cells.

Eggs and sperm each have 23 chromosomes.

19.4 Genetic disease

When does mutation happen? What causes colour blindness? Or sickle cell anaemia?

As well as genes for normal body development, we can sometimes inherit 'faulty' genes. Faulty genes can cause disease. They may come from the father, the mother or both. Quite often a faulty gene may be inherited through many generations.

Some genetic problems

Inherited or **genetic diseases** include sickle cell anaemia, cystic fibrosis, Huntington's disease and albinism.

Faulty genes can also cause:

- breast cancer
- heart disease
- diabetes
- colour blindness.

Mutation

Faulty genes happen because of **mutation**. A mutation is when a gene, or a whole chromosome, gets damaged. Mutation can be caused by X-rays, other kinds of radiation, and some chemicals. Once a mutation has happened, the change will be passed down the generations.

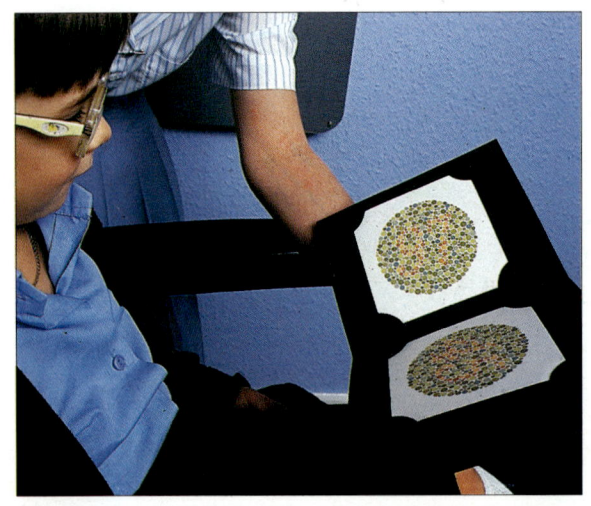

If you are colour blind you will not see the number.

Some heart disease may have genetic causes.

Two genetic diseases

Sickle cell anaemia is a genetic disease affecting the blood. Normal red blood cells are disc shaped. Someone with this disease has blood cells which can change shape or 'sickle'. If this happens the blood cells may get trapped in small blood vessels like capillaries. The body cells near the blockage are then starved of oxygen, and may be damaged. Sickle shaped cells are also less able to carry oxygen than normal red blood cells.

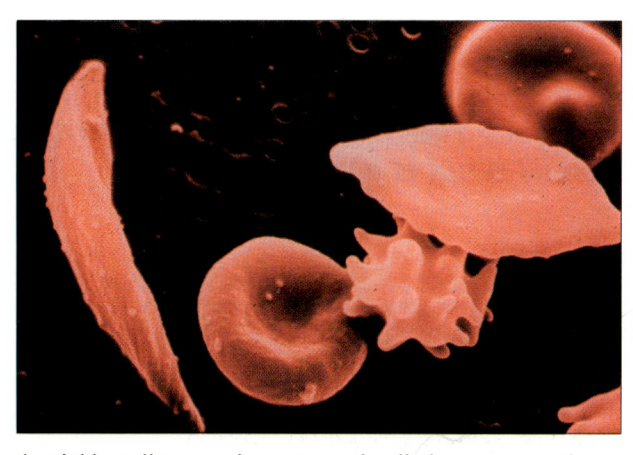

The girl in the photograph is getting help clearing her lungs. She is suffering from **cystic fibrosis**. She has inherited faulty genes, stopping the membrane of her lungs working normally. Mucus gathers, and infection becomes a danger.

In sickle cell anaemia some red cells have unusual shapes.

Carriers and sufferers

People who inherit a faulty gene from one parent and a healthy gene from the other parent may not suffer from the disease. They are called **carriers**.

Carriers are usually perfectly healthy but can pass on the faulty gene to their children. If two parents are carriers, then they might each pass on their faulty genes to a child – who will then be a sufferer.

Physiotherapy helps to dislodge mucus in the lungs of a person suffering from cystic fibrosis.

QUESTIONS

1. List four genetic diseases.
2. Which part of the body is affected by:
   a sickle cell anaemia
   b cystic fibrosis?
3. What causes mutation?
4. Carriers of cystic fibrosis do not suffer from the disease, but may have children with the disease. How do you explain this?

KEY IDEAS

Genes can be damaged by radiation and chemicals.

Faulty genes can cause disease.

A carrier is healthy but can pass on the disease.

CHAPTER 20: HUMAN REPRODUCTION

20.1 Girls

How does a girl's body make eggs? Where are they stored? What is a period?

Puberty

Sometime between 8 and 17 years, girls begin to change into adults. Puberty is the start of this change. At puberty a girl's body and mind are changing rapidly. These are the main changes in girls:

- your breasts get bigger
- your hips get wider
- you grow pubic hair
- your periods start
- your interests change.

Eggs are made in the ovaries

When a girl is born she already has two ovaries, each with thousands of eggs. The eggs are tiny and undeveloped and stay that way until the girl reaches puberty. When puberty happens, the eggs begin to mature. From then on one egg matures each month, ready for release, or **ovulation**. When an egg is released from the ovary it passes into the **oviduct**, or egg tube.

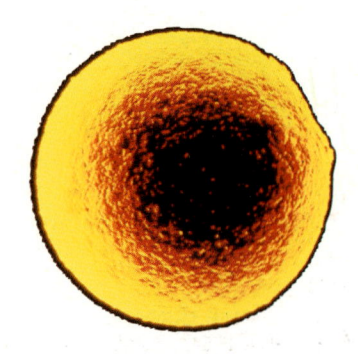

The female reproductive system.

The human egg.

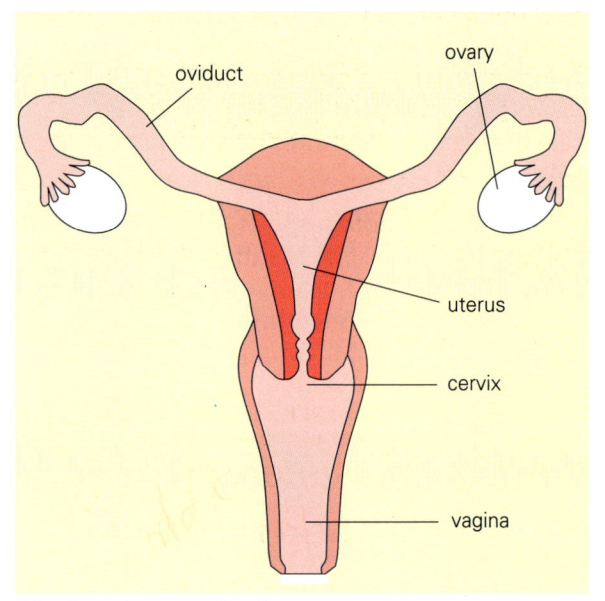

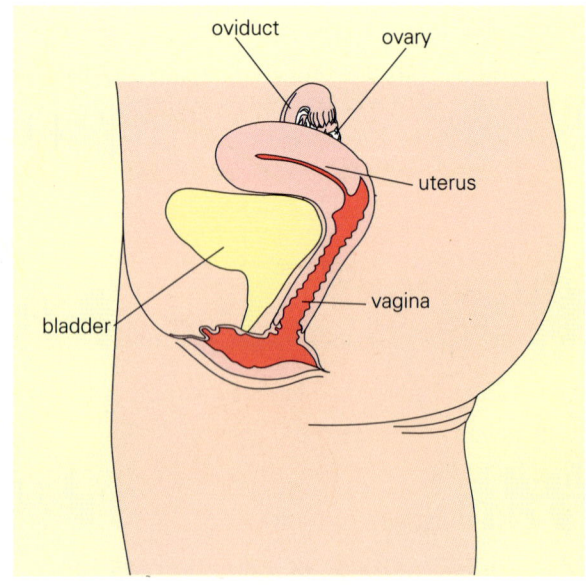

Side view of the female reproductive system.

154

Periods

During puberty the periods start. Each month the uterus wall builds itself up, ready to nourish a fertilised egg. When no egg is fertilised the wall breaks down and becomes thin again. For a few days, blood comes down out of the uterus and through the vagina. This is the period, and the monthly cycle of build up and then breakdown of the uterus wall is called the **menstrual cycle**.

In girls eggs are released once a month. The rhythm varies a little. For example when a girl has just started her periods, the time of the month varies before settling down.

The maturing of the eggs and the period are controlled by sex hormones. **Oestrogen** is a hormone made in the ovaries. One of the jobs of oestrogen is to build up the uterus wall after the period has finished.

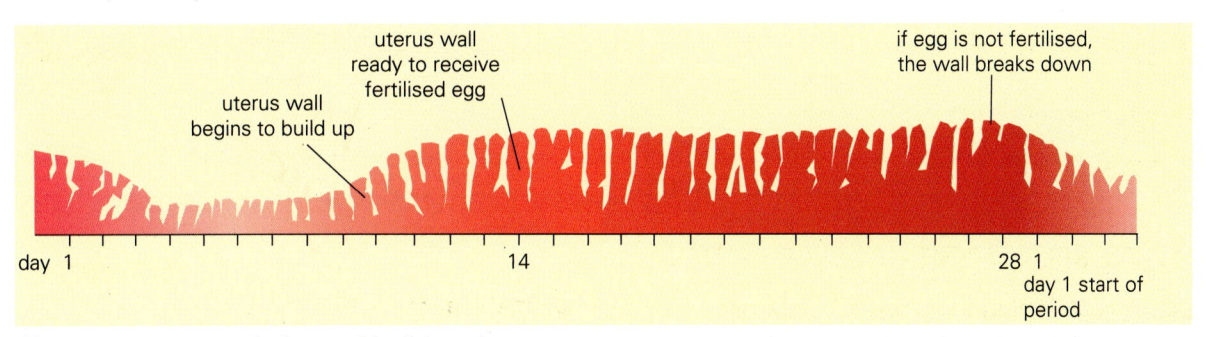

Hormones cause ovulation and build up the uterus.

QUESTIONS

1. In this diagram, what are the names of A, B, C, D, and E? 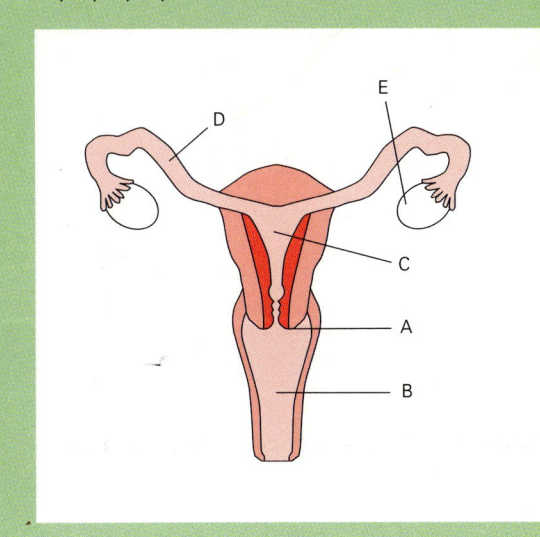
2. Where are eggs made?
3. How often are eggs released?
4. Explain why periods happen.
5. Why is the uterus wall built up again after a period?

KEY IDEAS

Eggs are made in ovaries.

Oestrogen is a female sex hormone. One of its jobs is to rebuild the uterus wall after a period.

20.2 Boys

What happens inside a boy's testicles? What does testosterone do? And where are sperm stored?

Boys usually reach puberty later than girls, between the ages of 10 and 18. Puberty is just as important for boys as for girls. These are the main changes in boys:

- your voice changes
- you become taller and more muscular
- you grow pubic hair
- you start to make sperm
- your interests change.

Testicles

When a boy reaches puberty his **testicles** start to produce the male sex cells or **sperm**. Millions are made each day. But to make sperm in such high numbers, the testicles need a temperature about 2°C lower than the rest of the body. This explains why testicles hang outside the body, where it is slightly cooler.

The testicles mainly consist of tubes, folded up to take up less space. Here, sperm are continuously manufactured and stored. The sperm live for a few days, before they are broken down again and absorbed by the body. They are then replaced by new sperm.

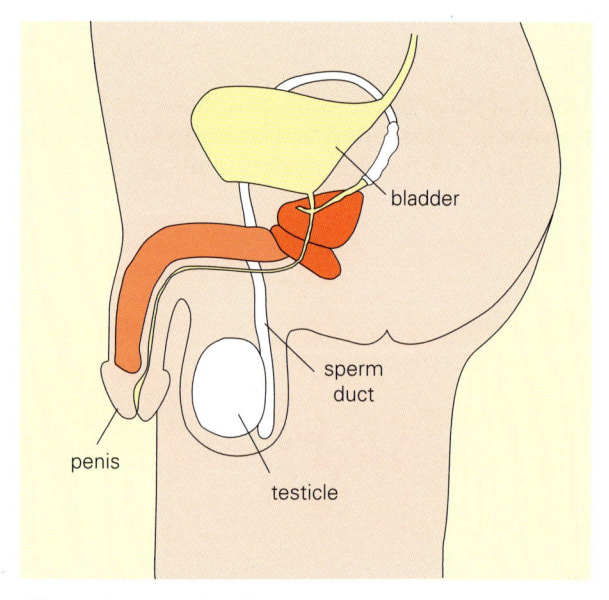

The male reproductive system.

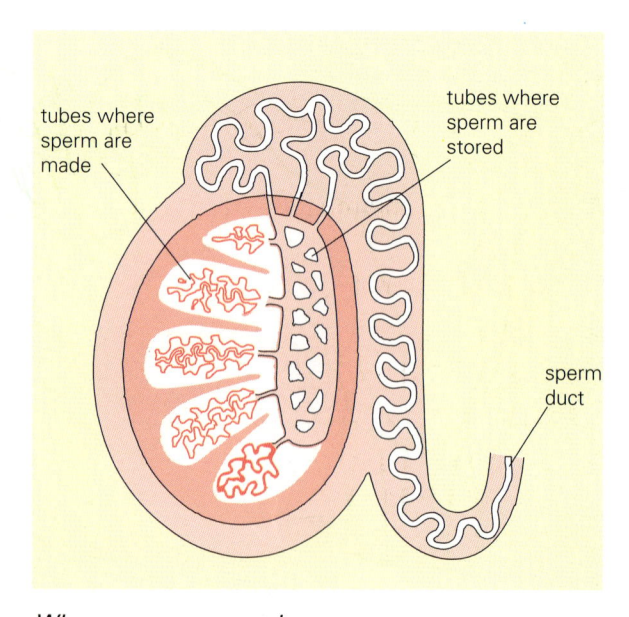

Where sperm are made.

156

Sperm

The diagram below shows the structure of a sperm. You can see there is a head, containing the nucleus. Inside the nucleus is the genetic material of the father. The tail is like a whip, and gives the sperm the ability to swim. This is extremely important because sperm have to swim if they are to reach an egg and fertilise it.

Sperm are extremely tiny and very numerous. Eggs are much bigger but far fewer. But eggs and sperm are the same in one way: they are both **gametes**. This means they contain only half the normal number of chromosomes – 23 instead of 46. If a sperm combines with an egg, then the new cell will have 46 chromosomes and will be able to grow into a baby.

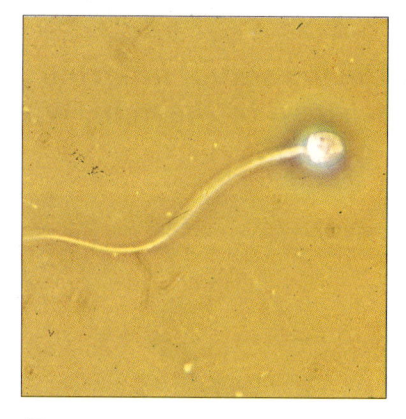

Human sperm cell.

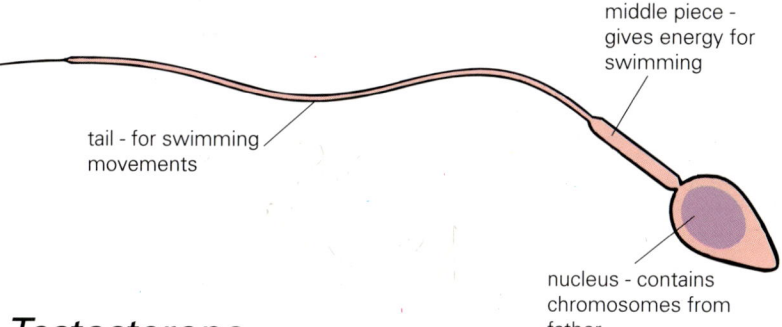

The structure of a sperm.

Testosterone

The male sex hormone which controls your puberty changes is **testosterone**. At puberty the testicles begin to make much more testosterone. Because of this sex hormone your body begins to change, growing larger and stronger and more adult.

QUESTIONS

1. Name three changes happening during male puberty.
2. How many chromosomes are there in each sperm?
3. Where is testosterone made?
4. Explain why:
   a sperm cells have tails
   b testicles hang outside the body.
5. What happens to sperm which do not leave the testicle?
6. In which way are:
   a sperm different from eggs
   b sperm similar to eggs?

KEY IDEAS

Sperm are the male sex cells.

Sperm are made in the testicles and have 23 chromosomes.

Testosterone is a male sex hormone. One of its jobs is to help sperm production.

20.3 Sexual intercourse

During sexual intercourse, up to 500 million sperm may be released by the man. Why so many? What happens to them?

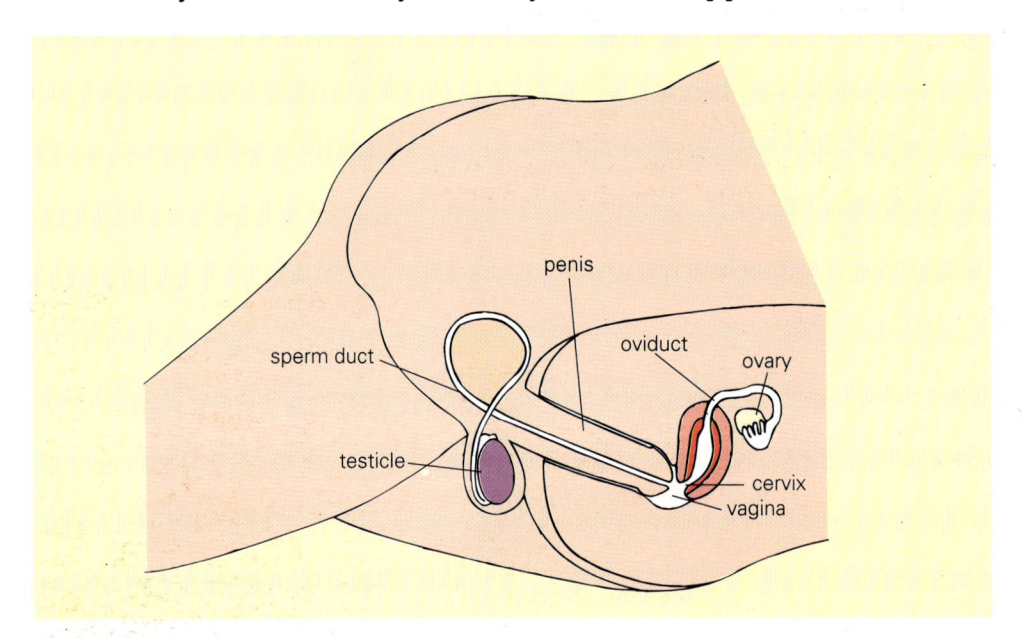

Sexual intercourse.

Sexual intercourse, or simply *sex*, is the body's way of helping one sperm to meet one egg.

The diagram above shows how sex takes sperm inside a woman. During sex, changes happen in both the woman's and the man's body. The vagina becomes moist and better able to receive the penis. In the man, high pressure blood makes the penis erect, so that it can enter the vagina.

The journey of the sperm

When the penis is inside the vagina, nerve signals start passing through the body. In the woman, the **clitoris** at the opening of the vagina is very sensitive to touch. In the man, the penis is sensitive. During sexual intercourse nerve signals to the brain produce feelings of pleasure. **Orgasm**, in both men and women, is when this pleasure is strongest.

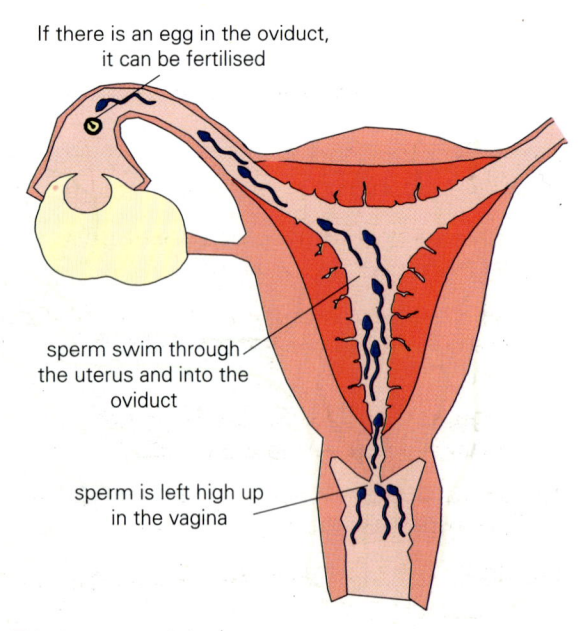

The journey of the sperm.

When the man has an orgasm, he ejaculates. Millions of sperm are suddenly pushed out of the testicles, through the penis, and into the woman's vagina.

Ejaculation leaves the sperm high up in the vagina, near the **cervix**. The cervix has a small hole in it. This is the entrance to the uterus. Now the sperm will start swimming through the cervix, up towards the oviduct.

Small contractions of the uterus help the sperm move towards the oviduct. Within a few hours, some surviving sperm – perhaps the strongest – are entering the oviduct. But out of a hundred million which left the penis, only a few thousand get this far.

The egg is surrounded

What happens next will depend on whether there is an egg in the oviduct. If there is an egg, the surviving sperm will quickly surround it. If there is no egg, the remaining sperm will remain in the oviduct for a few days, and then die.

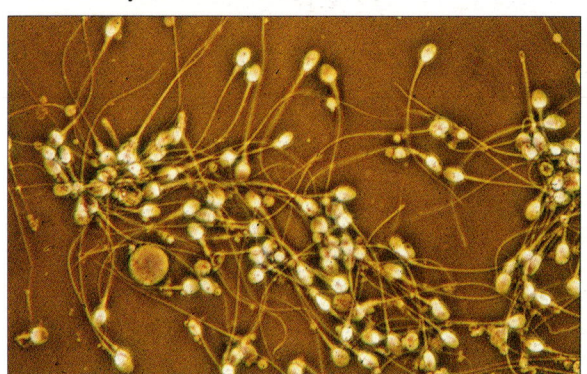

Sperm swim towards the egg.

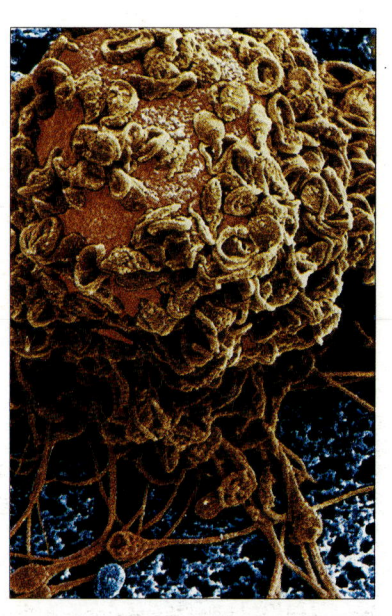

Sperm at the end of their journey.

QUESTIONS

1 How many sperm may be released during sexual intercourse?

2 The following is a list of the places in the sperm's journey. Put them in the right order:

vagina   testicle   uterus   penis   cervix   oviduct   sperm duct

3 Explain why the man produces so many sperm.

4 What happens when the sperm reach the oviduct?

KEY IDEAS

During sex, sperm are ejaculated into the vagina.

After sex the sperm swim towards the oviduct.

Only a few thousand sperm reach the oviduct.

20.4 Fertilisation

How many sperm fertilise one egg? What happens next? When does a woman actually become pregnant?

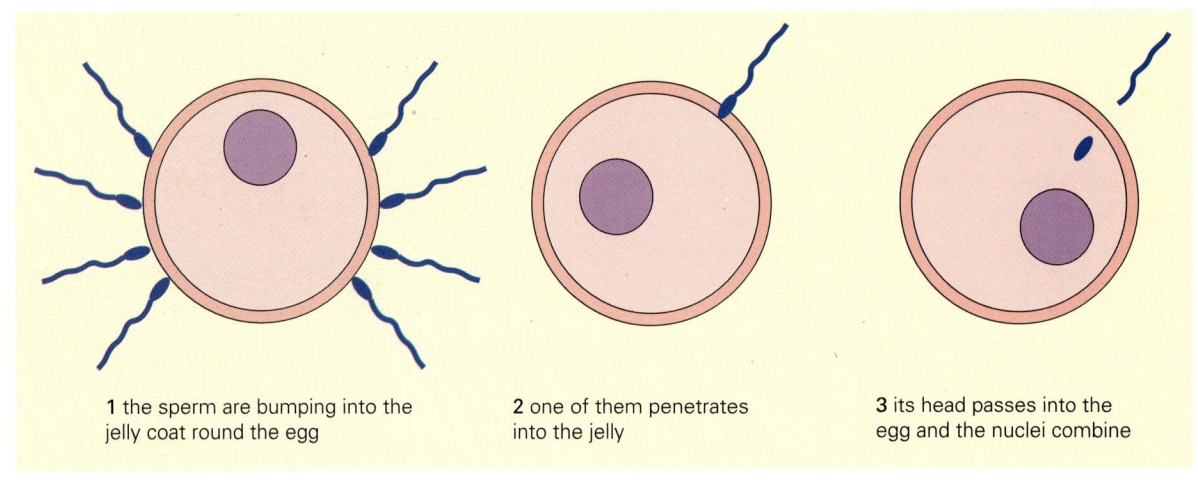

1 the sperm are bumping into the jelly coat round the egg

2 one of them penetrates into the jelly

3 its head passes into the egg and the nuclei combine

Egg surrounded by sperm.

Fertilisation is the moment a sperm enters an egg. The nucleus of the sperm joins the nucleus of the egg. Now the chromosomes from the mother are brought together with the chromosomes of the father.

In the diagram you can see that only one sperm enters the egg. The other sperm cannot enter, and will soon die.

Joining sperm with egg

Sperm and egg are the same in one important way. Unlike other cells, which have 46 chromosomes, they only carry 23. This is why gametes (eggs and sperm) cannot grow on their own. They do not have enough chromosomes (see 19.3).

At fertilisation, the egg joins with a sperm. This makes a **zygote**, or fertilised egg. The 23 chromosomes of the sperm join with the 23 chromosomes of the egg. Now there are 46 chromosomes, the normal number. This is why a fertilised egg can start to grow.

The journey of the fertilised egg

Once the egg is fertilised, it begins to grow. Within a few hours it has divided into two, then four, then eight cells. Quite soon the egg has turned into a ball of cells. It is growing fast, and is called an **embryo**.

Reaching the uterus

But the embryo must not develop in the oviduct – there is not enough room. So it keeps moving along the oviduct, towards the uterus. When it reaches the uterus it buries itself in the wall. This is called **implantation**. The embryo can now be nourished, protected and kept warm. At this point, the woman is pregnant.

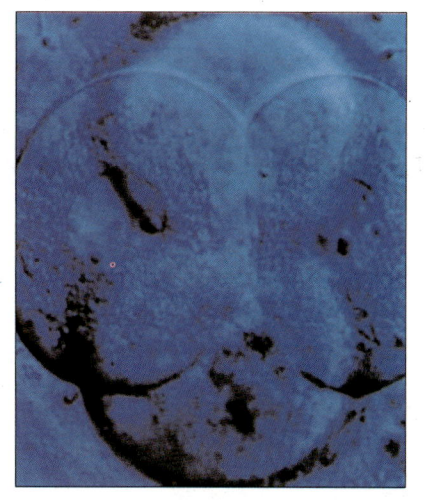

The early embryo is a ball of cells.

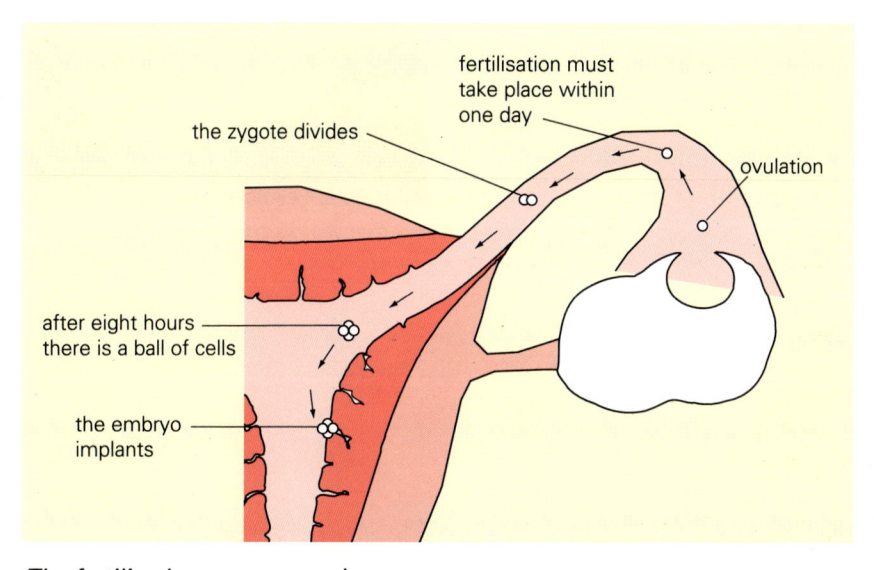

The fertilised egg moves and grows.

QUESTIONS

1. Where does fertilisation take place?
2. How many sperm fertilise one egg?
3. How many chromosomes are there in the human zygote?
4. Explain why the fertilised egg moves towards the uterus.
5. Why is implantation important for the growing embryo?

KEY IDEAS

Eggs are fertilised by sperm.

During fertilisation the chromosomes in the egg and sperm combine.

A fertilised egg is called a zygote.

20.5 The developing baby

You started your life as a tiny ball of cells. But nine months later you had bones, hair, eyes – and a name. What happened?

The placenta and umbilical cord

Five weeks after fertilisation, the embryo's heart begins to beat. In this picture you can see that the limbs have also begun to develop.

At nine weeks the embryo is called a **fetus**. It is growing fast, and needs a good supply of food and oxygen.

In the diagram you can see how the mother feeds the fetus. The **umbilical cord** takes blood from the fetus to the **placenta** in the uterus wall. In the placenta the blood of the fetus is very close to the blood of the mother. They do not mix but are close enough for materials to be exchanged. The fetus blood collects food and oxygen. It gets rid of carbon dioxide and other waste products in to the mother's blood. Then it returns to the baby in the umbilical cord. Nothing solid passes down the umbilical cord.

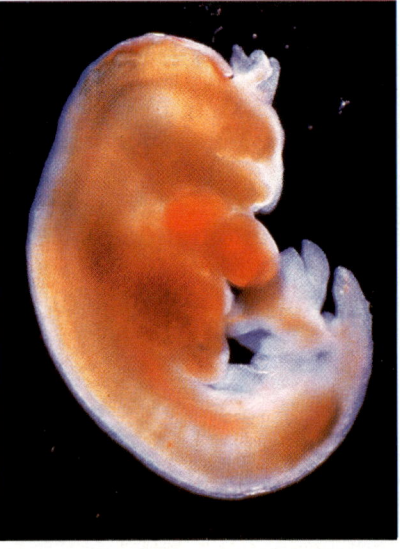

At five weeks the embryo is 1 cm long.

The developing fetus

This six-month fetus is 30 cm long. By now even the finger nails have formed. All the internal organs are fully developed, including lungs, heart and nervous system. Over the next three months the fetus will be getting larger and stronger, preparing for life outside.

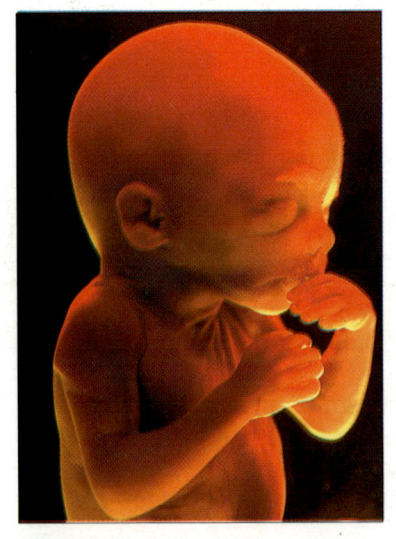

A fetus at six months.

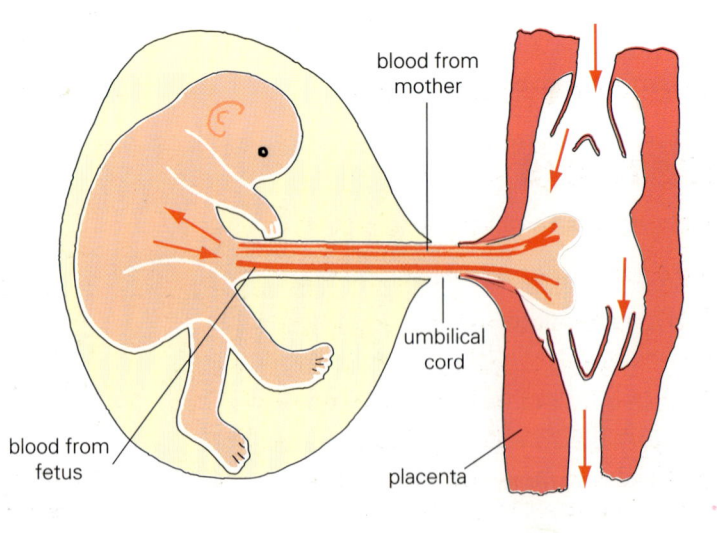

The placenta is made of blood vessels from mother and fetus.

Birth

When labour starts, the muscles of the uterus contract strongly. The baby is pushed out, head first. The cervix gets much wider, so that the head of the baby can get into the vagina. The hardest part for the mother is when the baby passes through the vagina. Although the vagina is stretchy it is a very painful time. After the baby is born the placenta is pushed out too.

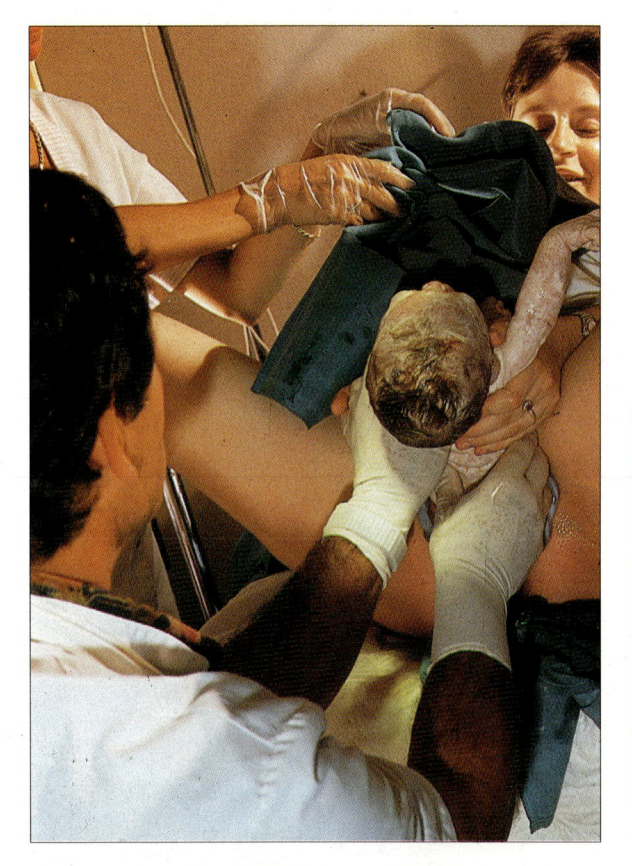

One minute after this photo was taken...

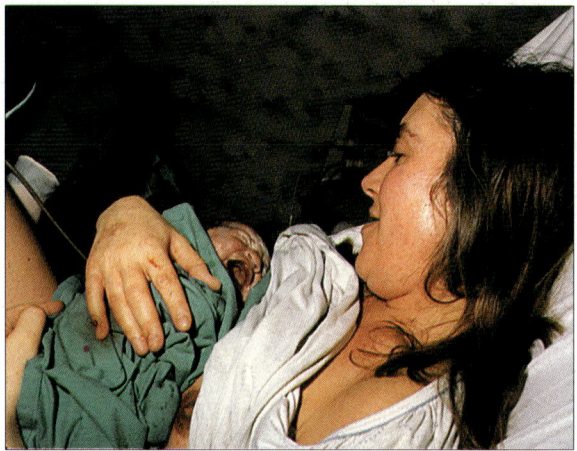

. . . the baby was being held.

QUESTIONS

1. How big is a five-week old embryo?
2. When does the embryo become a fetus?
3. How big is the six-month old fetus?
4. Name some of the materials which cross from the fetus's to the mother's blood.
5. How does the placenta make it easy for materials to cross from the mother to the fetus, and from fetus to mother?

KEY IDEAS

The growing baby inside the uterus is called the fetus.

The fetus is connected to the uterus wall by the placenta and umbilical cord.

In the placenta, food and oxygen pass into the blood of the fetus.

CHAPTER 21: REPRODUCTION

21.1 Sexual reproduction

What is meant by sex? Can bacteria have sex? Why is sex useful?

Sex results in combining a male's genes with a female's genes. For this to happen, the male and female produce their own sex cells or gametes. In animals, the males produce sperm and the females produce eggs.

Sexual reproduction is found throughout nature. Oak trees, poppies, salmon, frogs and elephants – even worms – all reproduce sexually. All of them have their own way of combining male and female genetic material, so as to make new offspring.

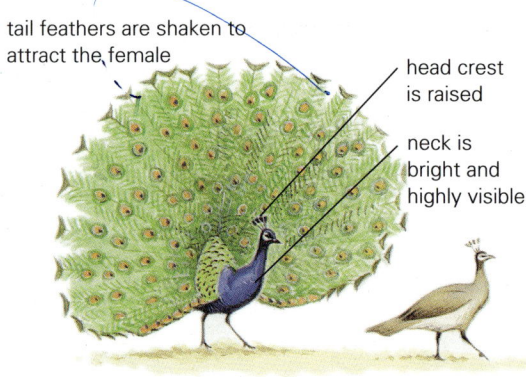

A male peacock attracts the female.

Sex increases genetic variety

Sexual reproduction increases genetic variation. One way this is helpful is in fighting disease. If there is an outbreak of disease, some animals may by chance have genes which make them **resistant**, or protected.

Internal fertilisation

In mammals, birds and reptiles, the egg and the sperm combine inside the mother. This is called **internal fertilisation**. Birds lay their eggs soon after fertilisation and look after them in the nest.

The giant tortoises in the photograph are trying to mate. They sexually reproduce using internal fertilisation. If fertilisation *does* occur, the baby tortoise will inherit genes from both its parents.

Keeping the baby inside the mother until it is strong helps it to survive after birth. Zebra, gazelle and wildebeest must be able to run from danger soon after they are born.

Genetic material from these two tortoises will combine inside the mother.

In half an hour this baby African wildebeest will be able to run.

External fertilisation

When fish have sex the males and females release their eggs and sperm straight into the water. This is called **external fertilisation**. Loose in the water, many of the eggs may die or be eaten. To increase the chance of fertilisation many fish release huge numbers of eggs and sperm.

male frog is able to fertilise eggs as they leave the mother

tadpoles are small and easy prey for other animals

frog spawn is easily eaten by other animals

Frogs have external fertilisation and produce many frog spawn.

QUESTIONS

1. Name four organisms which reproduce sexually.
2. What is the male gamete?
3. Which of the following have external fertilisation?
    a salmon
    b peacock
    c human
    d frog
    e tortoise.
4. Explain how the following can increase the chances that an egg will develop into an adult.
    a Internal fertilisation.
    b Growing offspring inside the mother until quite well developed.
    c Good parental care.

KEY IDEAS

Sexual reproduction increases genetic variety.

Internal fertilisation takes place inside the mother.

External fertilisation takes place outside the mother.

21.2 Reproducing without sex

Why do most organisms need two to reproduce?
Elephants, humans, mice and insects – they all need to find partners before they can reproduce and make new offspring. Wouldn't it be simpler if organisms could make offspring by themselves?

Asexual reproduction

Many plants and some animals can reproduce without sex. This is called **asexual reproduction**. In the diagram of the plant *Bryophyllum*, you can see that the edge of the leaf is turning into baby plants. They are about to drop off. When they do, they will quickly grow roots and start an independent life.

In asexual reproduction there is no need to make gametes. The new organism just grows out of the old organism. You can see this happening in the photograph of the water organism *Hydra* below. A new animal is growing out of the side of the parent and will soon drop off. This is called **budding**.

New plants are forming along the edge of the leaf on this Bryophyllum plant.

The best of both worlds

Aphids can reproduce sexually or asexually, depending on conditions. In asexual reproduction, every organism can make offspring, not just females. This way a population can rise very rapidly indeed, and this is what you can see with aphids, in the summer. With warmth and plenty of flowers in the gardens, the aphids quickly boost their population.

Aphids reproduce sexually when conditions are hard and a big population cannot be supported. Sexual reproduction is slower, but it produces genetic variation. Genetic variation can help animal populations survive through frost, drought and famine.

A new Hydra is forming on the side of the parent.

Asexual reproduction will quickly increase the population of garden aphids.

Clones

Asexual reproduction produces genetically identical organisms or **clones**. This is useful in farming where good quality, identical fruit will get the best prices. This strawberry is cloning itself by sending out 'runners'. The runners will grow into new, identical plants – clones. If the parent strawberry produced good-tasting strawberries, so will the clones.

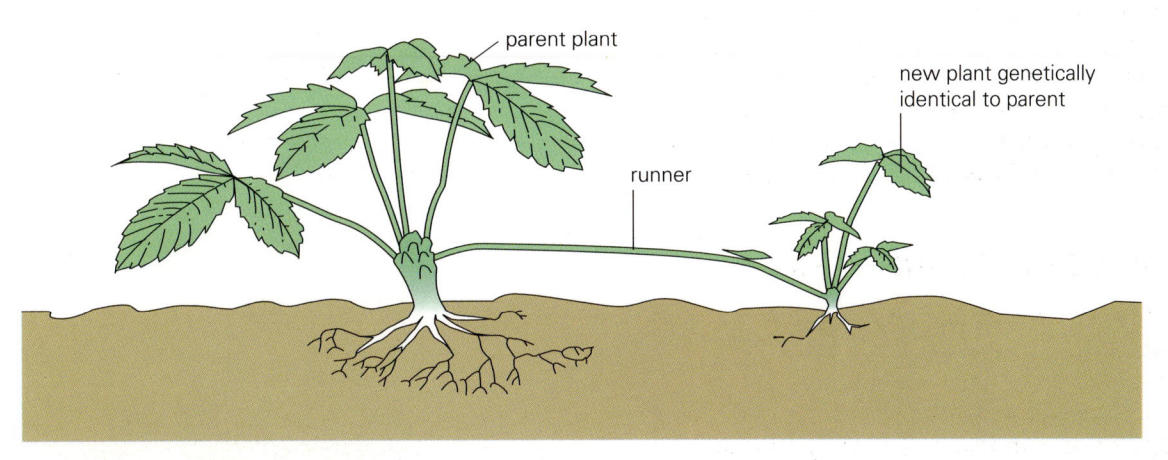

Strawberries reproduce asexually.

QUESTIONS

1. Name three organisms which can reproduce asexually.
2. Which part of the *Bryophyllum* plant produces offspring?
3. Explain why asexual reproduction is useful to a farmer.
4. Explain why aphids sometimes reproduce asexually, sometimes sexually.

KEY IDEAS

Asexual reproduction requires one parent only.

Gametes are not produced in asexual reproduction.

The offspring of asexual reproduction are genetically identical.

CHAPTER 22: THE EVOLUTION OF LIFE

22.1 Life on Earth

Which animals existed 300 million years ago? Has life on Earth always been the same?

The history of life

Life on Earth began three and a half billion years ago. The first living things were simple cells, like bacteria. Today the Earth is populated not just by bacteria, but by large and complicated species, including *Homo sapiens*, the human species.

The way life on Earth has changed over time is called **evolution**. During many millions of years, some species have disappeared or become **extinct**, and new ones have formed. The chart gives a simple history of fish, amphibians, reptiles, birds and mammals. You can see that the mammals and the birds were the latest to evolve.

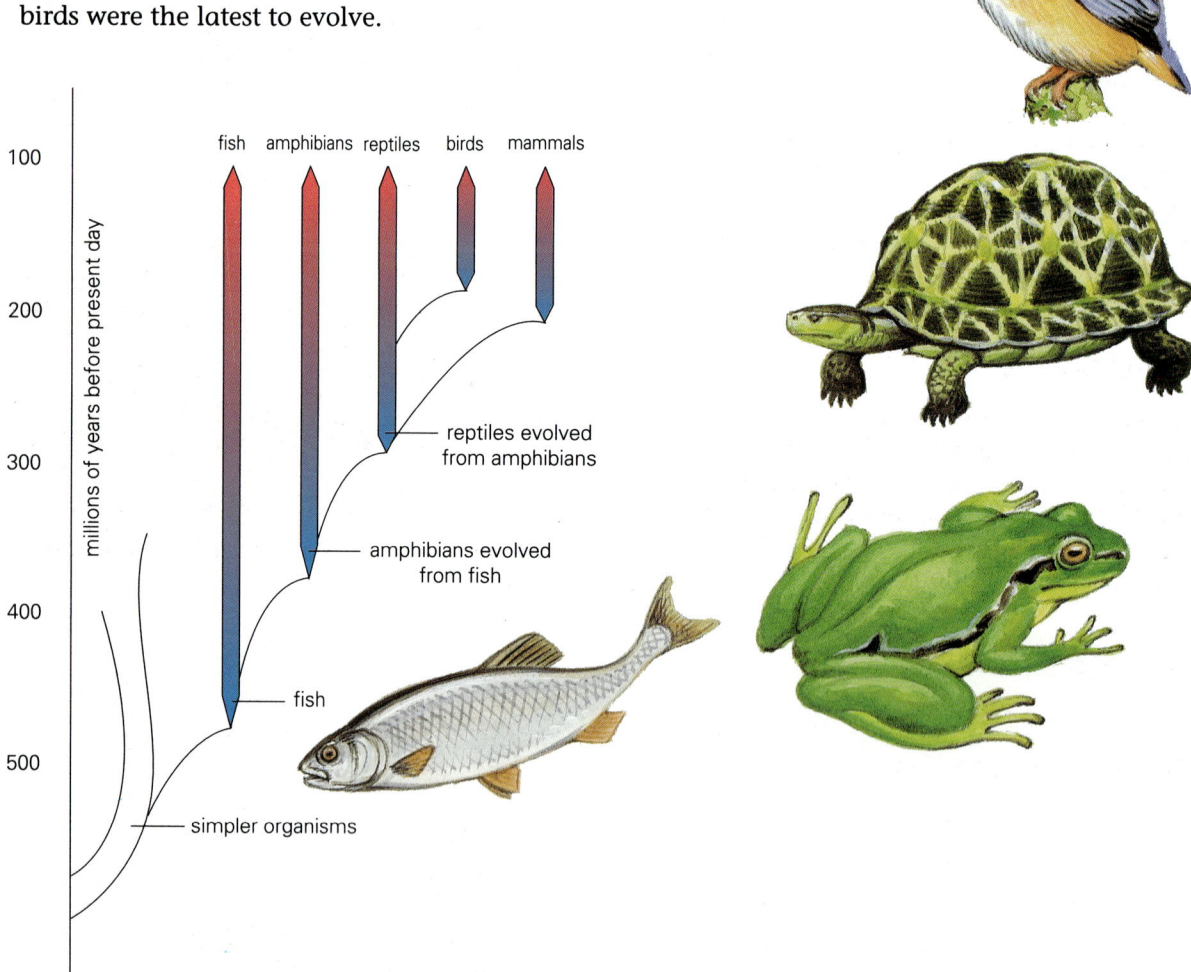

All animals with backbones evolved from fish.

168

Going, going, gone

Homo sapiens is a young species. We arrived only about three million years ago. But we have had a big effect on the species around us. Today the activities of humans are contributing to the extinction of many thousands of species.

Some species become extinct because of **habitat destruction**. This is when the homes of animals and plants are destroyed. Habitat destruction is one reason that tigers, gorillas and pandas are so rare. All over the world forests are being turned into farmland, roads and towns. Habitats for animals are being turned into habitats for people.

Habitat destruction drives many species to extinction.

Endangered species

The rhinoceros is rare, but not yet extinct. **Poaching** or illegal hunting has made it **endangered**. This means it is at risk of extinction. In the last 30 years 40 000 rhinos have been shot by poachers, who can make money by selling the horn. In a few countries the rhino horn is used to make traditional medicines, for treating fever and flu. Today there are only 10 000 rhinoceros left.

This rhino was killed for its horn.

Undiscovered species

One and a half million species have been found so far. But most of the world's species have not yet been discovered. There may be as many as 30 million more. Most new species will probably be found in tropical rain forests, where the warm, moist conditions are perfect for growth.

Most of the world's species live in tropical rain forests.

QUESTIONS

1. When did life on Earth begin?
2. What were the first living things?
3. Birds evolved from which organisms?
4. Describe two ways in which animals can become extinct today?
5. Most species discovered today are small. Why do you think this is?

KEY IDEAS

Life on Earth has changed over billions of years.

Most of the world's species are undiscovered.

Human beings are making many species become extinct.

22.2 Fossils

How do we know about extinct animals?
How can we investigate the Earth's past?

Fossils give clues about the history of life. Fossils are pictures of dead animals and plants, preserved in mud or rock. Fossils are snap-shots of life as it used to be, millions of years ago.

This fish was alive millions of years ago.

The photograph above shows a fossil of a fish. The fish died and sank to the bottom of the sea. Its bones rested on the sand and then got covered by more layers of sand. Over time the bones were slowly replaced by rock. Now the fossil can be used to give information about life millions of years ago.

Fossils are rare. When an animal or plant dies it usually rots, or is eaten. Only sometimes are conditions right for making fossils. Although fossils have been collected for over 200 years, not very many have ever been found. So scientists still have more questions than answers.

Amber fossils

Amber is a yellow stone, formed over millions of years from the sap of pine trees. Insects were trapped in the sap as it hardened, and so were preserved. Amber stones today often contain the bodies of insects which were alive 60 million years ago.

This piece of amber contains an insect from the past.

Ice fossils

Whole frozen mammoths are sometimes found in the ice of Alaska. The ice keeps the body preserved for 10 000 years. Ice fossils are unusual because the soft parts such as skin and muscle are preserved as well as the hard parts.

The story of evolution

The animal *Archaeopteryx* lived 150 million years ago. You can see teeth and feathers and a bony tail in the photograph. The fossil is bird-like because of the feathers and the beak, but reptile-like because of the teeth and the long bony tail.

Archaeopteryx is a clue. It is half a bird, half a reptile. This suggests that birds evolved from reptiles. So fossils do more than show which animals and plants have become extinct. Fossils like *Archaeopteryx* show how life on Earth has changed over millions of years.

This mammoth was excavated from Russian icefields.

Archaeopteryx, the bird-reptile.

QUESTIONS

1. Which extinct animals are sometimes discovered buried in ice?
2. Which animals are sometimes preserved in amber?
3. Why are fossils rare?
4. How can a fossil give information about evolution?

KEY IDEAS

Dead animals and plants are sometimes preserved as fossils.

Fossils can form in rock, amber and ice.

Fossils give clues about evolution.

22.3 Extinction

What happened to the Tyrannosaurus rex, the mammoth and the sabre-toothed tiger? What is likely to happen to the human species?

The dinosaur disaster

All the dinosaurs died 64 million years ago. One explanation is that a huge asteroid hit the Earth. Dust from the explosion went high into the atmosphere and blotted out the Sun. A fall in the temperature then killed off the dinosaurs.

An asteroid may have killed off the dinosaurs.

Hunting the mammoth

Mammoths lived through the ice age. Their woolly coats helped them survive. Mammoths survived the cold, but they couldn't survive the human race. When the great ice sheets retreated northwards 12 000 years ago, early human hunters travelled on to the great North American plains. They found mammoths everywhere – and started hunting them. The last mammoth died 10 000 years ago, driven to extinction by humans.

Mammoths were hunted to extinction.

Adaptation of species

The surface of the Earth is always changing, but slowly. You don't expect to see a mountain build up overnight – or a desert turn into an ocean. But if you could wait hundreds of thousands of years, that is what would happen. All species are affected by this slowly changing environment. Over time, new species arise, able to cope with the new environment. When an organism or species is well-suited to its way of life and environment, it is **adapted**. Species which are not well-adapted die out.

The future of the human race

Humans have only been here for a few million years. Our adaptation is our intelligence. We are clever enough to build aeroplanes, computers, central heating systems and food mixers. We can warm ourselves up by pressing a switch. We can survive underwater by carrying a tank of air so we don't need gills. We can even fly into space. Humans are a very successful, very well-adapted species – at the moment.

These flowers are adapted for attracting insects.

No one knows the future of the human race.

QUESTIONS

1. Name three extinct animals.
2. What might have made the dinosaurs extinct?
3. How did the end of the ice age bring about the end of the mammoths?
4. Explain how environment change can cause extinction.
5. What do you think humans will be like in a million years time?

KEY IDEAS

An asteroid impact could have made the dinosaurs extinct.

Hunting by humans could have made the mammoths extinct.

The human species is a young, well-adapted species.

22.4 New species

Species die out, but how do new ones appear? If people evolved from apes, will today's apes one day turn into humans?

In the past there were many species in the horse family. Most are now extinct. Our modern horse is the living descendent of the early horse. It has characteristics which helped it survive in its grassy environment.

The ancestor of this horse was the size of a fox.

The history of the horse

The diagram shows some of the ancestors of the horse. You can see there are several branches. The modern horse is the end of just one branch. Early versions of the horse were small and had teeth suitable for nibbling at fruit and bushes. They lived in woodland, not on grassy plains. Later versions of the horse lived in grassland. Their adaptations were good eye sight, long legs and teeth good at chewing grass.

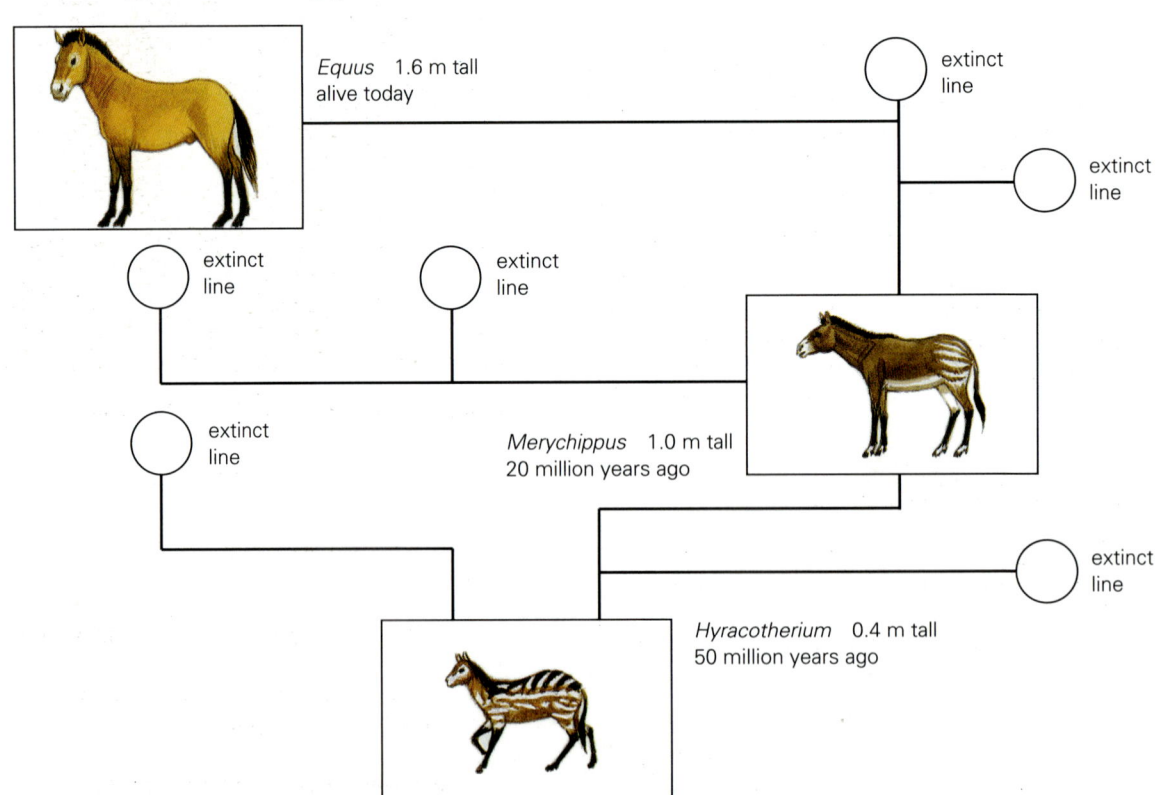

Equus 1.6 m tall alive today

extinct line

extinct line

extinct line

extinct line

Merychippus 1.0 m tall 20 million years ago

extinct line

extinct line

Hyracotherium 0.4 m tall 50 million years ago

A horse family tree.

Evolution is the survival of the fittest

The extinct horses may have died out because of climate change or because other animals started eating their food. But variation among horses probably meant that some had slightly longer legs and slightly harder teeth, good for grinding grass. These animals would be better able to survive in grassland, where food was still plentiful for animals which could run away fast from hunting animals. The longer-legged horses were adapted to the grassland and therefore survived.

Humans evolved from apes

Humans also have ancestors, the apes. Apes live in forests but early humans lived in open grassland. Perhaps, millions of years ago, a group of apes moved out from the forest into grassland, searching for food. But the grassland is home to fast-running predators. For apes it would be a dangerous place.

No one knows how those adventurous apes survived. Perhaps they had larger brains, or were better organised, than the cousins they left behind. Perhaps they could stand on their back feet quite easily, and so see further. Scientists disagree amongst themselves about the story of human evolution.

It isn't likely that today's apes could repeat the experiment. There is no space left. The open grassland has been taken by the humans, and is under their control.

Horses evolved among the dangers of the grasslands.

Todays apes will not turn into humans.

QUESTIONS

1. What was the habitat of the early horse?
2. How tall was *Hyracotherium*?
3. Why is open grassland sometimes dangerous for animals?
4. How might humans have evolved?
5. Explain why modern apes will not evolve into humans.

KEY IDEAS

New species form out of old species.

Horse ancestors were small and lived in the forest.

Humans evolved from apes.

SECTION E: QUESTIONS

1. A group of school students makes a survey of the way they vary. Which of the following characteristics vary continuously, and which vary discontinuously?

   a sex   b height   c weight
   d left or right handedness   e tongue rolling
   f blood group   g hair length.

2. The table shows the length of a growing fetus.

Age in months	1	2	3	4	5	6	7	8	9
Length (cm)	2	5	11	18	28	35	38	40	42

   a Draw a graph to show this information.
   b When did the fetus grow most quickly?
   c When was the growth of the fetus slowest?

3. The diagram below shows the chromosomes inside an animal cell.

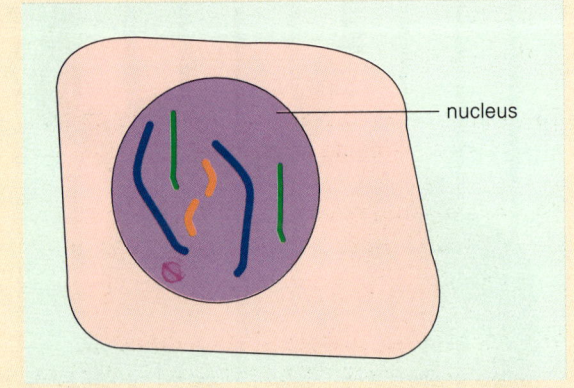

   a How many pairs of chromosomes are there?
   b The cell is *not* a sex cell. Why?
   c Draw a diagram showing the chromosomes of a sex cell of this animal.

4. Copy out and complete the following table.

Type of cell	No. of chromosomes
human sperm	
human egg	
brain cell	
skin cell	

5. This is a diagram of three pairs of chromosomes found in three different people, A, B and C. The cystic fibrosis gene can be found on these chromosome pairs.

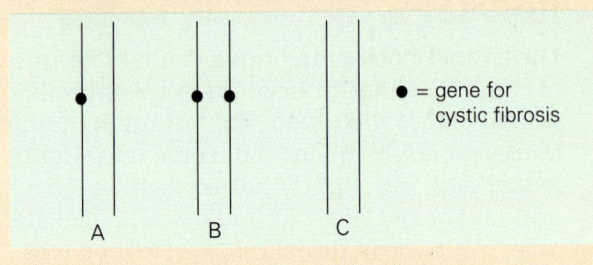

   ● = gene for cystic fibrosis

   a Who is a carrier of cystic fibrosis?
   b Who is a sufferer of cystic fibrosis?
   c Who is certain not to pass on the disease?

6. It is believed that some people, because of their genes, are more likely to get heart disease. What advice about diet and lifestyle might be given to such people?

7. Name one inherited disease which affects the red blood cells.

8. The diagram below shows how the uterus wall changes during the woman's menstrual cycle.

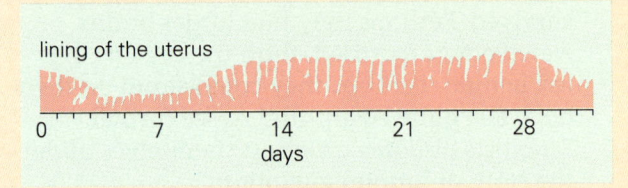

   a How long does each menstrual cycle take?
   b When does the 'period' take place?
   c When does ovulation take place?
   d Which hormone helps rebuild the wall?
   e When is the wall ready to receive a fertilised egg?
   f If a fertilised egg implants, periods stop. Why is this important?
   g Name two substances the embryo needs from the mother.

9 Look at the diagrams and match up the labels with the letters.

Female reproductive system
uterus   ovary
vagina   cervix
oviduct

Male reproductive system
penis   sperm duct
testicle

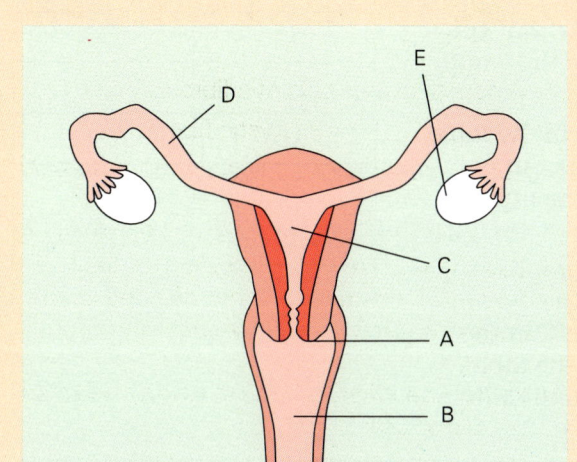

female reproductive system

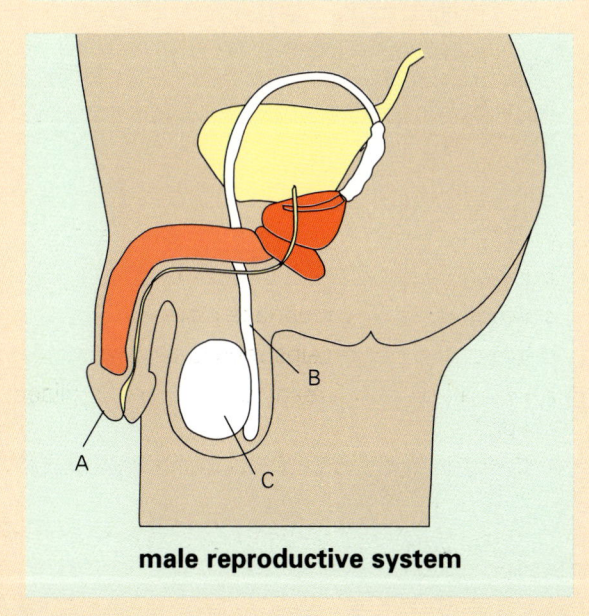

male reproductive system

10 Explain the following:
  a sperm have tails
  b the uterus is muscular
  c millions of sperm are made
  d in the placenta, the blood of the fetus and the mother come close together.

11 Here is a list of events in the male and female reproductive systems. Where do they occur?
  a fertilisation of the egg
  b manufacture of oestrogen
  c implantation of the egg
  d manufacture of sperm
  e manufacture of testosterone
  f storage of eggs.

12 How long ago did these organisms appear?
  a bacteria
  b fish
  c birds
  d mammals.

13 Asexual reproduction involves one parent. How can this be an advantage?

14 Asexual reproduction produces identical offspring. How can this be useful for a farmer?

15 Most organisms are able to reproduce sexually, resulting in variation. How might variation be helpful for organisms in the wild?

16 How would you explain the following?
  a People who work with X-rays are careful to protect themselves.
  b The wing bones of a bird are similar to the arm bones of a reptile.
  c The rate of extinction is faster now than at any time in the last few million years.
  d People who carry genetic diseases often seek genetic counselling when they want to have children.

177

DATA SECTION

Drawing line graphs

A line graph is a way of showing your results so that you can see what they mean more clearly.

Use the table of results and a piece of graph paper. Follow the steps below to produce a line graph.

Length of time pototoes were boiled for (mins)	Amount of vitamin C in potatoes (mg)
0	43
5	40
10	36
15	30
20	20
25	8
30	2
35	2

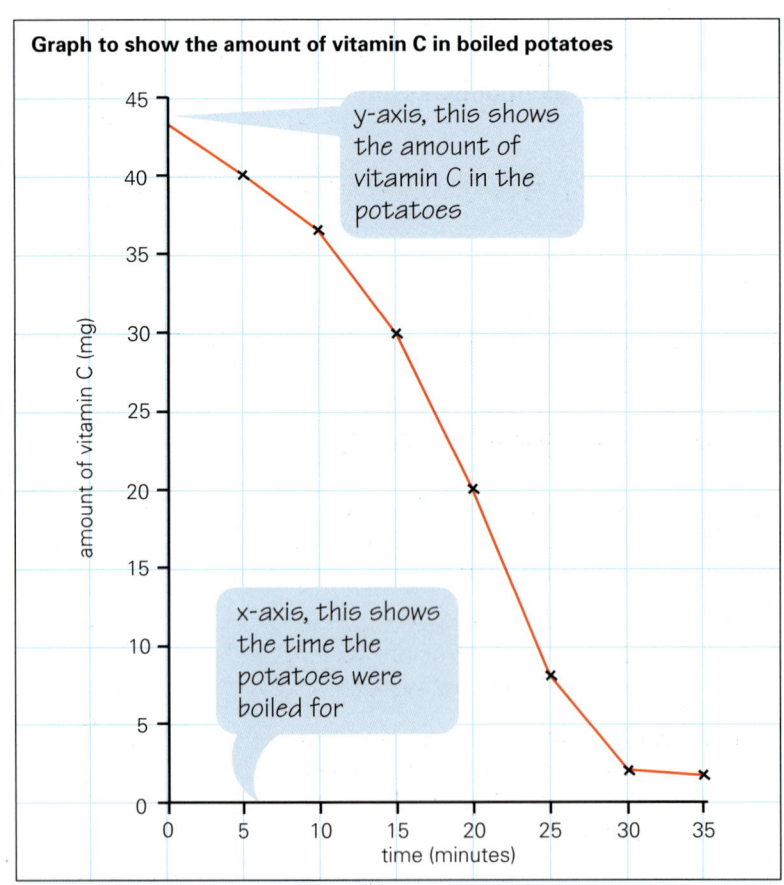

Step 1 The graph is made up of two sides. These are the axes. The x-axis along the bottom is the quantity that you decided before the experiment; in this case the length of time the potatoes were boiled for.

Step 2 Look at the biggest and smallest numbers in the table. Use the squares on the graph paper to work out a scale for the x-axis. You must have the same number of squares for the same time interval.

Step 3 The quantity that goes up the side of the graph, on the y-axis, is the one you found out from the experiment. This is the amount of vitamin C in the potatoes. Choose a scale for the results in the table and make sure you have equal spacing all the way along the axis.

Step 4 Label each axis of the graph and show what measurements are being used.

Step 5 Put a title at the top of the graph to explain what the graph is showing.

Step 6 Mark each point on the graph clearly with a cross, making sure the middle of the ✗ is exactly on the right place.

Step 7 Draw a smooth line through the points.

Graph to show the amount of vitamin C in boiled potatoes

y-axis, this shows the amount of vitamin C in the potatoes

x-axis, this shows the time the potatoes were boiled for

178

Measuring in biology

Measurement	Unit	Abbreviation
mass The mass of something is how much it weighs. The unit of mass is the gram (g). 1 kg = 1000 g	kilogram gram	kg g
length The unit for length is the metre. $1 \text{ cm} = \frac{1}{100}$ m $1 \text{ mm} = \frac{1}{1000}$ m $1 \text{ } \mu\text{m} = \frac{1}{1000000}$ m	metre centimetre millimetre micrometre	m cm mm μm
area The area of something is its **length** × its **width**. A field of 150 m long and 400 m wide has an area of 150 × 400 = 60000 m² (metres squared).	metre squared	m²
volume The volume is the amount of space inside an object. The volume of a cube is **length** × **width** × **height**, measured in metres cubed (m³). A liquid is measured by the amount of space it uses up in a measuring cylinder. The volume of liquids is measured in litres.	metre cubed millilitre litre	m³ ml l

Important equations in biology

Photosynthesis: carbon dioxide + water $\xrightarrow{\text{energy from the Sun}}$ glucose + oxygen

Respiration: glucose + oxygen ⟶ carbon dioxide + water + energy

How to make a table

Tables are a simple way to show information clearly. They are useful for recording the results from an experiment.

Step 1 A table has rows and columns. Decide how many columns you need. Give each column a heading.

Step 2 Make sure you have enough rows. This table can be used to record the pulse rates of two students after exercise.

Step 3 During the experiment write each result neatly in the table.

Minutes after exercise	Student 1 Number of pulses per minute	Student 2 Number of pulses per minute
0	94	104
2	80	90
4	75	82
6	65	75
8	65	70
10	65	70

Put your headings in this row.

Use this column to show when the measurements are taken.

Put your results in here.

GLOSSARY

acidic gases   5.1
these dissolve in water to make acids.

adaptation   1.1, 3.1, 22.3
the features of an organism which help it live in its environment.

addicted   16.2
physically dependent on a drug.

alveoli   12.1, 12.2
(sing., **alveolus**)
air sacs in lungs responsible for gas exchange.

amphibian   1.1
an animal with moist skin but no scales, e.g. frog.

amylase   11.6
digestive enzyme used to break down starch.

anaemia   11.2
lack of red blood cells. Can be caused by too little iron in the diet.

antibiotics   16.1
medicines which stop bacteria growing.

antibodies   18.2
chemicals made by white blood cells which stick to germs.

antitoxins   18.2
chemicals made by white blood cells which neutralise poisons produced by germs.

artery   13.3, 13.5
blood vessel leading high pressure blood away from heart.

asexual reproduction   7.2, 21.2
type of reproduction with only one parent, producing genetically identical offspring.

atherosclerosis   13.5
disease of the arteries in which they become narrower.

auxin   10.1, 10.2
plant hormone, important in growth.

bacteria   4.1, 16.1, 18.1
microbes, some of which can be harmful and some helpful.

balanced diet   11.1
a diet containing the right mix of the seven basic food types.

bronchi   12.1
the two tubes branching off from the trachea.

bronchitis   12.4
infection of the lungs.

capillary   13.3, 17.2
the smallest blood vessels.

carbon   4.3
a very important chemical found in all living things.

carbohydrate   11.1, 11.6, 14.1
one of the food types, used by the body as a source of energy.

carnivore   2.1, 2.2, 7.1
an organism which feeds on other animals.

carrier   19.4
someone who carries a genetic disease but does not suffer from it.

cell membrane   6.1
a thin layer which surrounds the cytoplasm of every living cell.

cell wall   6.2
found around the outside of plant cells.

central nervous system   15.4
the control centre for the nervous system, made up of the brain and spinal cord.

cervix   20.3
the entrance to the uterus. Found at the top of the vagina.

chlorofluorocarbons, 5.2
CFCs
chemicals used in fridges and aerosols which break down ozone.

chlorophyll   9.1, 9.2
green pigment used by plants to capture the Sun's energy.

chloroplasts   6.2, 9.2
green particles inside leaf cells, containing chlorophyll.

chromosomes   6.2, 19.2, 20.2
threads of genetic material found in the nucleus of cells.

classification   1.2
grouping organisms to identify them.

clitoris   20.3
sensitive area of female genitalia

clones   21.2
genetically identical offspring, produced by asexual reproduction.

community   1.3
all the organisms living in a particular habitat.

competition   3.3, 3.4
organisms struggling against each other for the same thing.

consumer   2.1, 2.2
an organism which cannot make its own food and feeds on other organisms.

continuous variation   19.1
smooth variation, as with height.

contracting   6.3
becoming shorter.

cornea   15.2
part of the eye which helps to focus light.

coronary artery   13.5
artery supplying wall of heart.

cutting   10.2
a way of growing a new individual by taking a piece or 'cutting' from one parent plant.

cystic fibrosis   19.4
an inherited disease, affecting the lining of the lungs, and the digestive system.

cytoplasm   6.1
jelly-like material found inside every living cell.

DDT   5.4
a pesticide, widely used in the 1940s and 1950s.

deciduous   1.4
trees which lose their leaves in winter.

decomposer   4.1, 4.2
organism which breaks down the dead bodies of plants and animals.

decomposition   4.1, 4.2, 8.4
the breaking down of dead plant and animal bodies.

deforestation   5.5
cutting down large areas of forest to make land for growing crops or building.

dehydration   11.7
too little water in the body.

diabetes   15.5
condition caused by too little insulin being produced by the pancreas.

diabetic   15.5
a person suffering from diabetes.

dialysis   17.3
filtering of the blood by an artificial kidney machine.

diameter   17.2
the distance across a circle – for example, the distance across a capillary.

dietary fibre   11.3
food type, important for preventing constipation.

digestion   11.5, 11.6
breaking down large molecules in the gut into small molecules, ready for absorption.

digestive system   7.1, 11.4, 11.7
the group of organs carrying out digestion and absorption.

discontinuous variation   19.1
variation involving a few distinct types. Tongue rolling and blood grouping are examples.

donor   17.3
person who gives their organ(s) for transplants.

drug   16.1–16.2
a chemical taken by humans which changes the way the body works.

ecology   1.1
studying an organism and its environment.

egg   19.3, 20.1, 21.1
the female sex cell or gamete.

ejaculation   20.3
the muscular spasm forcing sperm out of the testicles and penis.

embryo   20.4
the ball of cells that implants in the uterus at the start of pregnancy.

endangered species   22.1
any species threatened with extinction.

environment   1.3, 1.4
the physical conditions and living things that surround an organism in its habitat.

enzyme   11.5, 11.6
large molecule used by body for helping chemical reactions.

epiglottis   11.5
small flap preventing food from entering trachea during swallowing.

erosion   8.1
the loss of soil from fields or hills.

evolution   21.1, 22.2
the changes in life on Earth over long periods of time.

excretion   7.1, 17.3
getting rid of unwanted materials from the organism.

excretory system   7.1, 17.3
system made up of organs, which carries out the job of excretion.

external fertilisation   21.1
sexual reproduction in which the egg is fertilised outside the mother.

extinction   7.2, 22.1, 22.3
the complete and irreversible disappearance from the Earth of a species.

faeces   11.7
a mix of undigested waste and bacteria.

fat   11.1, 11.6
one of the food types, used by the body as a source of energy, or for storage and heat insulation.

feedback system   17.1, 17.3
system used in organisms for keeping conditions constant.

fertilisation   7.2, 19.2, 20.4
the moment when a sperm combines with an egg.

fertiliser   5.4, 8.4
a mix of extra minerals put on soils to increase crop growth.

fetus   20.5
name given to the baby in the womb, after nine weeks of pregnancy.

focusing 15.2
altering the rays of light that come into the eye so that they hit the back of the retina.

food chain 2.1
a chain of organisms which shows the feeding relationships between them.

food type 11.1
part of a balanced diet, for example carbohydrate.

food web 2.2
a diagram to show the feeding relationships between different species in a community.

fossils 22.2
preserved and ancient remains of living things.

frostbite 17.2
damage to tissue in very cold conditions because of lack of food and oxygen.

fungi 4.1
a group of decomposers.

gamete 20.2
a sex cell, for example the egg or sperm.

gas exchange 12.2
exchange of oxygen and carbon dioxide, for example inside lungs.

genes 19.2, 19.4
found on chromosomes. They carry instructions for making proteins.

genetic disease 19.4
a disease caused by faulty genes. Cystic fibrosis is an example.

genetic variation 19.1, 21.1
the kind of variation caused by genes.

germinate 3.4, 7.2, 10.1
the process by which a seed begins to grow into a plant.

glandular tissue 6.3
tissue which secretes digestive enzymes and hormones.

global warming 5.3
gradual warming of the Earth's surface.

glucagon 15.5
hormone which increases the amount of sugar in the body.

glucose 9.1, 11.6, 14.1
substance produced by photosynthesis. The fuel for respiration.

gut 11.4
the whole of the digestive tract from mouth to anus.

habitat 1.2, 1.3, 1.4, 5.4
the place where an organism lives.

habitat destruction 22.1
the loss of an area where animals and plants live, often leading to the organisms becoming rare or extinct.

haemoglobin 13.4
pigment in red blood cells, for carrying oxygen.

hallucinogen 16.2
drug which makes people imagine they are seeing or hearing things which are not really there.

herbivore 2.1, 2.2, 7.1
an organism which feeds on green plants.

homeostasis 17.1
keeping conditions constant in the body.

hormones 15.5, 20.1, 20.2
chemicals which are released by glands and act as messengers in the body.

hygienic 18.1
so clean that there are few germs around.

immunised 18.2
injected with dead germs, so the white blood cells produce antibodies to protect you from catching the disease in the future.

implantation 20.4
the moment at the start of pregnancy when the embryo buries itself in the female uterus.

infectious 18.1
carrying germs which can be passed on to someone else, giving them a disease.

inheritance 19.1
the passing on of genetic information from one generation to the next.

insulin 15.5
hormone which reduces the amount of glucose in the body.

internal fertilisation 21.1
sexual reproduction in which the egg is fertilised inside the mother.

iris 15.2, 15.3
a ring of coloured muscle around the pupil, which controls how much light can enter the eye.

key 1.2
a set of descriptions of what different organisms are like.

large intestine 11.4, 11.7
last part of the gut. Used for absorbing water and storing faeces.

leaf 8.1, 8.3, 9.2
green photosynthetic organ of plant, used for making food.

lens 15.2
part of the eye which can change its shape and helps focus light.

life processes 7.1
seven processes which every living organism carries out.

limiting factor 9.3
anything which limits the rate of photosynthesis.

magnesium 8.4
mineral used by plants to make chlorophyll.

mammal 1.1
a group of organisms which all have hair on their body and feed their young with milk from mammary glands.

microbe 4.2
very small organisms whose spores float in the air, e.g. fungi and bacteria.

migrate 3.2
travel large distances once a year to escape difficult environmental conditions.

mineral 8.4, 11.2
food type needed in small quantities

mucus 18.2
sticky substance produced in the lungs which traps germs.

mucous membranes 18.2
the tissue that produces mucus.

multi-cellular organism 6.1, 6.2
organism made of many cells.

muscle tissue 6.3
tissue which is capable of contracting to bring about movement.

mutation 19.4
damage to genes or chromosomes, caused by radiation or chemicals.

nerve impulse 15.4
electrical signal sent along neurones.

neurone 6.1, 15.4
nerve cell.

nitrate 8.4
mineral used by plant for making protein.

nitrogen oxides 12.4
polluting gases, produced especially by cars.

nose 12.1, 12.4
part of the respiratory system with an ability to clean incoming air.

nucleus 6.1
the part of the cell containing genetic material.

nutrients 3.3
chemicals which are used for building the bodies of living things.

oesophagus 11.4, 11.5
muscular tube connecting mouth to stomach.

oestrogen 14.1, 15.5, 20.1
female sex hormone, which controls the sexual development of females.

optic nerve 15.2
the nerve which carries impulses from the eye to the brain.

organ 6.3
a group of tissues working together to do the same job.

organ system 6.4
a collection or organs carrying out a function.

organic farming 8.4
farming without the use of pesticides or artificial fertiliser.

organism 1.1
a living thing.

orgasm 20.3
climax of pleasure during sexual intercourse.

oviduct 20.1, 20.3
the tube connecting the ovary to the uterus.

ovulation 20.1
the release of an egg from the ovary. In humans ovulation happens once a month.

oxygen 9.1, 12.1, 13.1, 14.2
gas needed for respiration. Waste product of photosynthesis.

oxyhaemoglobin 13.4
haemoglobin combined with oxygen.

ozone layer 5.2
a layer of gas which surrounds and protects the Earth from the Sun's harmful UV rays.

painkillers 16.1
medicines which relieve pain.

pancreas 11.6, 15.5
small organ near gut that makes enzymes necessary for digestion.

penicillin 16.1
a kind of antibiotic.

peristalsis 11.3
muscular action of gut, responsible for keeping food moving.

pesticides 5.4
chemicals which kill pests.

pests 5.4
organisms which slow down the growth of crops.

phloem 9.4
cells in plants for transporting sugars, proteins and other dissolved chemicals.

phosphate 8.4
mineral important for the health of plants.

photosynthesis 2.1, 4.3, 7.1, 9.1
the process by which plants make their own food using the Sun's energy.

physically dependent on a drug 16.2
lack of the drug makes the person physically ill.

placenta　　　　　　20.5
organ used for exchange of materials between mother and fetus.

plasma　　　　　　13.4
yellowish liquid part of blood, containing minerals and glucose.

platelets　　　　　　13.4, 13.5
small fragments of cells, floating in blood, important for clotting.

poaching　　　　　　22.1
illegal hunting, for instance of rhinoceros.

pollution　　　　　　3.5, 3.6, 5.1
things which are added to the environment which are harmful to life.

population　　　　　　1.3
the number of one type of organism living in a particular habitat.

predator　　　　　　3.5
animal which catches and kills other animals.

prey　　　　　　3.5
animal which is caught and killed by a predator.

primary consumer　　　　　　2.1
organism which feeds on producers.

producer　　　　　　2.1, 2.2
an organism which makes its own food.

products　　　　　　9.1
what a chemical reaction produces.

protein　　　　　　11.1, 11.6
one of the food types; used by the body for growth.

psychologically dependent on a drug　　　　　　16.2
the person has cravings for the drug.

pulse　　　　　　13.3
pressure wave from heart contraction

pupil　　　　　　15.2, 15.3
the black hole through which light enters the eye.

pyramid of biomass　　　　　　2.2
the amount of living material at each level of the food chain, represented as a pyramid.

pyramid of numbers　　　　　　2.3
the number of organisms at each level in the food chain, represented as a pyramid.

reactants　　　　　　9.1
starting ingredients of a chemical reaction.

receptor　　　　　　15.1, 15.3, 15.4
part of an organism which can detect stimuli.

rectum　　　　　　11.7
part of large intestine, where faeces are stored.

red blood cells　　　　　　13.4
cells in blood which transport oxygen.

reproductive system　　　　　　7.2
system made up of organs, which carries out the job of reproduction.

reptile　　　　　　1.1
an animal with dry, waterproof skin which lays eggs on land, e.g. crocodile.

respiratory system　　　　　　7.2, 12.1–12.4
the body system including lungs, trachea and diaphragm, used for taking in oxygen and getting rid of carbon dioxide.

respond　　　　　　7.3
to react in some way to a particular stimulus.

retina　　　　　　15.2
a layer of light-sensitive cells at the back of the eye which act as the receptors for light.

root hairs　　　　　　8.1, 8.4
microscopic roots, important for absorption of water and minerals.

rooting hormone 10.2
a type of powdered plant hormone used by gardeners to encourage root growth by cuttings.

roots 8.1, 10.1
underground part of plant, used for absorbing water and nutrients, and for giving anchorage to the plant.

scurvy 11.2
deficiency disease caused by lack of vitamin C.

secondary consumer 2.1, 2.2
organism which feeds on primary consumers.

sedative 16.2
also called depressant, a drug which slows down the brain.

sense 7.3, 15.1
to find out about and use information about the world.

sensitivity 7.3
the life process involving sensing information.

sensory organs 7.3
organs used for sensing information about the world.

sex 21.1
process in which the male and female genes are combined.

sex chromosome 19.3
an X or Y chromosome. A chromosome involved in determining sex.

sex pair 19.3
the sex chromosomes in a cell. In humans, males have the sex pair XY and females the sex pair XX.

sexual reproduction 7.2, 21.1
type of reproduction needing two parents, producing genetically varying offspring.

sickle cell anaemia 19.4
an inherited disease that affects red blood cells.

single-celled organism 6.1, 6.2
organism made of one cell only.

skin 17.2
a waterproof, germ-proof layer which separates our body from the outside environment.

small intestine 11.4, 11.6
part of the gut, starting after the stomach. Main area for digestion and absorption.

soda lime 9.3
chemical which absorbs carbon dioxide.

specialised cell 6.1
a cell which has a special shape for doing a particular job.

species 1.1, 22.1
a group of organisms of the same kind.

sperm 19.3, 20.2, 21.1
the male sex cell or gamete.

spinal cord 15.4
part of the central nervous system which runs up the back to the brain.

spore 4.2
a tiny particle which germinates in warm, moist conditions. Ferns, mosses, and microbes produce spores.

stem 8.1, 8.3
main supporting part of plant, usually holding the leaves.

stimulant 16.2
a drug which speeds up nerve impulses in the brain.

stimuli 15.1
things in the environment that organisms can sense, like sound, light and smell.

stomach 11.4, 11.5
organ in digestive system. Stores food, and starts digestion of protein.

stomata 6.2, 7.2, 8.3, 9.2
holes found in the surface of plants through which gases and water vapour can move.

sucrose 9.4
a type of sugar.

target organ 15.5
the organ on which a particular hormone acts.

tertiary consumer 2.1, 2.2
organism which feeds on secondary consumers.

testicle 20.2
the male sex organ. Responsible for making sperm and testosterone

testosterone 15.5, 20.2
male sex hormone, responsible for the sexual development of males.

tissue 6.3
a group of similar cells which together perform a particular function.

trachea 12.1, 12.4
the wind pipe.

transpiration 8.3
the evaporation of water from leaves

transpiration stream 8.3
the flow of water through a plant.

turgid 8.2
when a plant cell has a stiff cell wall because the vacuole is full of water.

ultraviolet rays 5.2
rays of light from the Sun.

umbilical cord 20.5
cord connecting the fetus to the placenta. Part of the fetal blood circulation, not the mother's.

urea 17.3
poisonous waste product which makes up part of the urine.

urine 17.3
made up of water, salt and urea. It is produced in the kidney.

vacuole 6.2, 8.2
a small sac surrounded by a membrane and filled with fluid. It is found in plant cells.

variation 19.1
differences between members of a population.

vascular bundles 9.4
the collection of xylem and phloem running through roots, stems and leaves.

veins 13.3
blood vessel leading blood back towards heart.

viruses 18.1, 18.2
a type of microbe, causing disease.

vitamin 11.2
food type needed in tiny amounts. Often involved in the body's chemical reactions.

vitamin deficiency disease 11.2
disease caused by lack of vitamins.

white blood cells 13.4, 13.5, 18.2
cells in blood, important for preventing disease.

withdrawal symptoms 16.2
physical symptoms, like vomiting and muscle pain, that happen when an addicted person does not take the drug.

zygote 20.4
a fertilised egg.